THE WOKE OPIATE

The Progressive Left's "Long March Through the Institutions"

KERRY D. MCROBERTS

Ark House Press
arkhousepress.com

Cataloguing in Publication Data:
Title: The Woke Opiate
ISBN: 978-1-7636468-0-3 (pbk)
Subjects: [REL067030] RELIGION / Christian Theology / Apologetics; [PHI040000] PHILOSOPHY / Movements / Critical Theory; [PHI008000] PHILOSOPHY / Good & Evil;

Design by initiateagency.com

CONTENTS

ENDORSEMENTS

"Dr. Kerry McRoberts skillfully addresses the powerful influence of woke ideas upon our culture and institutions that we thought were rock solid. His thorough research and keen insight offers the reader a clear understanding of how we arrived at today's woke ideology that permeates our culture. This work gives new meaning to the apostle Paul's warning in Colossians 2:8, 'Beware lest anyone cheat you through philosophy and empty deceit, according to the tradition of men, according to the basic principles of the world, and not according to Christ.' The consequences of accepting or ignoring the current CRT and DEI policies from the left are nothing short of catastrophic for our culture and the church. This work is a must-read for anyone who seeks to discern the times and be ready with an informed response."

Joe Holden, *Ph.D., President, Veritas International University*

"Dr. Kerry McRoberts is an astute spiritual and social analyst who has written on Christian discipleship and cultural apologetics for more than thirty years beginning with his critique of the New Age movement in 'New Age or Old Lie?' (1989). Since then, his books have addressed a wide range of relevant issues, including America's disturbing cultural trends in 'A Letter from Christ' (2012), Christianity's missional mandate in

'Living Missionally Beyond Sunday (2023), and practical counter-cultural Christian discipleship in 'Insanity' (2018).

In keeping with the apostle Paul's warning in Ephesians 6:10-13, 'The Woke Opiate' focuses on the 'spiritual forces of evil' that constitute modern cultural Marxism (a.k.a. neo-Marxism) in contemporary America, and how this ideology has infiltrated and infected every area of our society and culture through its systematic, resolute and unrelenting 'culture war of attrition.' Based on extensive research, McRoberts traces the evolution of anti-Western, anti-American and anti-Christian secular socialist ideology from its 19th century origin in the writings of Hegel and Marx to influential 20th century proponents such as Antonio Gramsci, Herbert Marcuse and the Frankfurt School – culminating in the toxic 'woke' agenda manifest in contemporary socio/moral disorders such as Critical Race Theory and the cult of DEI (Diversity, Equity and Inclusion). The author's warning, and our mandate, is clear: unless Christians awaken and become proactive in combating these insidious trends, America is doomed. Our nation's social, cultural, religious, legal and political foundations are cracking and crumbling, and the residual Christian influences are eroding. Just as Karl Marx proclaimed that 'Religion is the opiate of the masses,' Antonio Gramsci declared that "Socialism is precisely the religion that must overwhelm Christianity." As Dr. McRoberts notes, their solution to the Christian opiate is the 'woke' opiate. This book exposes the cultural and ideological pathologies that are devastating Western civilization and America in particular – and what Christians can and should be doing in faithful response. All those who understand the consequences of this Satanic assault on everything that is True, Good and Beautiful will greatly benefit from Dr. McRobert's analysis."

Jefrey D. Breshears, *Ph.D. Historian, founder and president of The Areopagus, Inc., and author of "American Crisis: Cultural Marxism and the Culture War – A Christian Response" and "C. S. Lewis on Politics, Government, and the Good Society" Jefrey D. Breshears, Ph.D., "The Areopagus"*

For,

Kari & Traci

DR. PHIL FERNANDES, PH. D
FOREWORD

UNDERSTANDING THE SPIRIT OF THE AGE

The year was 1998. I was presenting a paper at the Northwest regional meeting of the Evangelical Theological Society in Portland, Oregon. I titled my paper: "The Death of Man: The Coming Death of Western Civilization." In my paper, I examined the thought of atheist Friedrich Nietzsche, as well as the ideas of Christian thinkers C. S. Lewis and Francis Schaeffer to show that with the death of God (i.e., the rejection of Christianity in Western Civilization), the death of man will follow. In his writings, Nietzsche argued that if God is dead, truth, morality, and meaning are dead as well. He called for a group of "supermen" to arise with the courage to create their own truth, morality, and meaning through their "will to power."

But Christian thinkers Lewis and Schaeffer understood that if God is dead this will lead to the death of man, not the superman. Lewis sounded the alarm with his 1940s work *The Abolition of Man*, whereas Schaeffer coined the phrase "the death of man" in his booklet *Back to Freedom and Human Dignity*. Lewis was appalled concerning the teaching of moral relativism in British schools. He believed this would lead to science, law, and education to become arbitrary. These fields would no longer have any concern for truth, morality, and the dignity of human life. Instead, science, law, and education would be used as mere tools to protect those in position of power. The few "man-molders of the new age" would rule over the billions and treat humans as sub-humans, thus creating a race of men without chests—men without moral consciences.

Schaeffer opposed the behavioral psychology of B. F. Skinner who believed that humans do not have non-material souls, and that our choices are biologically and environmentally determined—there is no free will. Skinner believed he and his colleagues should control, genetically and environmentally, humanity to bring about the best possible future (whatever that would mean in an atheist world without truth and morality). Both Schaeffer and Lewis warned Western Civilization of the disastrous consequences of a world without God.

I tried to pick up where Lewis and Schaeffer left off; I attempted to warn academic evangelicals about the coming death of Western Civilization. The late Dr. Stanley Grenz, a leading theologian at the time, contested the thesis of my paper. This led to a friendly, but passionate debate. Two scholars sided with him and attacked my arguments. But two young students boldly came to my aid and argued for the validity of my case. (I later found out the two young students who came to my defense were former students of Dr. J. P. Moreland. Hence, I suspected Moreland was also aware of the dangers facing the West.)

Dr. Grenz asked me "Don't you think that what Lewis and Schaeffer said was right for their time, but not now?" I responded that that was not a possibility since they were predicting what would happen in our day if the West did not return to the God of the Bible and His moral laws. And I saw no evidence of this repentance in the West. Numerous pastors and professors thought I was being too pessimistic, maybe even conspiratorial. (In 2020, I received quite a few apologies from pastors and professors who regretted not taking my warning in a serious manner.) Slightly depressed after the presentation of my paper, a theology student asked me, "Now that Lewis and Schaeffer are with the Lord, is there any scholar who will pick up the mantle for them?" I had no answer—I knew of no one with the brilliance and, more importantly, the spiritual insight, to understand the spirit of the age and sound the alarm.

Years later, I began to read the works of a Christian thinker named Dr. Kerry McRoberts. Way ahead of his time, he had written a book refuting the New Age Movement back in the 1980s. He even had the courage to research and write about "Burning Man" from a Christian perspective. He was well aware of the damages that both Modernism and Postmodernism were causing for the future of Western Civilization. Scholars like McRoberts and Gene Edward Veith, Jr. see the writing on the wall. They understand the times and offer sound advice as to how the church of the Lord Jesus should respond. They follow in the footsteps of Lewis and Schaeffer—they have the prophetic insight and the prophetic voice to sound the alarm. I pray they are not voices crying in the wilderness of American Christianity, for there is a remnant, and the remnant needs spiritual wisdom and discernment to face the dark days ahead.

In the American Church's attempt to find common ground with the world, we have become the world. We thought we could change our culture by changing leaders and changing laws; yet, the best way to change a culture is by changing hearts. And the best way to change hearts for the good is by the preaching of the Gospel and doing quality discipleship. We are facing what Lewis called "the abolition of man," what Schaeffer called "the death of man," and what I call "the deification of the state" (i.e., when the government tries to replace God and seek for itself, through technology, omniscience, omnipotence, omnipresence, and complete control over its citizens). The real battle, as Dr. McRoberts tells us in this book, is not merely political or moral; it is a spiritual battle (Ephesians 6:12) and it must be fought spiritually.

True, there is "nothing new under the sun." Anti-Christian, even demonic, ideologies have come and gone in the West. But we must discern the signs of the times. This is no longer grandpa's America. The changes that have occurred in America in the past decade are far more radical and pervasive than possibly all the changes that have occurred in the previous one-hundred years. Dr. McRoberts has researched the detrimental transformation of our society; he has earned the right to be heard. Though he has never claimed to be a prophet, God has given him the biblical knowledge and the spiritual wisdom to help us understand the times in which we live. Let us sit at the feet of this great cultural apologist and learn about the forces that are presently destroying America and the West: Gramscian Communism, the Frankfurt School, cultural Marxism, Critical Race Theory, DEI (Diversity, Equity, and Inclusion), the rapid loss of freedoms of speech and religion for Christians, etc. We must not be ignorant of the schemes of the devil.

Though McRoberts acknowledges the horrible, unethical mistakes of America's past, he promotes realistic solutions rather than the so-called solutions proposed by anti-American, globalists—solutions that will certainly bring about the death of man and the deification of the state. McRoberts shows us that, in a similar fashion to the treatment of the pigs in George Orwell's *Animal Farm*, Christians are still free in America, just not as free as non-Christians. This points to a very dark future for the West.

But McRoberts reminds us that God has left us with a remnant. And, God will protect and empower His remnant, preparing us for the coming days.

The Western church has rejected the warnings of C. S. Lewis and Francis Schaeffer. I pray that we heed the warnings in this book given to us by Kerry McRoberts. We now live in the days Isaiah warned about, when "evil is good, and good is evil" (Isaiah 5:20). This book is a call to fight the good fight of faith, for this is a spiritual battle against Satan and his minions. Concerning the spirit of the age and the demonic agenda we face, there is a great lack of knowledge by Christian professors, pastors and their flocks. McRoberts has sounded the alarm, and, by God's grace, wisdom, and power, he has given us our biblical battle plans. He who has an ear, let him hear what God's Spirit says to the churches. Prayerfully read this book, take its words to heart, and allow the God of Abraham, Isaac, and Jacob to prepare you for the present battle and the battles to come. To God be the glory.

ACKNOWLEDGEMENTS

A primary purpose for my writing, *The Woke Opiate, The Progressive Left's "Long March Through The Institutions"* is to make a case for believers in churches ranging from congregations of 20 to 20,000 people to respond to their biblical calling to combine their vocation and mission, and as missional practitioners, they will begin to turn back the overwhelming tide of Woke Identity Marxism one community at a time (See Chapter 11, 'The Priesthood of All Believers'— *Living Missionally Beyond Sunday*). *The Church can achieve this outcome for a self-evident reason: America, and the West's "superstructure" was not built on the ingenious foundation of secular government but on the traditional values of, primarily, Christians who both believed in the Scriptures and possessed a vision for the most unique experiment in human history.* (Please see Chapter 10, "The Meaning Of Truth," Subtitle: "America's Superstructure").

Insightful scholars, well-acquainted with the subject matter of the *Woke Opiate*, have each contributed to my writing in very significant ways: Joe Holden, Ph.D., a prestigious Christian leader, and "renaissance scholar" specializes in numerous subjects though archeology and apologetics appear most prominent in his work. Dr. Holden is a co-founder and President of Veritas International University. H. Wayne House, Ph. D., is a distinguished scholar and prolific writer on numerous topics to include archeology, apologetics, theology and law. Jefrey Breshears, Ph.D. is a distinguished historian and dynamic Christian scholar; his tome, *American Crisis: Cultural Marxism and The Culture War: A Christian Response,* was among the first texts I turned to, to gain understanding of the Woke Identity Marxist invasion of the West, and particularly, America. Dr. Breshears' work has been foundational to mine. And Phil Fernandes, Ph.D., is a prolific writer and distinguished apologist; he is listed among: "The Top 100 Apologists" ("Apologetics For Life") and he is the author of the foreword of this book.

George Yancey, Ph.D., is a Professor of Sociology at Baylor University. He has published several research articles on the topics of institutional racial diversity, and racial identity. Dr. Yancey graciously extended time to review two chapters in *The Woke Opiate,* Chapter 6, "Critical Race Theory— Two Histories," and Chapter 12, "Racial Reconciliation— An Introduction." I am very grateful for Dr. Yancey's insights.

Finally, *The Woke Opiate* is dedicated to my Wife's (Vicki) and my two daughters, Kari and Traci— "*You are altogether beautiful, my [lovely daughters]; there is no flaw in you*" (Song of Solomon, 4:7, ESV).

INTRODUCTION

"What's happening to my country?"
"Will this 'madness' pass or will it continue until it radically transforms Western Civilization in irreversible ways?"

The eminent British theologian, J.I. Packer, used to say of the primitive church, "They were a people who lived their lives with their bags packed and ready to go home."

Os Guinness speaks of the "astonishing growth of the premodern churches in the Global South," primitive like churches, compared with the spiritually "poor condition of the churches in the West, largely because of their capitulation to the distorting power of modernity."[1] Over the course of the last fifty (plus) years, the Evangelical Church's capitulation has resulted in the cultural repositioning of the church to downstream from culture; and consequently the church has imperceptibly *conformed* to Western culture. Guinness specifically describes the spiritually "poor condition" of the church in the West: "At the heart of the crisis of the church in the advanced modern world, we need to recognize how modernity has had the effect of shifting the church from an integrated faith to a fragmented faith, from a

1 Os Guinness. *Renaissance, The Power of the Gospel However Dark The Times.* Downers Grove, IL.: Inter-Varsity Press, 2014. 34; 36.

stance under authority to a stance of preferences, and from a supernatural sense of reality to a purely secular perspective."[2] *We have unpacked our bags and made ourselves at home in our secularized thinking and way of life.*

Guinness solemnly presides over the church's present condition: "The overall challenge of modernity is summarized in the gravedigger thesis—the idea that the Western church was the single strongest source of the ideas has become culturally captive to the world to which it gave rise. In so doing, it has become its own gravedigger."[3] But although the Church is, at present, "flatlined," God, in His great faithfulness, has not abandoned His covenant people— Despite her condition, this is a battle the Church needs to lead; the *real* enemy is not the "Progressive Left" but "… *the powers of this dark world and … the spiritual forces of evil in the heavenly realms"* — Eph. 6:12.

"At least five times …," observes G.K. Chesterton, beginning with "Feudalism's passing away …," followed by the passing of "The whole Medieval order…", and then, "the Renaissance;" followed by "the Age of Reason;" and "… after the "Enlightenment," Darwin;" the Christian faith was expected to pass with each age— the Faith "… had to all appearance gone to the dogs" but "… in each of these five cases it was the dog that died."[4]

How complete was the collapse and how strange the reversal— it seemed to most "… like a river turning backwards from the sea and trying to climb back into the mountains."[5] But the point is, what is happening now in Western Civilization, has happened again, and again, and "though we can only see in detail in the case nearest to our own time"[6] — Indeed, we can

---

2 Ibid. 37.

3 Ibid.

4 G.K. Chesterton. "The Five Deaths of Faith." Part 2. Chapter 6. https://www.worldinvisible.com/library/chesterton/everlasting/part2c6.htm

5 Ibid.

6 Ibid.

clearly see that Western Culture has been demoralized by the Progressive Left, "under the flag" of Woke Identity Marxism, and the Groom has once again been "widowed...."[7]

God forbid that Christians, in their complacency, would resign themselves to the regrettable notion that, "This too shall pass," as we continue to depend on the GOP to fill the role of the nation's prophetic conscience, a role the Church was ordained to fill, not the state. If the Church refuses to wisely and responsibly recover her vocation as the prophetic conscience of each of our cultural contexts, and together, the nations, we will surely turn Western Culture over to "the dogs" (viz., Woke Identity Marxism) without a fight (*et. al.* Matthew 5:1-16; Romans 13:1-7).

In the face of all the madness, Western Culture's answer is: "Jesus Christ," and no other. As you read this book, please keep in mind three questions: "*Where is Jesus Christ in all the madness?*" "*What is Jesus doing?*" And *"how can we/I join Him?"*

---

[7] Ibid.

PART—1

THE WOKE MARXIST REVOLUTION

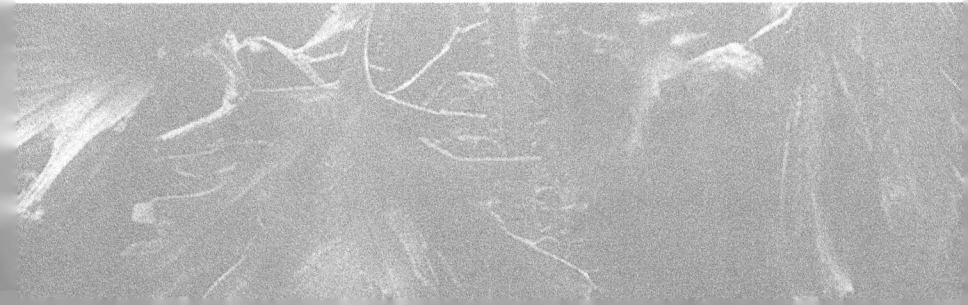

PROLOGUE— CHAPTER 1

A TRIP TO THE FARM— AN INTRODUCTION TO "THE REVOLUTION"

Why do Americans, and conscientious people throughout Western Culture, need to read this book and understand classic and contemporary Marxism? The answer requires only a single sentence: In the preface of a 1947 Ukrainian edition of *Animal Farm,* George Orwell expressed, "… *how easily totalitarian propaganda can control the opinion of enlightened people in democratic countries*" [8] Our search for clarity and meaning in a world obsessed with deliberately coloring outside the lines of reality begins with a trip to an allegorical farm.

---

8 Ian Robertson, February 2019. *"George Orwell's Preface to the Ukrainian Edition of Animal Farm | The Orwell Foundation". www.orwellfoundation.com. Retrieved 6 March 2021.* Quoted in *Animal Farm.* https://en.wikipedia.org/wiki/Animal_Farm. Downloaded: 06/19/2023. (The italics are the author's).

"ALL ANIMALS ARE EQUAL BUT SOME ARE MORE EQUAL"

"A lie told often enough becomes the truth"
— Vladimir Lenin.

Animal Farm is a classic allegory written in 1945 by George Orwell. A critic of Joseph Stalin, Orwell described *Animal Farm* as a satirical tale written against the ruthless Soviet leader.

The intention of the story under the subheading: "All Animals Are Equal But Some Are More Equal," is for the reader to become familiar with socialist/communist terms and ideology through "Marxist lens," both by reading the Animal Farm allegory and carefully studying the definitions of Marxist's terms and thought in footnotes 10-28. As the reader continues through Chapters 1-8 (Section One: The Marxist Revolution) of the book, they will grow in their understanding of the implications and nuances of Marxist thought, and propaganda.

ANIMAL FARM: THE ANIMALS REVOLT AGAINST HUMAN OPPRESSION

In former times, Manor Farm was a productive, prosperous enterprise, but in more recent years, under the management of an alcoholic farmer, Mr. Jones, the farm had fallen on hard times— The neglected farm animals were suffering, and they were becoming restless.[9]

An aged boar named "Old Major" called the farm animals together to plan a rebellion against their oppressor, farmer Jones. The farm animals hoped to create a society in which they could be equal, free, and

9 "Manor Farm is symbolic of the hegemony of the "Privileged."

happy.[10] The "Old Major" (an allegorical combination of Marx and Lenin) announced that all animals will live by seven commandments:[11]

(1) Whatever goes upon two legs is an enemy; whatever goes upon four legs, or has wings, is a friend.
(2) No animal shall wear clothes.
(3) No animal shall sleep in a bed.
(4) No animal shall drink alcohol.
(5) No animal shall kill any other animal.
(6) All animals are equal.

"Old Major" closed the meeting by teaching the animals a revolutionary song, "Beasts of England."[12] But before the animals finished singing their newly declared anthem, a stumbling, hung over, gun-toting farmer Jones inadvertently fired a round into the barn striking Old Major in the head and killing him.

Adding to the animals' grief, farmer Jones neglected to feed the animals the following morning. The animals then broke into the storehouse and fed themselves. When the tyrant farmer awakened and attempted to bring the animals under his control, they revolted and drove Jones off the farm. They then abruptly renamed the farm, "Animal Farm."[13]

---

10 The farm animals are *"Woke,"* that is, they are awakened to the need of Revolution.

11 Politically Correct "New Realities" depend on what serves the Party's ends, the "New Realities," are therefore, subject to change.

12 "Beasts of England" corresponds to the famous socialist anthem, The Internationale. In the "Animal Farm," story, "Beasts of England" serves as a metaphor for the Communist Manifesto of Marx. Old Major explained his dream to the farm animals of an animal-controlled society three nights before his death.

13 "Animal Farm" is symbolic of the "counter-hegemony" of the "Elites" on behalf of the Oppressed.

The animals then removed every trace of farmer Jones' incompetency and cruelty, especially the weapons he inflicted them with. And they reaffirmed that they would not live in the now abandoned farmhouse. However, Napoleon, a power-hungry boar took interest in the vacated house and a litter of puppies left without their mother.

Snowball, a young pig, taught himself how to read and write; he then committed himself to teach the other animals how to read and write. Food was plentiful on the farm and the animals began to enjoy their newfound freedom. But, almost immediately, the ambitious pigs began appointing themselves to leadership roles, and selecting for themselves choice food items, claiming that they need to stay healthy as leaders. And Napoleon made himself busy training the pups to serve him in his leadership ambitions.[14] Snowball, faithfully working in the best interests of all the animals, announced his idea for a windmill. A windmill will help in the production of more food, while reducing the long hours of hard labor for the animals.

The animals were very receptive of Snowball's idea, but Napoleon opposed it, and commanded his dogs to chase Snowball away from the farm.[15] Once Snowball was out of the way, Napoleon elevated himself to the animals' leader and he began making changes.

Instead of all animals coming together for meetings, a select group of pigs will oversee the operations of the farm— Squealer, a young pig, became Napoleon's spokesperson.[16] Through Squealer, Napoleon communicated his plans for his regime.

---

14 The Revolution begins, and the "Ruling Elites" (the pigs) take charge.

15 Snowball is symbolic capitalism and traditional values.

16 "The Ruling Elites" is a reference to the self-appointed leadership of the Revolution. Throughout this book, "The Ruling Elites," "The Party," and "The Progressive Left" are synonymous terms.

Old Major had the Seven Commandments of "Animalism" painted on the side of the barn for all to see.[17] The most conspicuous commandment is the seventh one, "All animals are equal."[18] And therefore, all animals work together, though Boxer, the powerful workhorse, and Benjamin, a young donkey, work the hardest.

But as Napoleon and the "ruling pigs" abused their power by imposing greater levels of control over the other animals, they simultaneously began revising the Seven Commandments for the purpose of justifying their exceptional privilege. For example, after the pigs were discovered sleeping in the farmhouse, they revised the fourth commandment: "No animal shall sleep in beds" to say, "No animal shall sleep in beds with sheets." And after imbibing the farmer's whiskey, "No animal shall drink alcohol," the fifth commandment, was altered by the "ruling pigs" to state, "No animal shall drink alcohol to excess"[19]— And consequently, the most important of the commandments became, *ex de facto, "All animals are equal, but some are more equal."*[20]

Although Napoleon's revisionist history regarding Old Major's seven commandments is precipitated by his willing embrace of a "*false conscience*" —i.e., he has exchanged thinking like an animal for thinking like a man— most of the animals never question their leader, instead they continue to believe that he and the ruling party of pigs are acting in all the

---

[17] "Animalism" is a system of thought based on "Major's" proposed Seven Commandments.

[18] The 7th Commandment is "equity." "Equity" refers to the leveling of society and the eventual reign of the "Workers" (Socialism/Communism).

[19] A Synopsis of George Orwell's Animal Farm, "Animal Farm Plot." https://www.imdb.com/title/tt0047834/plotsummary/ Downloaded: 06/16/2023. (No author is mentioned for this synopsis. It is necessary to state that this synopsis was a guide for me as I worked through multiple resources for this account of Orwell's "Animal Farm" to illustrate the content of Section One of this book).

[20] Political Correctness serves the power-crazed "ruling elites;" **not** the "Underprivileged/Oppressed."

animals' best interest—*The "Party's interest is to be treated as a reality that ranks above reality itself."*[21]

Napoleon's insatiable appetite for more power and wealth drives him to become a business associate with Mr. Whymper for jellies and jams. Napoleon unilaterally offers Mr. Whymper all the hens' eggs as payment for the jellies and jams. But the hens promptly reject such a business arrangement, and they revolt by throwing their eggs at the pigs to turn them away from following through with Napolean's dealings[22]— (The hens' dissent will not go unpunished).

Napoleon subjects the hens to an inquisition by the pigs. To instill fear in the chickens, or any animal that dares to dissent from his commands, Napoleon chooses a duck and sheep and accuses them of treachery. The animals are then taken outside and mauled to death by the dogs. The blood of the duck and sheep is used to revise the sixth commandment, "No animal shall kill any other animal," to, "No animal shall kill any other animal except with cause."[23]

THE 'POLITICALLY CORRECT' FARM

"If there is no absolute by which to judge society, society is absolute"
— Francis Schaeffer.

---

[21] Angelo M. Codevilla. "The Rise of Political Correctness." November 28, 2016. Originally published in *Claremont Review of Books* on November 8, 2015. p. 1 of 12 pages. https://claremontreviewofbooks.com/the-rise-of-political-correctness/ Downloaded: 06/16/2023.

[22] The hens protest Napoleon's socialist agenda. The hens want "free market" enterprise wherein private business ownership, "free enterprise," will flourish.

[23] Angelo M. Codevilla. "The Rise of Political Correctness." The identity of the ruling elites must be affirmed often to ensure that the masses will "bite their lip" and not express their dissent publicly. 3 of 12 pages.

"The Animal Farm dream is finally a reality," declares Napoleon, and therefore, "Beasts of England" is no longer appropriate, it must be banned.[24] Political Correctness is a weapon the ruling party uses on its own loyalists— to keep them loyal— as well as to manipulate and control their enemies.

As Mr. Whymper continues to profit from his trading with Animal Farm, the other farmers become increasingly disgruntled with his success each passing day. The farmers decide to attack the farm. Jones wants to join them, but they want nothing to do with him. An angry Jones then blows the windmill to pieces with himself inside of it.

The animals defeat the hostile farmers but at great cost; many of them are wounded, including Boxer. And though he must struggle, because of his wounds, Boxer continues his hard work until he collapses while working on the windmill. Napoleon arranges for a van to come and take Boxer to the veterinarian. But as the van drives away, Benjamin notices that it belongs to Whymper's glue factory! Benjamin attempts to rescue Boxer, but he fails.

Squealer, a typical politician for whom lying is the norm, speaks with ease of conscience as he shares his being at Boxer's side to hear his dying words of praise and admiration for Napoleon. Squealer is also quick to renounce any rumors having to do with Boxer being sold for money. The grieving animals, however, are very familiar with Napoleon's dishonest ways; they see through his lies. But before they can act in the face of Napoleon's duplicity, the animals are driven away by a pack of snarling dogs.[25]

---

24 Despite limits imposed by reality, "the elite" force the working class to celebrate the party's pseudo-realities and "affirm things they know are not true and deny others they know to be true." Ibid. 4 of 12 pages.

25 The Ruling Elites' power will not be challenged.

A TRANSFERRING OF POWER TO THE UNDERPRIVILEGED?

A "pure" (utopian) Communism has never succeeded, and among the primary reasons for its lack of success is the inviolable commitment of the Ruling Elites to perpetually hold onto their power.[26]

As the years pass, the pigs appear to have been transformed into man's image; they walk upright and wear clothes. Napoleon, in the likeness of Nikita Khrushchev, dresses in a suit with medals attached above his left breast pocket. And the Seven Commandments have been reduced to only one: "All animals are equal, but some animals are more equal than others."[27]

Napoleon enjoys hosting dinner parties and hearing his guests, who are exclusively pigs, commend him on how hard his animals work for so little food. Napoleon toasts his guests as they envision a world in which pigs own and operate farms everywhere.

As Benjamin overhears the conversation between Napoleon and his guests, he imagines the pigs' faces as replicas of farmer Jones' face. Realizing that life has become worse than it was before the animals rebelled, the animals all come together and plan their overthrow of Napoleon— The Animal Farm story closes with Napolean being overwhelmed by the farm animals and beaten to death.

Animal Farm is an allegory about Communist (totalitarian) regimes: The "Ruling Elites" (portrayed by the pigs) shepherd "the working class," the Proletarians or "Underprivileged" (portrayed by the "other" farm animals), through the revolution.[28] As we venture forward in Section

---

26 Paulo Freire. "The Pedagogy of the Oppressed." Edited: Myra Berman Ramos. Translated: New York: Continuum. 1968.

27 *Political Correctness creates "new realities" conformed to the dictates of the Party.*

28 In the eyes of the "Woke," today's "Proletariat," is the "Underprivileged/Oppressed" and the human farmers are the "Privileged/Oppressors."

One: "The Woke Marxist Revolution," introduced in this chapter as the allegorical world of "Animal Farm," will transform into an alternative reality where truth still perseveres, but perversions of the truth consistently seem to work better.

CHAPTER 2

"WE THE PEOPLE"

Every morning, I (the author) drove 5.1 miles from my home, two blocks off highway 99, which merges onto NW 3rd Street, a one-way, two laned street, enroute to my church on NW Circle Blvd. Once I merged and entered the flow of traffic onto NW 3rd Street, inevitably a certain car would be just ahead of me, in the right-hand lane, displaying a bumper sticker with large black embolden letters on a bright yellow background demanding: **"TAX THE CHURCHES!"**

Why aren't churches taxed? Churches are not taxed because America is a Democratic Republic. An explanation of this assertion begins by briefly introducing Benjamin Franklin's challenge and then continuing with "The Higher Law & The Republic."

"A REPUBLIC ... IF YOU CAN KEEP IT"

Kevin D. Roberts' commentary on American History begins with a brief, profoundly invaluable story that in his words, "distills the challenge before

America today."[29] The story is only a sentence more than a single paragraph, but wisdom does not require much space:

> At the end of the Constitutional Convention, as delegates emerged from their secret deliberations, a Philadelphia woman— one "Mrs. Powell" — asked Pennsylvania delegate Benjamin Franklin what kind of government the convention had given them.
>
> Franklin answered her: "A republic … if you can keep it."[30]

How do we "keep" the Republic?

"THE HIGHER LAW"

We hold these truths to be self-evident, that all men are created equal, that they are endowed by their Creator with certain unalienable Rights, that among these are Life, Liberty, and the pursuit of Happiness. That to secure these rights, Governments are instituted among Men, deriving their just powers from the consent of the governed

— Preamble: The Declaration of Independence.

The principal point of the preamble of the Declaration of Independence is its "higher law," founded in God's revelation: *So, God created mankind in his own image, in the image of God he created them; male and female he created them*— Genesis 1:27.

---

29 Kevin D. Roberts. *America Must Reclaim What The Left Has Attempted To Destroy.* The Heritage Foundation. July 25, 2023. https://www.heritage.org/american-founders/commentary/america-must-reclaim-what-the-left-has-attempted-destroy. Downloaded: 03/11/2024

30 Ibid.

Humanity's creation in the image of God means, we are in a special (unique) relationship with God— *All human beings, Black, Brown, Yellow, Red, and White, are "a meaningful reflection of God."*[31] And, concludes Kierkegaard, the relationship between God and man (the "likeness-image," Gen. 1:26-27) is what makes man a man[32]— *The image of God is the "self-evident" basis for human equality, and personal dignity.*

Moreover, Adam's creation (Genesis 1 and 2) is described in terms of a corporate entity: "*Adam* here refers not only to a single man named Adam but also to humanity as a whole"[33] — The unity of the human race is revealed in both Testaments, Old and New— ***26*** ***"****From one man he made all the nations, that they should inhabit the whole earth; and he marked out their appointed times in history and the boundaries of their lands"* (Acts 17:26).

"Because of these ideas," write John Stonestreet and Glenn Sunshine, "Christianity is the sole historical source of concepts now taken for granted: human dignity, human equality, and universal human rights." [34] The origins of these virtues are acknowledged even by prominent atheists, viz., Tom Holland, Jurgen Habermas, and Luc Ferry: "… these ideas are at the root of our modern concern for the poor and oppressed."[35] The Declaration of Independence, the Constitution, the Bill of Rights, and the Federalist Essays acknowledge— *Holy Scripture reveals to humanity that we are universally united on the sacred foundation of our special creation in the image of God.*

---

31 John F. Kilner. *Dignity and Destiny, Humanity in the Image of God.* Grand Rapids, MI: William B. Eerdmans, 2015. 128-29.

32 Soren Kierkegaard. *The Point of View.* Translated by W. Lowie. London: Oxford University Press. 1939. 114.

33 Kilner. *Dignity and Destiny.* 85.

34 BREAKPOINT, Colson Center. "Why Wokeness is a Christian Heresy—2021 Year in Review." John Stonestreet and Glen Sunshine. 3 of 4 pages. Downloaded: 12/10/2022.

35 Ibid.

THE HIGHER LAW & RELIGIOUS FREEDOM

Congress shall make no law respecting an establishment of religion or prohibiting the free exercise thereof; or abridging the freedom of speech, or of the press; or the right of the people peaceably to assemble, and to petition the Government for a redress of grievances— The First Amendment of the Constitution of the United States of America.

"America is the most deliberate nation in history— it was built for reasons that are stated in the legal documents that form its founding."[36] The lynchpin of the longest enduring and greatest ever composed legal document, The Constitution of the United States, is "Religious Freedom," that is, "Congress shall make no law respecting an establishment of religion or prohibiting the free exercise thereof…."

"Religious Freedom" does not refer to a particular religion; it refers to *freedom of conscience*. Regardless of any person's religion, or any person's lack of religion, Religious Freedom means American citizens are free to exercise freedom of religious belief or no belief— And flowing from Religious Freedom are Freedom of Speech, Freedom of the Press, The Right to Peaceably Assemble, and to Petition Government for a Redress of Grievances. In *Federalist* 63, James Madison contended, "'that ours will be the first purely representative government.' This doesn't just mean that instead of a king being sovereign, as in England, we would elect our rulers. It means that no one inside the government— none of the people carrying on the activities of the government— would be sovereign. The sovereign would be *outside* the government. As Lincoln would later put it, the constitutional majority is the only true sovereign of a free people. All powers are

[36] Larry Arnn, President, Hillsdale College. "Orwell's 1984 and Today," 2. *Imprimis*, Hillsdale.EDU. December 2020, Vol. 49, No. 12.

to be delegated from the society to the government"[37] — Americans, have been given "A republic … if [we] can keep it."

What is the balance between the interests of the state and Religious Freedom—*That is, between the state and individual freedom of conscience?* Western liberal democracies have been confronted by the supposed conflict between secularism and religious freedom for centuries. The First Amendment of the Constitution implies that for individual freedom— for self-government to exist— the state must be secular. "Simply put, the state is to have no interest in matters of religion"[38] — For freedom to be truly free, it must originate through, and be sustained by, religious faith (i.e., a "transcendent authority,"[39]), and virtue: *Faith and Virtue are integral to Religious Freedom— That is, "The Higher Law" is integral to the balancing of the interests of the state and freedom of conscience and thus, for the sake of avoiding an imbalance, churches are not taxed.* Grant Atkinson, Alliance Defending Freedom, firmly states the implication behind the "Higher Law": "While the First Amendment does not explicitly mention taxes for

---

37 Ibid.

38 Barry W. Bussey. Law and Religion, Religious Liberty, Religious Freedom. "Fides et Libertas," 2011. Fides et Libertas 2011.pdf. Downloaded: 04/09/2024. A second exception to the First Amendment's establishment clause prevents the government from creating a church, endorsing religion in general, or favoring one set of religious beliefs over another. In 1947, *Everson v. Board of Education of Ewing Township*, the U.S. Supreme Court decided that the establishment clause was intended to erect "a wall of separation between church and state" (of course, the degree to which government should accommodate religion in public life has been debated in numerous Supreme Court decisions since then). The point here is two-fold: (1) The Constitution *does not* explicitly make any reference to the "separation of church and state," and (2) the U.S. Supreme Court decision in 1947 (*Everson v. Board of Education of Ewing Township*) was clearly for the purpose of keeping the state "out of the church," *not* keeping the church out of the state.

39 A "transcendent authority" is language used by the postmodernist, Jean-Francois Lyotard, Chapter 9, "Woke Moral Subjectivity & The Abolition of Man," under the subheading: "The Woke 'Opiate.'"

churches, it is well understood that taxation often serves as a way for a ruler to control his subjects. Thankfully, we do not have 'rulers' or 'subjects' in our form of government, but as the U.S. Supreme Court said in the 1819 case *McCulloch v. Maryland*, 'the power to tax involves the power to destroy.'" [40]

THE REPUBLIC & AMERICAN "EXCEPTIONALISM"

Our nation's free Republic originated in and has been sustained by a robust religious freedom as evidenced not only in the words of our founders, but within the government buildings themselves. For example, the Ten Commandments hang over the head of the Chief Justice of the Supreme Court. In the House and Senate Chambers appear the words, "In God We Trust." On the walls of the Capitol dome appear the words, "The New Testament according to the Lord and Savior Jesus Christ." Engraved on the metal cap on the top of the Washington Monument are the words, "Praise be to God," and numerous Bible verses line the walls of the stairwell. And the Eighty-Third Congress set aside a room in the Capitol Building exclusively for the private prayer and meditation of members of Congress.

Our nation's most foundational documents, especially the Declaration of Independence, point to our Creator as our source of rights: "We hold these truths to be self-evident, that all men are created equal; that they are endowed by their Creator with certain unalienable rights; that among them

[40] Grant Atkinson, Alliance Defending Freedom. **"No Strings Attached: Why the Government Shouldn't Tax Churches."** https://adflegal.org/article/no-strings-attached-why-government-shouldnt-tax-churches?sourcecode=10016058_r500&utm_source=grant&utm_medium=ppc&utm_campaign=GRANT&gad_source=1&gclid=Cj0KCQjwwO20BhCJARIsAAnTIVRkmlV87LYFxqvD4S-2FgB20upttUykRvIUjOT7Vl3w4M3ePwd7uMsaAll6EALw_wcB. Revised: Oct. 5, 2023.

are life, liberty, and the pursuit of happiness"— *Our unalienable rights are founded on moral absolutes and our special creation in God's image.*

Barry Bussey stresses, "In principle, so the argument goes, the state cares only for the public safety and well-being of its citizenry irrespective of the religious persuasion of the citizen."[41] Certainly, each nation is unique regarding its history and culture, but the rich complexity of the ethnic and religious diversity of America, and the First Amendment's understanding of Religious Freedom (i.e., freedom of individual conscience) is, in a word, "exceptional."

America's "exceptionalism," therefore, does not refer to its superiority over any other nation or culture but rather, its multi-layered ethnic and religious diversity, is not only preserved but flourishes in the American context— American exceptionalism is the coexistence of religious freedom, the basis for self-government, and secular governmental interests balanced by her inherent traditional values, the whole of which are succinctly described by reference to the "Golden Rule": "*So in everything, do to others what you would have them do to you ...*" (Mt. 7:12).

WHAT IF WE CANNOT "KEEP" THE REPUBLIC?

"Governments are instituted among Men, deriving their just powers from the consent of the governed"— The moment "We the People" ("the governed") lose our *unalienable* right to "consent" to be governed, the sovereign would no longer be outside the government (Lincoln) but centralized in it— We would have failed to keep our Republic and "We the People" will be found living under the oppression of a totalitarian socialist state.

---

41 Ibid.

Without the need to speculate, if a viral [Marxist] evil from within, "snaked" its way into Western cultural institutions that socialize people into believing and behaving according to the norms of the Republic, it would first strike the nation's traditional values, founded on religion, in general, and Christianity, in particular, infusing its venom (propaganda) into America's and Western Civilization's "superstructure."[42] The People's Republic of China (The Chinese Communist Party— CCP) followed the Marxist cultural transforming path of Antonio Gramsci. And, following the "CCP," the Progressive Left is determined to employ Gramsci's pathology throughout American and Western Civilization.

ANTONIO GRAMSCI

"Socialism is precisely the religion that must overwhelm Christianity"
— Antonio Gramsci.

Antonio Gramsci (1891-1937), an Italian (Communist) Marxist, is a critical historical link between classical Marxism and the present-day infiltration of American and Western Civilization by Woke Critical Identity Marxism.

GRAMSCI'S "PRISON NOTEBOOKS"

Although Antonio Gramsci worked closely with Benito Mussolini for a season in 1926, he was, however, imprisoned by the Italian Fascist Government— (In the 1920s and '30s, Communists and Fascists were

[42] In relation to the Marxist "virus," the "superstructure" is religion, family, education, law, and the media. See Antonio Gramsci, the next subheading, under: "The Long March Through The Institutions."

ideological enemies). Gramsci was considered a threat to Mussolini's regime.

The prosecutor stressed that Antonio Gramsci should be sentenced to 20 years to "silence his mind." But Gramsci was released from prison in 1934 because of ill-health (he died 3 years after his release at the age of 46). While in prison, Gramsci's mind was not silenced, he copiously wrote, producing a voluminous collection of "Prison Notebooks." Gramsci's work was influential for the critical theorists in the Frankfurt School (Chapter 5), and likely, also the French postmodernists, e.g., Lyotard, Derrida, Baudrillard, Camus, etc.[43] Gramsci's notebooks were not published until 1948, and it was not until the 1970's that they were translated into French, German, and English.[44]

In his Prison Notebooks, Gramsci challenges classic Marxism— "Why have Marxist predictions of proletarian rebellion failed throughout Western Civilization? Why hasn't the Russian revolution of 1917 been repeated in Western European nations?"

Karl Marx argued that predetermined economic relations were the only "reality" underlying civil society. The political sphere was merely a part of the "superstructure," the ideologies that serve to justify the mode of production, those who own the mode of production, and the role of the disenfranchised laborers.[45] Marx's attention was therefore on class, not the superstructure of ideas.

---

[43] Jim Lindsay, Antonio Gramsci, Cultural Marxism, Wokeness, and Leninism 4.0.

[44] Robert S. Smith, "Cultural Marxism: Imaginary Conspiracy or Revolutionary Reality?" 442. (The translation into English of Gramsci's Notebooks was led by Joseph Buttigieg at Notre Dame University).

[45] Kevin Slack, Hillsdale College. "The American Left: From Liberalism to Despotism." Lecture 8: "Radicals March Through the Institutions." https://online.hillsdale.edu/courses/american-left. Downloaded: 03/11/2023.

Gramsci, however, viewed Marx's dialectic between "historical materialism" and "economic determinism" and the inevitability (predetermination) of a proletarian revolution as backwards. The implication of this profound observation is simply, "culture is not downstream from economics, but economics is downstream from culture."[46]

Gramsci's reversal of Marx's dialectic means, "... if you want to change the economic structure of society, you must first change the cultural institutions," the "superstructure" or ideologies "that socialize people into believing and behaving according to the dictates of the capitalist system."[47] How is such an undertaking to be accomplished? By Marxist's intellectuals creating a culture-war and infiltrating the foundations of Western Civilization, beginning with Judeo-Christian values— *"... unless and until Western Culture is dechristianized, Western society will never be decapitalized."*[48]

'THE LONG MARCH THROUGH THE INSTITUTIONS'

Gramsci believed in a two-staged revolution, in which there is, initially, a cultural revolution that demoralizes and weakens the civil sphere of culture beginning with religion— In Western Civilization, Judeo-Christian values and faith must be uprooted; then the family—The nuclear family is the primary domain of traditional values, morality, and social norms passed down through generations; then education, law, and media follow. Once the pillars of civil culture have been sufficiently weakened, a "hard revolution" (the

46 Robert S. Smith, "Cultural Marxism: Imaginary Conspiracy or Revolutionary Reality?" 442.

47 Ibid.

48 John Fulton, "Religion and Politics in Gramsci: An Introduction," *Sociological Analysis* 48 (1987): 197-216. Quoted in: Robert S. Smith, "Cultural Marxism: Imaginary Conspiracy or Revolutionary Reality?" 442.

second stage) overtakes the political sphere through, ideally, a "soft coup" but if that doesn't work, a forceful revolution must take place.

In the 1920's and into the 1940's, Chinese Marxists followed Gramsci's pathology and waged a two-stage cultural revolution. In the first stage, the civil culture of China (Gramsci's "superstructure")— religion, viz., Confucianism and Taoism, followed by the family, then education, law, and media were demoralized, and dismantled. The breaking down of Chinese culture involved the obliteration of the "four old's" — (1) "old values," (2) "old ideas," (3) "old customs," and (4) "old ways of thinking." [49] The "four old's" were replaced with Marxist's values, ideas, customs, and ways of thinking.

Through Marxist infiltration, China was divided into the Privileged/ Oppressors, the Hans were the majority population (91.6% of the population), and the Underprivileged/Oppressed, the non-Han minority groups consisted of Tibetans, Mongols, and Uyghurs (Tibet, Inner Mongolia, and Xinjiang).

Mao Zedong[50] was able to then take-over the political sphere— severely weaken by the breaking down of the civil sphere— and establish the People's Republic of China and lead it as the Chairman of the Chinese Communist Party from 1949 until his death in 1976.

GRAMSCI: THREE CRITICAL MARXIST THEORIES

First, Marx predicted in *Das Capital* that the working class would *inevitably* become conscious of the need to violently revolt against the supposed

49 Jim Lindsay, Antonio Gramsci, Cultural Marxism, Wokeness, and Leninism 4.0 https://www.youtube.com/watch?v=VdsSIWh_VkQ. Downloaded: 09/26/2022.

50 While the pinyin-derived spelling Mao Zedong is increasingly common, the Wade-Giles-derived spelling Mao Tse-tung is still used in modern publications.

machinations of capitalism. But Gramsci disagreed with the Marxist view of the predetermination of "historical materialism" and "economic determinism," proceeded by the inevitable awakening of the working class to their need to revolt.

Second, Gramsci "was among the first to understand that a 'successful' Marxist Revolution depended on the infiltration and demoralizing of key cultural institutions and the gradual changing of a society's values—A process that required a long-protracted culture war of attrition.[51]

Third, Gramsci's "Prison Notebooks" link aspects of Leninist style revolution[52]— viz., Lenin believed the Proletariats were *not* going to wake up by themselves (as Marx predicted), so they needed a group of elites, rich people within the Bourgeoisie who are deep into the ideology of Marxism, to "shepherd" the "working-class" through the Revolution.[53]

The theoretical need of a group of elites to "shepherd" the working class is seen as a legitimate need by Gramsci, but he would have rejected Lenin's brutality—*Changing a person's thinking about communism is much more permanent than attempting to beat them into submission to the communist vision.*

---

[51] Jefrey D. Breshears. *American Crisis, Cultural Marxism, and the Culture War: A Christian Response.* Centre Pointe Publishing, 2020.

[52] Re: "… aspects of the Leninist style revolution include Lenin and his Bolshevik contingent's argument that the ideas of Marx had to be cultivated and practiced by a professional revolutionary class that would shepherd the proletariat through the various stages of Marxism. Lenin and his Bolshevik Party believed that majority of the proletariat lacked the intellectual capability and foresight to guide the revolution through the various phases, as outlined by Marx. Therefore, Lenin built the Bolshevik wing of the Social Democratic Party as a professional revolutionary cadre that worked to foster and implement the proletarian revolution on behalf of and in conjunction with the workers of Russia and ultimately the world." Russian Revolution of 1917: The Essential Reference Guide Page xvii (18 of 298). https://publisher.abc-clio.com/9781440850936/18 Downloaded: 11/29/2022

[53] Re: Footnote #117.

CHAPTER 3

'UNDERSTANDING THE TIMES OF UNCERTAINTY IN WHICH WE LIVE'

"We are living in a country that has no resemblance to the vision of the founding fathers in the first two-hundred years of its history; we are losing that ability with tribal politics, wokeness and cancel culture"
—Victor Davis Hanson, Senior Fellow, Hoover Institution, Stanford, University.

Freedom of Speech is literally being "canceled" every day in multiplied Western cultural institutions from the corridors of academia to include every major public university, and high schools, middle schools, and elementary schools; and virtually all levels of governmental agencies, especially where diversity training takes place, and corporate life, where the gods of equity are continually sacrificed to. *Who or what exactly is behind all the craziness?*

MARXIST CRITICAL THEORY

The fiercest of the forces behind the "madness" is, "Woke Marxist Critical Theory."[54] Critical Theory is a Marxist technique used to evaluate the ways liberal societies fail to live up to their ideals, especially regarding how they continue to oppress certain underprivileged people groups. (The multi-sided, diverse techniques of Woke Marxist Critical Theory are diffused throughout Section 1 of this book. Whereas Woke Critical Theory is fully defined in Chapter 4, "The Frankfurt School," Chapter 2 introduced, by way of Gramsci's pathology, how Critical Theory works).

And "Woke," briefly introduced above, will also be a prominent feature of our culture's present social crisis as presented in Section 1, "The Woke Marxist Revolution." For now, a succinct definition will suffice: Woke refers to "the Underprivileged," who have been "awakened" to the cultural oppressive dominance of "the Privileged" and their consequent need to join the cultural revolution: The dismantling and replacing of America's Republic (i.e., America's alleged "oppressive hegemony") with a Woke Marxist Socialist State.

THE "HEGEMONY" OF "THE PRIVILEGED"

The "Cultural Hegemony" of the Privileged requires the Underprivileged to live under the power and control of their Oppressors.

[54] I am constrained to caution contemporary Western Christians to not concentrate on the Progressive Left as the "fiercest enemy," but the "principalities and powers" as revealed in Ephesians 6:10-18.

Woke Critical Theorists divide present-day Western Civilization[55]—e.g., Europe, North America, South America, e.g., countries with European heritage,[56] Australia, and New Zealand,[57] into two classes: The **Privileged/ Oppressors** and the **Underprivileged/Oppressed.**

The majority, e.g., heterosexuals, whites (especially males) are identified as the Privileged/Oppressors— If you are white, no matter how you were raised, no matter what you have, or don't have—You are inherently privileged.[58] And people who do not match these descriptions (particularly "White") are the Underprivileged/Oppressed—No matter your socio-economic standing, professional background, or educational achievements, you are inherently "Underprivileged."

In what ways does the "hegemony of the Privileged" oppress the "Underprivileged"? The Privileged are accused of oppressing the Underprivileged on three principal socio-cultural fronts: (1) "Dominant Discourses;" (2) "Whiteness;" and, "Capitalism."

---

55 Western civilization refers to the art, literature, culture, and enduring ideas that emerged from the eastern Mediterranean basin in the centuries before the common era, that developed in myriad forms through the Middle Ages, and that ultimately took modern shape after the Renaissance.

56 "European heritage" refers to South American countries influenced by European values through immigration and/or colonization.

57 David Rozado, "The Great Awokening As A Global Phenomenon," reports on the "prevalence of prejudice-denouncing terms and social justice associated terminology (diversity, inclusion, equality, etc) in over 98 million news and opinion articles across 124 popular news media outlets from 36 countries representing 6 different world regions: English-speaking West, continental Europe, Latin America, sub-Saharan Africa, Persian Gulf region and Asia." https://arxiv.org/ftp/arxiv/papers/2304/2304.01596.pdf. Downloaded: 07/07/2023.

58 Your politics (i.e., "left-wing") may make you underprivileged/oppressed.

DOMINANT DISCOURSES—THE PRIVILEGED OPPRESSORS

Who controls *access* to knowledge? Who controls *what* we think; and even *how* we think? In the cultural context of the West, knowledge is seen as socially constructed by the Privileged/Oppressors for their advantage— "*It is legitimized as knowledge by the powerful and this then becomes dominant discourses— The natural way of talking about things that is then perpetuated by everybody.*"[59] And thus, the Privileged *"are all complicit in maintaining these systems of oppressive power."*[60]

A prominent idea in Antonio Gramsci's *Notebooks* is "cultural hegemony." Cultural hegemony is the idea that cultural conformity requires everyone to be loyal to the ideologies of the dominant culture. And capturing the consciences of the "Oppressed" in the way of the thinking of the dominant culture's ideologies creates a "false consciousness" among the "Underprivileged," according to Gramsci.

A "false conscience," among the Underprivileged, then enables the Privileged to not only control access to knowledge, but also control *what* the Oppressed think and *how* they think—Dismantling the socially-constructed dominant discourses of the Privileged, and shifting all power imbalances away from the Oppressors is the expressed purpose of Woke Critical Theory's counter-cultural hegemony.

How are the consciousnesses of the Underprivileged conditioned in Western Culture, and particularly, the United States?

---

[59] Helen Pluckrose on confronting Critical Theory/Solutions with David Ansara Podcast #32. https://www.youtube.com/watch?v=xCMUa7pMA8/ Downloaded: 09/28/2022. Pluckrose's quote was "… we are all complicit." I inserted "the Privileged" to tell this story as the Underprivileged/Oppressed would tell it.

[60] Ibid. Helen Pluckrose's quote was "… we are all complicit." I inserted "the Privileged" to tell this story as the Underprivileged/Oppressed would tell it.

'WHITENESS'— WESTERN CIVILIZATION'S WOKE 'MATRIX'[61]

In his, *One Dimensional Man,* Neo-Marxist scholar, Herbert Marcuse contends that "white supremacy is an ideological manifestation of capitalism in the United States."[62] In Marcuse's *One-Dimensional Man* (1964) "white supremacy," and "capitalism" are both compared to the "proverbial grimness" of life under Stalin and his henchmen.

"Whiteness" is seen as representative of a flat epistemology ("epistemology" is a philosophical term for, *how we access reality*[63]) — And because flattened epistemologies are predetermined (according to Marxists), they "always progress towards the reproduction of capital and disallow critical engagement of the system."[64] "The Dominant" (The Privileged) thus place themselves above criticism.

And consequently, Woke Marxist Critical Theorists believe, "contemporary industrial society tends to be totalitarian"[65] — The "totalitarian" control of industrial society by white capitalists, in the thinking of Marcuse and Woke Marxists, is a means to Privileged hegemony.

Dolores Calderon's observation points to what is allegedly *unseen* by Whites: "Whiteness represents the normative practices and discourses upon which everything is measured, but this measurement is not an explicit

---

61 'MATRIX' is a reference to "The Matrix" released in 1999, starring Keanu Reeves. The Matrix is a computer simulation of the "realty" that Neo (Reeves character) is living in. The Matrix was created by an evil Artificial Intelligence (A.I.). In the thinking of the Underprivileged/Oppressed, the evil A.I. would be analogized to "Whiteness," i.e., the Privileged.

62 Herbert Marcuse. *One-Dimensional Man.* 2nd ed. Boston, MA: Beacon Press, 1991. (First published 1964). Quoted in: Dolores Calderon. "One Dimensionality and Whiteness." *Policy Futures in Education.* Volume 4, Number 1, 2006. 73.

63 Epistemology is commonly related to worldviews. And more specifically, epistemology has to do with both how we know and how we access truth.

64 D. Calderon, "One Dimensionality and Whiteness." 75.

65 H. Marcuse. *One-Dimensional Man.* 2-3. In Calderon, 75.

act. Rather, it remains an unseen, or invisible measure."[66] And because of its ascended (superior) invisibility, Professor Calderon further notes, "Whiteness silently pervades all sectors of life, both public and private."[67] "Whites" are incapable of "Wokeness"[68] because they are blinded by their privilege, and therefore, they not only resist cultural revolution, they also actively oppress the would-be revolutionaries, the Underprivileged.

Marcuse couples the ubiquity of "whiteness," as observed by Calderon, with capitalism: "Mass production and mass distribution claim the *entire* individual ... The result is, not adjustment but *mimesis*: an immediate identification of the individual with *his* society and, through it, with the society as a whole."[69] Marcuse's implications are made more explicit by Dolores Calderon in her remarks regarding Critical Theorists' view of the relationship between "white supremacy" and capitalism: "Whiteness, I argue, is the central organizing ideological component of advanced industrial society in the United States. It is not a static ideology, as it has shifted and been historically redefined to maintain the economic, political, and cultural advantages that whiteness has provided in the United States and globally."[70]

Woke Marxism attempts to counter "Whiteness" with Critical Theory—Critical Theory is a complex idea, but essentially, its aim is to unmask any ideology that seeks to falsely justify any form of social inequality, particularly involving class, race, gender, sex, and identity— *Critical*

---

66 Ibid.

67 Ibid.

68 The "Elites," the self-appointed—White— "shepherds" of the Underprivileged masses are exceptions, they are Woke. The "dictatorship of the proletariat" (White Elites) will be introduced in Chapter 3, "Where is History Going?" and Chapter 4, "Antonio Gramsci, The Woke Link." The "dictatorship of the proletariat" will be developed in Chapter 5, "The Frankfurt School— Neo-Marxism."

69 H. Marcuse. *One Dimensional Man.*

70 D. Calderon. "One Dimensionality and Whiteness." Endnote #1. 80

Theory's sights are fixed on the principal source of the Privileged hegemony in Western Civilization.

WESTERN CAPITALISM

"... unless and until Western Culture is de-Christianized, Western society will never be decapitalized."[71]

The Oppressor's hegemony creates "systems of oppression," viz., capitalism—Capitalism is rooted in the class order and thus it "maintains privilege" through an oppressive false conscience founded on "Whiteness" and Judeo-Christian (traditional) values which empowers the resistance of the Middle Class to the Marxist Socialist State (the prelude to communism) and thus, the ultimate ascendency of the Underprivileged in the thinking of Critical Race theorists.[72]

Capitalism is therefore a racist construct— Ibram X. Kendi proclaims, "*In order to truly be antiracist, you also have to truly be anti-capitalist.*"[73] Kendi explains that over the course of American history, there has been racial inequality—The establishment of slavery was from America's beginning. And "the origins of racism cannot be separated from the origins of capitalism, the life of racism cannot be separated from the life of capitalism— When you think about the slave trade, which was critical to the

[71] John Fulton, "Religion and Politics in Gramsci: An Introduction," *Sociological Analysis* 48 (1987): 197-216. Quoted in: Robert S. Smith, "Cultural Marxism: Imaginary Conspiracy or Revolutionary Reality?" 442.

[72] Critical Race Theory is the subject of Chapter 6.

[73] Quoted by Christopher F. Rufo, *Primus* Ibid. 3 of 7 pages.

accumulation of wealth in Europe, that was fundamentally a set of racist policies."[74]

If capitalism is intended to maximize profit, its operation inherently divides workers and extracts labor from communities of color, including enslaved people, indigenous people, and immigrants. Therefore, if you think of capitalism as "racial capitalism," then the outcome is you cannot eliminate capitalism without the complete destruction of white supremacy.[75]

The "totalitarian control," i.e., the "white supremacist dominance" of industrial society, in the thinking of Woke Marxists, anchors the Privileged hegemony. "Identity Politics," or "Marxist Identity," is therefore critical for both the definition and preservation of Black authenticity through diversity and segregation.

THE PRIVILEGED SUFFER FROM PHOBIC DISORDERS

According to Woke Critical Theorists, the Oppressors suffer from a variety of forms of subconscious sicknesses, i.e., phobias, that drives them to use their control of access to knowledge to oppress the Underprivileged for the sustaining of their cultural hegemony.

Therefore, Woke Social Justice activists' adjudication of their demoralizing "justice" involving the Privileged is, in their thinking, wholly legitimate. For example, if a resident in London is uncomfortable with a growing, isolated, thoroughly unassimilated Muslim community replacing

---

74 Ibram X. Kendi. "Antiracism, Anticapitalism, and the Eugenicist Origins of IQ & SAT Tests." Democracy Now! https://www.youtube.com/watch?v=_oQXki0hG9w. Downloaded: 04/12/2024.

75 Robin D.G. Kelley, "The Rebellion Against Racial Capitalism," interviewed by Jeremy Scahill, *The Intercept* (2020).

his or her neighborhood, they are accused (by Woke Social Justice counter-hegemonic activists) of being "Islamophobic." However, because the Muslims residing in the isolated, thoroughly Islamic, and unassimilated community, are included among the oppressed, they are then celebrated for their "multiculturalism."[76]

What is the origin of these "phobias" that drive the Privileged to oppress the Underprivileged? Angelo Codevilla shares an abbreviated explanation employed by Social Justice activists: "Beginning in the 1960's, from Boston to Berkely, the teachers of America's teachers absorbed and taught a new Cliff Notes style of sacred history: America was born tainted by Western Civilization's original sins— racism, sexism, greed, genocide against natives and the environment, all wrapped in religious obscurantism, and on the basis of hypocritical promises of freedom and equality"[77] — From the Woke Marxists' perspective, the phobic-ridden thinking of the Privileged merely reflects "society's basic structure."[78]

Any point of view that differs from Critical Theory's "Cliff Notes" is quickly dismissed as a "phobia." And if a member of the privileged demographic denies that they are oppressive towards anyone identified as a member of the underprivileged demographic, they are simply censored or

[76] Whereas *sociological* multiculturalism is at the heart of America's idea of citizenship and exceptionalism, i.e., America as a "melting pot," "From Many One" — *E Pluribus Unum, Ideological multiculturalism* is different; it asserts that all cultures and nations on earth are morally equivalent to American culture— *E Pluribus Unum* is fast becoming obsolete and with it, America's idea of citizenship and exceptionalism.

[77] Angelo M. Codevilla. "The Rise of Political Correctness." Originally published in *Claremont Review of Books,* November 8, 2016. Page 9 of 12 pages. https://claremontreviewofbooks.com/the-rise-of-political-correctness/. Downloaded: 09/30/2022.

[78] My quote is only a partial of Codevilla's point. Codevilla's full statement not only mentioned how progressive's reason, but it concludes by asserting that, "… *reality* forces *progressives* to admit that individuals often choose how they think or act despite lacking the 'structural' basis for doing so, or that they act contrary to the economic, social, or racial 'classes' into which progressive theories divide mankind."

"canceled"[79] because they suffer from a form of mental delusion brought on by at least one of many phobias. Therefore, in the thinking of Woke Marxists, they are justified in their censoring of any view expressed in opposition to Critical Theory by the Privileged.

Woke Marxism's counter-hegemony calls for the replacing of the present order of the Privileged cultural hegemony with "a new historical reality"[80] — "New ways of thinking and speaking" constitute "a new language."[81] Language "is the key to the mastery of consciousness— a mastery more secure than anything that force alone can achieve."[82]

[79] "Cancel Culture" refers to a celebrity or public figure being culturally blocked from a prominent public platform or career. A familiar pattern involves a celebrity or public figure doing or saying something offensive. A public backlash, often provoked by political progressive social media. "Then voices cry out to cancel the person, that is, to effectively end their career or revoke their cultural cachet, whether through boycotts of their work or disciplinary action from an employer." Re: VOX.COM - "Why we can't stop fighting about cancel culture. Is cancel culture a mob mentality, or a long overdue way of speaking truth to power?" By Aja Romano@ajaromano. Updated Aug 25, 2020. https://www.vox.com/culture/2019/12/30/20879720/what-is-cancel-culture-explained-history-debate.

[80] Angelo M. Codevilla. "The Rise of Political Correctness." Page 5 of 12 pages. I have extracted descriptions of political correctness from Codevilla's statements involving Gramsci and his application of Machiavelli's *The Prince* (Chapter V) to revolution and counter-cultural hegemony. (Gramsci was an Italian Communist who is the historical link between Karl Marx and contemporary Woke Identity Marxism).

[81] Ibid.

[82] Ibid.

'WOKE' POLITICAL CORRECTNESS— "NEW REALITIES"

The Woke Marxist revolution is, for many, simply "the unveiling of a clown world," but beneath the surface, it is sinister— Wokeness[83] is a "conscience raising" awareness of racial, gender, and identity issues — Critical Theory Wokeness has infiltrated and infected every layer of Western Culture— e.g., religion, family, education, law, and media— with the intent of disrupting and dismantling "bourgeois morality," that is, traditional Western Christian values and creating "new realities," i.e., new language and consequent new ways of thinking.

Towards Critical Theory's cynical ends, Woke shaped identity politics are endlessly promoted contrary to Western traditional values, ideas, customs, and ways of thinking— Marxist Identity values, ideas, customs, and ways of thinking have gone "crazy viral" resulting in the unbounded "progressive"[84] transformation of the Western conscience.

"Political Correctness," Critical Theory's propaganda organ, is effective in "persuading"—i.e., *inducing*[85] —"people who had never thought of such things to join in ways of life radically different from their own."[86] And "when it happens that the founders of the new religion speak a different

---

83 Woke Critical Theory's culturally destructive cache of theories is used in its assault on western culture, e.g., "The Frankfurt School of Critical Theory," is the subject of Chapter 5 and Critical Race Theory, Intersectionality and Standpoint Theory is discussed in Chapter 6. Critical Theory's Diversity, Equity, and Inclusion will be discussed more thoroughly in Chapter 7. For an outstanding study of Critical Theories, see: Helen Pluckrose & James Lindsay. *Cynical Theories, How Activist Scholarship Made Everything about Race, Gender, and Identity— and Why This harms Everybody.* Durham, NC: Pitchstone Publishing, 2020.

84 See: Mona Charen. (Nationally Syndicated Columnist). *Useful Idiots, How Liberals Got It Wrong in the Cold War and Still Blame America First.* Washington D.C.: Regnery Publishing, Inc. 2003.

85 Italics are mine.

86 Angelo M. Codevilla. "The Rise of Political Correctness." Page 5 of 12 pages.

language, the destruction of the old religion is easily effected"[87] — Critical Theory's effective use of political correctness to create "new historical realities" serves to delegitimize and dismantle the West's traditional values, that is, Judeo-Christian values, and consequently, the basic structural support of the pillars of Western Civilization: religion, family, education, law, and media.

IDENTITY POLITICS— 'WOKE DIGNITY'

Ancient Rome originated with three distinct ethnic groups. The Latin term "tribus" referred to these diverse ethnic groups— "Tribalism" is a derivative of *tribus*— Tribalism differentiated groups of people by their ethnicity and race.[88] In modern, Western Civilization, tribalism has morphed into Identity Politics/Critical Diversity.

Identity Politics is fundamentally opposed to the dream of Martin Luther King Jr. and the Civil Rights Movement that advocated people ought to be judged by "the content of their character" instead of by the color of their skin —The Civil Rights Movement was centered in humanity's universal unity and therefore, integration, assimilation, and equality were foundational.

Woke Critical Theory rejects notions of humanity's universal unity,[89] and instead, Woke Identity Politics are anchored in race, ethnicity, and gender as essential to a person's identity, instead of incidental to who

---

87 Machiavelli. *Discourses on Livy.* Book II, Chapter 5— "The Rise of Political Correctness, Ibid.

88 Victor Davis Hanson. "American Citizenship And Its Decline." Lecture 5— The Rise of Tribal Politics. https://online.hillsdale.edu/courses/american-citizenship-and-its-decline. Downloaded: 12/08/2022.

89 Universal Unity and its integral role in the Declaration of Independence will be discussed further in Chapter 6, Critical Race Theory.

they are. For example, Woke "gender politics" expands the definition of "woman" to be inclusive of those who identify as transgender. The newly revised Cambridge Dictionary now states that the term, "woman" describes "an adult who lives and identifies as female, though they may have been said to have a different sex at birth."[90] And likewise, man is defined as "an adult who lives and identifies as male, though they may have been said to have a different sex at birth."

Gender Identity is not sequestered to the halls of elite universities to be debated, to the contrary, they are very much cultural mainstream—Gender/Identity politics were front and center in the nomination process of Supreme Court Justice, Judge Ketanji Brown Jackson.

WHAT IS 'WOMAN'?

POLITICO's, Myah Ward covered Judge Ketanji Brown Jackson's Supreme Court Nomination. Ward's article is entitled, "Blackburn to Jackson: Can You Define 'The Word Woman?'"[91]

"Can you define the word woman"? Really? Is the definition of "woman" so controversial that a Supreme Court nominee, a celebrated female jurist, was asked what a woman is?! The spectacle that followed was confusing, astonishing, and shocking but, never-the-less, typically Woke.

As the confirmation hearing approached the 13th hour, Senator Marsha Blackburn (TN Republican) asked Judge Ketanji Brown Jackson to define

---

90 Tre' Goins-Phillips. "Cambridge Dictionary Bows to 'Woke Activists,' Changes Definition of 'Woman.'" 12/14/2022. https://www1.cbn.com/cbnnews/us/2022/december/cambridge-dictionary-bows-to-lsquo-woke-activists-rsquo-changes-definition-of-lsquo-woman-rsquo Downloaded: 12/15/2022.

91 Myah Ward. POLITICO. "Blackburn to Jackson: Can You Define 'The Word Woman?' 03/2022. https://www.politico.com/news/2022/03/22/blackburn-jackson-define-the-word-woman-00019543. Downloaded: 09/14/2022.

the word "woman." "I can't —" replied Judge Jackson. "You can't?" the Senator queried. "Not in this context. I'm not a biologist," said the honorable Jurist. "The meaning of the word woman is so unclear and controversial that you can't give me a definition?" — asked the Senator.

The Tennessee Senator's line of questioning nailed nearly every current controversial, politically correct issue, from Critical Race Theory to teaching children about gender identity in schools to Lia Thomas, a transgender swimmer on the University of Pennsylvania's women's swim team.[92]

The Supreme Court justice nominee attempted a defense by stating that her role as a judge would be to address disputes about a definition and to interpret the law. The Senator countered: "The fact that you can't give me a straight answer about something as fundamental as what a woman is underscores the dangers of the kind of progressive education that we are hearing about," Blackburn said, before turning to Lia Thomas, who has been at the center of the debate over policies for transgender athletes.

Senator Blackburn asked what message allowing Thomas to compete is sent to "girls who aspire to compete and win in sports?" "Senator, I'm not sure what message that sends; If you're asking me about the legal issues related to it, those are topics that are being hotly discussed, as you say, and could come to the court," Jackson said. Blackburn countered: "I think it tells our girls that their voices don't matter; I think it tells them that they're second-class citizens."

Critical Theory Wokeness' *moral subjectivity* lowers the status of girls in general, and the University of Pennsylvania women athletes in particular, to a far more diminutive status than "second-class citizens" —*Critical*

---

92 Ibid.

Theory's moral subjectivism is dehumanizing.[93] But under the persuasion of cult-like methods of psychological programming, i.e., "political correctness," many are rendered incapable of perceiving the deluding, dehumanizing effects of Woke— *Party ideology then replaces objective reality for those under the spell of Woke.*

Chapter 4 introduces the "dialectics" of Georj F.W. Hegel and Karl Marx. Whereas this chapter's content is less engaging than most of the chapters in this book, it is needed to prepare the reader for select chapters in the book (especially, 5-9) that relate to one's understanding of "Far Left Progressivism" as a "Woke Marxist equivalent to the "Party," and/or "the Ruling Elites."

---

93 C.S. Lewis' thought, regarding the dehumanizing effects of moral subjectivity is a principal theme in Section II, Chapter 9, "Woke Moral Subjectivity & 'The Abolition of Man.'"

CHAPTER 4

THE DIALECTICS OF GEORJ F.W. HEGEL & KARL MARX

A basic understanding of the dialectics of Hegel and Marx is critical for our understanding of contemporary Woke Marxism. [94]

A dialectic is when two seemingly conflicting things are true at the same time. For example, a Minnesotan informs a Californian that it snows in Springtime. The thesis, "in Minnesota it snows," is antithetical to "snows in Springtime," in the mind of the Californian. The synthesis, however, of the thesis and the antitheses does not negate the thesis, it elevates it— It may not snow in California in the Springtime, but there is a capacity for snow in the Springtime in Minnesota. The dialogue between the Minnesotan and the Californian introduces an elementary understanding of "dialectics."

94 Fundamentally, dialectics view nature as a connected whole. The Marxist Project. "Fundamentals of Marx: Dialectics." https://www.youtube.com/watch?v=GNHzVeC7jeY. Downloaded: 11/28/2022/.

Dialectics are generally understood as the collision of a thesis and an antithesis resulting in the forming of a new idea, i.e., the synthesis. The synthesis then becomes a new thesis which is opposed by an antithesis, and through that confrontation, another synthesis is formed which becomes a thesis that is confronted by an anthesis, and another synthesis is formed— The calculus of dialectics is, theoretically, *ad infinitum.* This is made clear in the idealistic dialectics of the Prussian philosopher, Georg F.W. Hegel.[95]

GEORG WILHELM-FRIEDRICH HEGEL'S DIALECTIC

Georg Wilhelm Friedrich Hegel (1770-1831) was born in Stuttgart, Germany, a city situated in a geographic context described as the "… cradle of more thinkers and poets than any other German region."[96] And, at least in terms of enduring philosophical influence, Hegel ascended all of them with his rare intellect and imagination. The preeminent philosopher's imagination is reflected in his dialectic of progressive history and final consummation in the "Absolute Idea."

HEGEL'S IDEALISM

Understanding Hegel's dialectic requires a preliminary introduction to three dynamically related concepts— First, *Geist* (spirit), second, *truth as process,* and third, *dialectic.* While a professor at the University of Jena (1801-1806), Hegel's highly acclaimed academic career reached a zenith

---

95 David Guignion. What is the Dialectic? | Plato, Kant, Hegel, Marx | Keyword https://www.youtube.com/watch?v=RY_rGJUpwsM. Downloaded: 11/28/2022.

96 Carl J. Friedrich, Introduction, in G.W.F. Hegel. *The Philosophy of Hegel,* ed. Carl J. Friedrich. New York, NY: Random House, 1954, xiv. Quoted in: Stanley J. Grenz & Roger E. Olson. *20th— Century Theology, God & the World in a Transitional Age,* 32.

when he began to reflect on the first of these concepts, *Geist* (spirit), a cornerstone notion towards the development of his philosophy. *Geist* is translated as "spirit" in English. But English fails to capture the whole meaning of the German term, *Geist.* Grenz and Olson explain: "It combines the concept of rationality reflected in the word *mind* with the dimension of the super-material bound up with *spirit.*"[97]

Thus, "Spirit," in Hegel's thought, *does not* relate to the third Member of the Holy Trinity, but rather it relates to a process, it is an "active subject."[98] Grenz and Olson provide clarity: "Although present in humans, it is not to be equated with the human spirit, for it is the inner being of the world, the Absolute, even the sole Reality."[99] The "Spirit" then, though in humans, transcends humans, "for the world process is the activity of the Spirit" — "Hence, Hegel viewed all processes in nature and history as forming a unified whole and as the manifestation of a spiritual principle underlying them."[100]

Secondly is "truth as process" — "Truth" is not a rational conclusion in Hegel's philosophy, but rather, "truth is the process itself." And when linked with the historical process, the "Spirit comes to self-awareness" — For Hegel, this is reality.

Regarding Hegel's dialectic, Grenz and Olson observe that, "The different epochs in human history are the stages through which Spirit passes enroute to self-discovery."[101] Truth, then, is history as revealed in the dynamic of the historical process (i.e. "the activity of the Spirit") which

---

[97] Stanley J. Grenz & Roger E. Olson. *20th— Century Theology, God & the World in a Transitional Age.* 33.

[98] Ibid.

[99] Ibid.

[100] Ibid— (Paraphrase).

[101] Georg Hegel. *Phenomenology of Mind.* Translated by J.B. Baillie. New York: Harper and Row, 1967. 807-808. In Grenz and Olson, Ibid., 34.

involves an unrelenting conflict between differing paradigms— "In each stage, the preceding stage is carried into the next as its foundation, but it is also negated."[102] In other words, "First a thesis arises. This immediately generates its antithesis"[103] —The historical process then involves thesis and antithesis continually opposing one another until a superior more accurate synthesis finally results from the conflict. The resulting synthesis then generates an antithesis, and the process is repeated unceasingly, until ultimately Hegel's understanding of reality emerges in the "Spirit's self-awareness," or the "Absolute Idea."[104] In Hegel's philosophical thought, the "Absolute Idea" — Reality— would be finally reached.[105]

Alasdair Elder observes that for, "Hegel, there was no distinction between the phenomenological and the numinous; reality was constructed and shaped by the mind. From Hegel onwards, philosophers started to think in terms of progress rather than in terms of individual minds."[106] Hegel's philosophical thought conceived a "sagacious methodology for appraising individual consciousness and personal freedom; personal freedom was perforce the freedom of socialized beings, so the development of personal freedom took the form of progressive societal states."[107] "Progressive societal states" presuppose a primitive state of consciousness among human beings, a notion, or hypotheses, that contained "at least a kernel of truth." And "based on these hypotheses, a particular social structure would be put in place that created two classes of people; masters and servants."[108]

---

[102] Ibid. 34

[103] Ibid. 35

[104] Hegel's philosophy laid the foundation for theological studies at his alma mater, the University of Tubingen.

[105] Alasdair Elder. *The Red Trojan Horse, A Concise Analysis of Cultural Marxism.* 18.

[106] Ibid. 19.

[107] Ibid. 19-20.

[108] Ibid. 20.

Hegel observed that the structure of ancient economies, e.g., Persians, Greeks, and Romans, required a mass number of slaves to maintain the economy. But eventually, feudalism replaced slavery and although peasants were not owned by their masters, they were still tethered to their master's land. Eventually, feudalism gave way to capitalism and with it, the right to private property ownership brought economic freedom. This process is for Hegel, the master-slave dialect.[109]

Hegelian thought, though antithetical to a Christian understanding of "Providence,"[110] nonetheless, stood as a philosophical stronghold in the world for almost three centuries.[111] The most prominent *misrepresentation* of Hegelian philosophy in world history is Karl Marx.

KARL MARX'S DIALECTIC

Although Karl Marx was a student of Hegelian philosophy, his dialectic contrasts with Hegel's *idealism*— "which regarded matter as dependent upon mind and history as the progressive self-realization of an absolute Mind." Marx's dialectic proposal is referred to as "dialectical materialism" — matter was primary, and change was inherent in the evolution of material reality.

---

109 Ibid.

110 In theological categories, God's sovereign providence essentially means: (1) God sees *all* things throughout the expanse of His creation, visible and invisible (e.g., Absolutely all parts of His creation, to include every thought that passes through the mind of every person, every moment, of every day, until their final thought before death); and (2) All that God sees, He sustains, He holds together; and (3) All that God sustains, He governs towards the ultimate end of human history (which is, "His-Story") to the New Heavens and the New Earth under the sovereign, eternal reign of the Son, Jesus Christ— Jesus Christ is the Alpha and the Omega of all that is (Jn. 1:3/Col. 1:17).

111 Though Hegel maintained that his "constantly alternating dialectic system would reach a final point of true knowledge," knowledge was always in a progressive flux, and therefore, history was unable to deliver absolute philosophical truth. Ibid. 19.

Marx's dialectic "turned Hegel upside-down;" but in his understanding, Marx turned Hegel "right side up":

> My dialectic method is not only different from the Hegelian, but is its direct opposite .... With me..., the ideal is nothing else than the material world reflected by the human mind, and translated into forms of thought... With him it is standing on its head. It must be turned right side up again if you would discover the rational kernel within the mystical shell.[112]

MARXIST MATERIALISM

Two factors shaped Karl Marx's (1818-1883) interest in economic theory. First, his exposure to the communist movement in Paris resulted in Marx's life-long relationship with, Friedrich Engels (1820-1895) and secondly, Marx began to see the fundamental human problem as consisting of oppression and alienation— "Oppression is a consequence of living in a society of stratified classes, an arrangement exacerbated by the exploitation inherent in capitalism."[113]

The class system— in Marxist thinking— has always created deep division between the "haves" and the "have-nots." However, the Marxist dialectic points to ultimate "hope" for the "have nots" — The Marxist dialectic presupposes Darwinian evolution and therefore, it begins with

[112] Karl Marx. "Afterword to the Second German Edition," in *Das Kapital* (1873), in *Capital: A Critique of Political Economy: Volume One.* Translated by Ben Fowkes. London: Penguin, 1976. Pp. 102-103. Quoted in: Robert S. Smith, "Cultural Marxism: Imaginary Conspiracy or Revolutionary Reality?" 438.

[113] Robert S. Smith, "Cultural Marxism: Imaginary Conspiracy or Revolutionary Reality?" 438.

matter, founded on the twin forces of "historical materialism" (Marx's thesis) and "economic determinism" (Marx's antithesis) — And the syntheses created by the merging of historical materialism and economic determinism will inevitably replace capitalism with a classless utopian society. This view infers "that the transition from capitalism to communism would be unstoppable due to the natural 'evolution of the material forces of production.'"[114] This is the consummation— the ultimate synthesis— of the Marxist dialectic.

The "private ownership of the means of production"[115] is finally put to death by the proletariat as workers unite and rise to oppose and overthrow their evil oppressors, the greedy capitalists — *The proletariat revolution results in the obliteration of "the evil bourgeoise"[116] capitalists.* And as the curtain closes on history, the struggle of the proletariat ends in the emergence of a new, classless society— "Marxism is a secularized vision of the kingdom of God," observes Klaus Bockmuehl, "It is the kingdom of man."[117]

The *inevitable* classless society— the "kingdom of man" — was the foundation for Marx's "unshakeable" predictions, "that social revolutions would first take place in the most advanced capitalist nations (Britain, America and France)" — *But they have not.* Instead, revolutions have taken place in under-developed (third world) regions of the world—Eastern Europe, Asia, and Africa.[118]

The Marxist Communist vision is founded on *pseudo-reality*— i.e., the idea that historic materialism and economic determinism are *predetermined.*

---

[114] Ibid. 439.

[115] Ibid.

[116] Ibid.

[117] Ibid. — (Marxist Communism's synthesis is the vision of "The Tower of Babel" — Gen. 11:1-9).

[118] Leszek Kolakowski. "What is Left of Socialism?" October 2002. *First Things. https://www.firstthings.com/article/2002/10/what-is-left-of-socialism.*

The Communist vision has failed to produce any classless societies under the rule of former "Proletarians." Instead, revolution after revolution has left breath-taking carnage (100 million dead) and mind-numbing destruction in its wake.[119]

THE MARXIST DIALECTIC AND COMMUNISM

The Marxist dialectic's synthesis results in an unstable, binary society of rich and poor, oppressor and oppressed, exploiter and exploited, victimizer and victimized.[120] There is no middle class, only a wealthy upper, privileged class, and a poor, lower, underprivileged class— Binary societies are 3rd world socialist/communist societies.

Thomas Sowell has wisely observed: "The history of the 20th century is full of examples of countries that set out to redistribute wealth and ended up redistributing poverty."[121] Sowell brings fuller enlightenment by explaining why countries end up redistributing poverty: "You can only confiscate the wealth that exists at a given moment. You cannot confiscate future wealth— and that future wealth is less likely to be produced when people see that it will be confiscated."[122]

In 3rd world socialist/communist societies, political power is centralized in the state— In a totalitarian regime, there is no private property ownership; the state regulates or owns all means of production, the distribution

---

[119] Robert S. Smith, "Cultural Marxism: Imaginary Conspiracy or Revolutionary Reality?" https://www.thegospelcoalition.org/themelios/article/cultural-marxism-imaginary-conspiracy-or-revolutionary-reality/. Downloaded: 2022. 439.

[120] Victor Davis Hanson. *American Citizenship and Its Decline.* Lecture 3: "The Disappearing Middle Class." https://online.hillsdale.edu/courses/american-citizenship-and-its-decline. Downloaded: 11/28/2022.

[121] Jefrey D. Breshears. *American Crisis, Cultural Marxism and The Culture War: A Christian Response.* P. 205.

[122] Ibid.

of goods and services, and the redistribution of wealth "in keeping with the left-wing ideals of 'social justice' and 'equality.'"[123]

"REVOLUTIONARY TERROR"

"... there is only one way in which the murderous death agonies of the old society and the bloody birth throes of the new society can be shortened, simplified and concentrated, and that way is revolutionary terror"
— Marx and Engels.

Marx's call for violent revolution stands out in bold relief in the closing of *The Communist Manifesto:* "The Communists disdain [the concealing] of their views and aims. They openly declare that their ends can be attained only by the forcible overthrowing of all existing social conditions. Let the ruling classes tremble at a Communistic revolution. The proletarians have nothing to lose but their Chains. They have a world to win. 'WORKING MEN OF ALL COUNTRIES, UNITE!'"[124]

From "the time of revolutionary terror" and the dawn of the utopian classless society, "a transitional government of the working class" — "the dictatorship of the proletariat," will need to lead.[125] For Lenin's Soviet regime, the ascendance of "the dictatorship of the proletariat" was commenced by "destroying nearly all churches, killing nearly all priests, punishing even the hint of dissent, as well as by making rejection of bourgeois cul-

---

123 Ibid. P. 199.

124 Marx and Engels. *The Communist Manifesto,* 39. Quoted in: Robert S. Smith, "Cultural Marxism: Imaginary Conspiracy or Revolutionary Reality?" 439.

125 Karl Marx. "The Victory of the Counter-Revolution in Vienna." *Neue Rheinische Zeitung,* 136. November 1848, https:///www.marxists.org/archive/marx/works/1848/11/06.htm. Quoted in: Robert S. Smith, "Cultural Marxism: Imaginary Conspiracy or Revolutionary Reality?" 439.

ture a condition for ascending to the ruling class" — Lenin "succeeded in pushing the old culture to near destruction."[126] The consequence of Lenin's terror included the destruction of "the very basis of Soviet power."[127]

REINFORCING THE PARTY'S IDENITY

Why would ruthless communist dictators spare some churches and some priests? For the pleasure of taking "young cadres" to church services to observe and mock the poor, elderly, "socially repulsive" disenfranchised outcasts— "In part, because each smiting of cultural enemies reinforced the cadre's identity. It made them feel better about themselves, and more powerful. Had there been no remnants of the old society, or dissidents, the party might have manufactured them."[128]

What does Marxist Communism have to do with "wokeness" in contemporary America and Western Civilization?

---

[126] Angelo M. Codevilla. "The Rise of Political Correctness." 3 of 12 pages.

[127] Ibid.

[128] Ibid.

CHAPTER 5

THE FRANKFURT SCHOOL OF MARXIST IDENTITY CRITICAL THEORY

"The history of all hitherto existing societies is the history of class struggles .... [In] a word, oppressor and oppressed, stood in constant opposition to one another .... Hitherto, every form of society has been based ... on the antagonism of oppressing and oppressed classes"
— Karl Marx, *Communist Manifesto.*

Classical Marxism is defined by class conflict, the struggle between the bourgeoisie and the proletariat, the "haves" and the "have nots." Contemporary Neo-Marxism (Woke Identity Marxism) is defined by social conflict, the struggle between the Oppressors and the Oppressed; those who are privileged and those who are not.

Marx believed that the awakening of "class consciousness" among the working class was predetermined— the working class would inevitably revolt and overthrow their oppressors, the bourgeois capitalists. And the Proletariat would then create a dictatorship and establish socialism as the next stage of history on their way to a classless, perfected society—Communism was the predetermined end of history.

Like Marx, Neo-Marxists believe in the ultimate failure of capitalism—capitalism is a transitional stage in history's progress. But contrary to Marx (and like Lenin) Neo Marxists *do not* believe the Underprivileged will rise-up and revolt against their Oppressors on their own, instead, "between the time of revolutionary terror" and the *reality* of a communist utopia (a classless society) they will require a "dictatorship of the proletariat,"[129] that is, "a transitional government of the working class"[130] to "shepherd" them through the Revolution.

Instead of Lenin's brutality, Neo-Marxists subscribe to Gramsci's two-staged revolution beginning, initially, with a "counter-hegemony" (or cultural revolution) that demoralizes and collapses the civil sphere of culture— e.g., religion, family, education, law, and media. And the destabilizing and inevitable toppling of the political sphere will follow—*Antonio Gramsci's historic bloc, the transforming of America's Democratic Republic into a Marxist Socialist State, will emerge for an indeterminate period of history until it gives way to the perfected classless society of Communism.* [131]

---

[129] Robert S. Smith, "Cultural Marxism: Imaginary Conspiracy or Revolutionary Reality?" 439. Please note, in his article, Robert S. Smith references Karl Marx, "The Victory of the Counter-Revolution in Vienna," *Neue Rheinische Zeitung,* 136 (November 1848, http://www.marxists.org/archive/marx/works/1848/11/06.htm for the purpose of providing context for his remarks relating to revolutionary terror. The author's quoting of short phrases is primarily for the purpose of documenting the use of a "dictatorship of the proletariat" in the context of a "transitional government." Robert Smith further footnotes (#9, 439) a clarification regarding Marx's use of the phrase, "dictatorship of the proletariat" as a reference by Marx to "socialism" — See "The Class Struggles in France, 1848-1850" (1895) in *Karl Marx and Friedrich Engels: Selected Works* (Moscow: Progress Publishers, 1969), 1:139-242.

[130] Ibid.

[131] The term "socialist state" is widely used by Marxist–Leninist parties, theorists, and governments to mean a state under the control of a vanguard party that is organizing the economic, social, and political affairs of said state toward the construction of socialism. *Marxists often refer to socialism as the first, necessary phase on the way from capitalism to communism.*

THE FRANKFURT SCHOOL— HISTORICAL OVERVIEW

Critical Theory is not simply a theory it is a school of thought— The Frankfurt School of Critical Theory is a philosophical/sociological movement influencing many universities around the world.[132] The school was founded in 1923 as the Institute for Social Research (*Institut für Sozialforschung*).[133] On June 22, 1924, the Institute officially opened at Victoria Allée 17 in Frankfurt am Main.[134] (An endowment from Hermann Weil financed the opening of the ISR).[135]

The Institute was attached to Goethe University in Frankfurt, Germany. The school's aim was the development of Marxist studies in Germany. Not long after its founding, the Institute for Social Research was formally acknowledged by the Ministry of Education as an entity attached to Goethe University in Frankfurt, Germany.[136]

Carl Grünberg (1923-1929) was the Institute's first director. Grünberg's celebrated contribution to the Institute was the "Archive for the History of Socialism and the Labor Movement." In 1930, Max Horkheimer

---

132 Internet Encyclopedia of Philosophy—A Peer-Reviewed Academic Resource. "The Frankfurt School and Critical Theory." https://iep.utm.edu/critical-theory-frankfurt-school/. Downloaded: 11/01/2022. https://www.google.com/search?q=the+-frankfurt+school+of+critical+theory&sxsrf=ALiCzsYltsstivSeHVy0kvHjJ1K7j6U-jtw%3A1667079082695&source=hp&ei=qptdY_DkJ_Gt0PEPmP6DAs&iflsig=A-JiK0e8AAAAAY12pupzFRk6my0VnLcd1TiIKecrdDt7R&oq=Th (See this fuller presentation of the history of the Frankfurt School).

133 The Bolshevik Revolution in Moscow in 1917 led to the founding of the Institute for Social Research. Lenin died in 1924.

134 Stuart Jeffries' *Grand Hotel Abyss: The Lives of the Frankfurt School.* The Frankfurt School: A Timeline. September 29, 2017. https://www.versobooks.com/blogs/2844-the-frankfurt-school-a-timeline. Downloaded: 11/04/2022.

135 In the same year, Frankfurt elected its first Jewish mayor. The city was renowned as the headquarters of the world's largest chemicals conglomerate IG Farben, which would later develop Zyklon B, the cyanide-based killing agent used in Nazi concentration camp gas chambers to murder Jews. Ibid.

136 Internet Encyclopedia of Philosophy—A Peer-Reviewed Academic Resource. "The Frankfurt School and Critical Theory."

succeeded Grünberg. Horkheimer determined that the Institute's mission would concentrate on a Marxist interpretation of the "interdisciplinary integration of the social sciences."[137] As directed by Horkheimer, the school studied horoscopes, movies, jazz, sexual repression, the sado-masochistic impulses at the heart of fascism, and the reconfiguration of Marxist theory as inspired by the publication in the early 1930s of Marx's early Economic and Philosophical Manuscripts.[138] Further, under Horkheimer's direction, psychoanalysis was made a critical part of the school's academic foundation.

Eric Fromm (1900-1980) significantly advanced the academic discipline of psycho- analysis at the school. Fromm's aim involved a synthesis of Marxism and psychoanalysis—Fromm was seeking "the missing link between ideological superstructure [e.g., religion, family, education, law, and media] and socio-economic base" —i.e., capitalism.[139] The school's interest in psychoanalysis, particularly, Freud's instinct theory, was a preoccupation in the works of both Adorno (*Social Science and Sociological Tendencies in Psychoanalysis,* 1946), and Marcuse (*Eros and Civilization: A Philosophical Inquiry into Freud.* 1955).[140]

THE INSTITUTE'S EXILE IN AMERICA

In 1933, Hitler became chancellor of Germany. On May 13, 1933, the swastika flag was raised over Frankfurt town hall. The Nazis forced the closure of the Institute for Social Research.

---

[137] Ibid.

[138] Stuart Jeffries. *The Lives of the Frankfurt School*: A Timeline.

[139] Jay, Martin. *The Dialectical Imagination*, Berkeley: University of California Press, 1996, p. 92.

[140] Internet Encyclopedia of Philosophy—A Peer-Reviewed Academic Resource. "The Frankfurt School and Critical Theory." Marcuse's book imagined a society no longer motivated to work because of the subversive potential of sexual desire.

Horkheimer moved the ISR to Geneva. And in 1935, the Institute was moved to the United States where it was well received by Columbia University in New York City. (Erich Fromm, while in the United States, persuaded Columbia University to give refuge to the Institute for Social Research).[141] A large contingency of the Institute, including Horkheimer, Adorno, and Marcuse, moved to Morningside Heights in New York, where they established the Frankfurt School in exile.[142]

In 1927, Horkheimer published, *The Impotence of the German Working Class.* The book argued that Germany's "proletariat" was incapable of waging a socialist revolution (as Marx predicted in *Das Capital*).[143] And in 1937, Horkheimer published his *Traditional and Critical Theory* — Horkheimer's work became the Institute's ideological manifesto.[144] An imposing theme in Horkheimer's work—connected to his, *The Impotence of the German Working Class*— speaks of trapping the consciousness of the Oppressed in the way of the thinking of the dominant culture's ideologies and the creating of a "false consciousness" among the Oppressed.[145]

---

141 Stuart Jeffries. The Frankfurt School: A Timeline.

142 Adorno became a researcher on the Princeton Radio Research Project led by Viennese sociologist Paul Lazarsfeld to study the effects new forms of mass media on American society. Ibid.

143 György Lukács' 1922 publication, *History and Class Consciousness,* essentially made the same argument. Lukács' work had become a source of inspiration for the Frankfurt School.

144 In 1938, November 9-10, Kristallnacht took place in German cities and Jewish homes, hospitals, synagogues, and schools were destroyed. Hundreds of Jewish people were killed and tens of thousands were arrested to be imprisoned in concentration camps. Ibid.

145 Max Horkheimer. "Traditional and Critical Theory." Translated By: Matthew J. O'Connell. Pages 197-98. https://books.google.com/books?hl=en&lr=&id=YiXUAwAAQBAJ&oi=fnd&pg=PR3&dq=horkheimer+traditional+and+critical+theory&ots=uxU-Gjo6xp0&sig=CnhUgMYORCyZgTi9jAlAJzB- IvE#v=onepage&q=horkheimer%20traditional%20and%20crit... Downloaded: 11/14/22. (Article extracted from the book, Max Horkheimer. *Traditional and Critical Theory.* New York, N.Y.: The Continuum Publishing Co. 1972).

In 1941, Horkheimer moved to Pacific Palisades, a community near Los Angeles. He built a home within the vicinity of other German intellectuals. Among the German intellectuals were Bertold Brecht and Thomas Mann, who, along with others, were interested in working for the film industry.[146]

In 1944, the same year Allied Forces invaded Normandy, Adorno and Horkheimer published *Dialectic of Enlightenment.* This book became a seminal text of the Frankfurt School's Critical Theory; the book forecasts a pessimistic view to the possibility of human emancipation and freedom.[147] In 1946, the Institute was officially invited to join Goethe University Frankfurt.[148]

On November 14, 1951, Horkheimer gave his inaugural speech for the reopening of the Frankfurt School. One week later, as the new Rector, Horkheimer inaugurated the University's academic year.

In 1955, Adorno succeeded Horkheimer as director of the Frankfurt School, and in 1957 he was appointed full professor in philosophy and sociology. Although Adorno was a significant influence in philosophy, his most innovative contribution was in the field of music theory and aesthetics. Some of his most influential works included *Philosophy of Modern Music* (1949) and later *Vers une Musique Informelle.*[149]

---

146 Wiggershaus, Rolf. *The Frankfurt School*, Cambridge: Polity Press, 1995. P. 292. In: Internet Encyclopedia of Philosophy—A Peer-Reviewed Academic Resource. "The Frankfurt School and Critical Theory."

147 Stuart Jeffries. The Frankfurt School: A Timeline.

148 1941-45: The Holocaust: Six million Jews are murdered by the Nazis. Among them is Walter Benjamin's brother Georg, killed at the Mauthausen-Gusen concentration camp in 1942. During this time, exiled Frankfurt School thinkers Marcuse, Neumann and Otto Kirchheimer work as intelligence analysts for the OSS, the forerunner of the CIA, while Pollock and Löwenthal also support the war against Nazism by working in other US government departments. Ibid.

149 "Towards a Re-conceptualization." Ibid.

The 1960's were marked by student protests throughout Europe and North America. Amid Western culture's chaos, Adorno's seminal work, *Negative Dialectics* was published in 1966. *Negative Dialectics* is neither materialistic nor metaphysical, it's described as an "open and non-systemic" notion of dialectics. Adorno's work appeared two years after Marcuse's influential work, *One Dimensional Man* (1964). Marcuse introduces the notion of "educational dictatorship" suggesting a strategy "for the advancement of material conditions aimed at the realization of a higher notion of the good."[150] Whereas Adorno assumed a more moderate profile, Marcuse was at the forefront of the student radicalism in the '60s.

In his work, *Grand Hotel Abyss: The Lives of the Frankfurt School,* Stuart Jefferies, a left-wing author, acknowledges the impressive expanse of the work and influence of the collective critical theorists representative of the Frankfurt School: "These men (the Frankfurt School) … bore witness to everything from the rise of capitalism's mass production techniques, the birth of Hollywood, World War I, the failed German revolution, the Soviet experiment, the Weimar Republic and the rise of Hitler, the Holocaust, the era of mass European exile, sexual liberation, the swinging 60s and student radicalism, Germany's post-war travails, the rise and fall of the Berlin Wall, 9/11, and the development of multicultural multi-religious western societies."[151]

---

[150] Internet Encyclopedia of Philosophy—A Peer-Reviewed Academic Resource. "The Frankfurt School and Critical Theory."

[151] Stuart Jefferies, *Grand Hotel Abyss: The Lives of the Frankfurt School.* New York: Verso, 09/2017.

THE FRANKFURT SCHOOL OF CRITICAL THEORY

Critical Theory is defined in a narrow and a broad sense in philosophy, and the history of the social sciences.[152] The first generation of Critical Theorists associated with the Frankfurt School of Critical Theory included Max Horkheimer (1895-1973), Theodor Adorno (1903-1969), Herbert Marcuse (1898-1979), Walter Benjamin (1892-1940), Friedrich Pollock (1894-1970), Leo Lowenthal (1900-1993), and Eric Fromm (1900-1980).[153] In the 1970s, a second generation surfaced with Jürgen Habermas. Habermas led the Frankfurt School into global influence through its involvement with methodological approaches in other European academic contexts and disciplines.[154] Richard Bernstein, a philosopher and contemporary of Habermas, embraced Critical Theory and significantly contributed to its development in American universities, beginning with the New School for Social Research in New York.[155]

In the Frankfurt tradition, Critical Theory is distinguished by three practical dynamics: A theory is *critical* relative to: (1) Human "emancipation from slavery," (2) Its activity as a "liberating influence," and (3) How it "works to create a world which satisfies the needs and powers of" humanity.[156] The purpose of Critical Theory, in the Frankfurt School tradition, is social transformation. The Frankfurt School's primary philosophical preoccupations concentrated on cultural studies, particularly

---

[152] *Stanford Encyclopedia of Philosophy.* Critical Theory. First published Tue Mar 8, 2005. https://plato.stanford.edu/entries/critical-theory/. Downloaded: 11/01/2022.

[153] Internet Encyclopedia of Philosophy—A Peer-Reviewed Academic Resource. "The Frankfurt School and Critical Theory." https://iep.utm.edu/critical-theory-frankfurt-school/. Downloaded: 11/01/2022.

[154] Ibid.

[155] Ibid.

[156] Max Horkheimer. Translation: Kritische Theorie. *Traditional And Critical Theory.* 1972, p. [ ] horkheimer_traditional-and-critical-theory.pdf. Downloaded: 11/07/2022. [246, 1992]

modernity, and capitalist society, social emancipation, and "the detection of societal pathologies"— *What is wrong with Western Civilization? And what are "clear norms for criticism and achievable practical goals for social transformation"?*

What are the "practical goals" prescribed by the Frankfurt tradition— That is, Woke Marxist ideology— for "social transformation"? First generation Critical Theorists asserted that human beings are "self-creating producers of their own history"[157] — Consequently, the Frankfurt School's Woke Marxist view is to "transform contemporary capitalism into a consensual form of social life."[158] In Horkheimer's view, "a capitalist society could be transformed only by becoming more democratic, to make it such that all conditions of social life that are controllable by human beings depend on real consensus in a rational society."[159] Critical Theory's approach to social inquiry sets its sights on "the transformation of capitalism into a 'real democracy' in which such control could be exercised."[160] What is Horkheimer's understanding of a "real democracy"? The framing of Horkheimer's "democracy" in Critical Theory and the vision of a Marxist classless, binary society,[161] produces a "direct democracy."[162] A direct or "real" democracy is a totalitarian state "that eliminates the very possibility of cultural resistance to progressivism."[163]

---

157 *Stanford Encyclopedia of Philosophy.* Critical Theory.

158 Ibid.

159 (Horkheimer 1972b [1992, 250])

160 *Stanford Encyclopedia of Philosophy.* Critical Theory.

161 For both Classical Marxism and Neo-Marxism, there is no middle class, only a wealthy upper, privileged class, and a poor, lower, underprivileged class— Binary societies are 3rd world socialist/communist societies.

162 The first examples of direct democracy can be found in the ancient Greek city-state of Athens, where decisions were made by an Assembly of some 1,000 male citizens. During the 17th century, similar people's assemblies were used in many Swiss towns and town meetings in colonial America.

163 Angelo M. Codevilla. "The Rise of Political Correctness." 1 of 12 pages.

For Marxists, like Horkheimer, democracy is, therefore, a single party system; a "direct democracy" centralizes societal control in government[164]— "... more democratic" thus points in the direction of totalitarianism— And thus, capitalism is "flattened" into first, socialism, and eventually, communism.

[164] Gramsci's Prison Notebooks link aspects of a Leninist style revolution, viz., Lenin and his Bolshevik contingent argued that the ideas of Marx had to be cultivated and practiced by a professional revolutionary class that would shepherd the proletariat through the various stages of Marxism. Lenin and his Bolshevik Party believed that the vast majority of the proletariat lacked the intellectual capability and foresight to guide the revolution through the various phases, as outlined by Marx. Therefore, Lenin built the Bolshevik wing of the Social Democratic Party as a professional revolutionary cadre that worked to foster and implement the proletarian revolution on behalf of and in conjunction with the workers of Russia and ultimately the world. Russian Revolution of 1917: The Essential Reference Guide Page xvii (18 of 298). https://publisher.abc-clio.com/9781440850936/18 Downloaded: 11/29/2022

CHAPTER 6

CRITICAL RACE THEORY—A TALE OF TWO HISTORIES

Despite the Civil War (1861-1865), the bloodiest war America has ever fought— 618,222 Americans were killed— 360,222 Union Soldiers, and 258,000 Confederate Soldiers— and the Emancipation Proclamation, which eventually freed slaves across the reunited nation, and the three Amendments to the United States Constitution— The 13th Amendment abolished slavery in the United States, the 14th Amendment guaranteed that citizens would receive "equal protection under the law," and the 15th Amendment granted Black men the right to vote, the postwar "White South" continued in a racist ethos.

BLACK CODES & JIM CROW LAWS

Black Codes restricted the freedom of African Americans in extreme ways.[165] Jim Crow Laws were dehumanizing for African Americans,[166] and violent hate groups, to include the KKK terrorized Black communities (The cowardly KKK organization included members at the highest levels of government and in the lowest echelons of criminals).

---

165 Under Black Codes, many states required Black people to sign yearly labor contracts and if they refused, they risked being arrested, fined, and forced into unpaid labor.

166 "Blackface" became popular in the U.S. after the Civil War (white actors smeared shoe polish, greasepaint or burnt cork and paint on their faces). The white actors then performed as characters that were demeaning and dehumanizing to African Americans. Among the black-faced white actors was one referred to as "Jim Crow," a foolish, clown-like individual, wearing tattered, scarecrow like, clothes and dancing as though he was being blown in circles by a strong wind.

Jim Crow Laws were a collection of state and local statutes that legalized segregation (These laws remained in effect from 1865 to 1968, slightly over one-hundred years). Early in the 1880s, large cities in the South were not wholly supportive of Jim Crow laws and therefore, large Black populations began moving to large cities. But, as the decade progressed, white city residents began to demand more laws to limit opportunities for African Americans.

Jim Crow laws soon spread around the country with increasing force. African Americans were forbidden to enter parks, theaters, and restaurants. Additionally, segregated waiting rooms in bus and train stations were required, as well as water fountains, restrooms, building entrances, elevators, cemeteries, and even amusement-park cashier windows.

African Americans were— under Jim Crow Laws— forbid from living in white neighborhoods. And further, segregation was enforced for public pools, phone booths, hospitals, asylums, jails, and residential homes for the elderly and handicapped. Some states required separate textbooks for Black and White students. New Orleans even mandated the segregation of prostitutes according to race. And in Atlanta, African Americans in court were given a different Bible from White people to swear on. And marriage and cohabitation between White and Black people was strictly forbidden in most Southern states. It was not uncommon to see signs posted at town and city limits warning African Americans that they were not welcome there. HISTORY. Black Codes. https://www.history.com/topics/black-history/black-codes. Jim Crow Laws. https://www.history.com/topics/early-20th-century-us/jim-crow-laws.

The three "Reconstruction Amendments" — The 13th, 14th, and 15th— were passed into law by Congress, January 31, 1865. Why then did the United States Government tolerate Black Code and Jim Crow Laws for more than a century beyond the Civil War?

1787—THE "THREE-FIFTHS COMPROMISE"

The so-called "Three-fifths Compromise" was an agreement between delegates from the Northern and Southern states at the United States Constitutional Convention in 1787.[167] The "compromise" stipulated that only three-fifths of the "slave population" would be counted for the purpose of "direct taxation" and "equal representation in the House of Representatives."

Many of the Founding Fathers acknowledged that slavery violated the "ideal of liberty" that was central to the American Revolution, "but because they were committed to the sanctity of private property rights, the principles of limited government, and the pursuit of intersectional harmony, they were unable to take bold action against slavery."[168] The Continental Congress was confronted with a Republican dilemma— If the Republic was to have equal representation in the House, the Northern and Southern States would need to make compromises.

Smaller states, e.g., New Jersey proposed equal representation in Congress for each state. And larger states, e.g., Virginia, proposed congressional representation should be based on population and/or wealth.

---

167 Three-Fifths Compromise. United States History. The Editors of *Encyclopaedia Britannica*. (The most recent edition of my source was revised and updated by Adam Augustyn). https://www.britannica.com/topic/three-fifths-compromise. Downloaded: 08/14/2023.

168 Ibid.

The Connecticut, or "Great Compromise," was the resolve: A "bicameral legislature" called for proportional representation in the "lower house," and in the "upper house," there would be equal representation.[169]

The matter of "proportional representation" was challenging: The Northern States' delegates, restricted by the priority they placed on private property rights, principles of limited government, and intersectional harmony, over the abolition of slavery, attempted to make the size of a state's free population the determinant for congressional representation. Southern delegates, however, threatened to leave the congressional proceedings if their enslaved population was not counted.

Finally, another compromise was reached that called for representation in the House of Representatives to be apportioned on the state's free population plus three-fifths of its enslaved population. The compromised agreement then read: *"Representatives and direct Taxes shall be apportioned among the several States which may be included within this Union, according to their respective Numbers, which shall be determined by adding to the whole Number of free Persons, including those bound to Service for a term of years, and excluding Indians not taxed, three-fifths of all other Persons."*[170]

Although the "Three-Fifths Compromise" appeared to preserve the rights of many Americans, it "violated the ideal of liberty." The "resolve" of the Continental Congress was to remove, "Thomas Jefferson's statement regarding the injustice of the Slave Trade (and, by implication, slavery) from the final version of the Declaration of Independence."[171]

---

169 Ibid.

170 It ought to be noted that the terms, "slave" or "slavery" do not appear anywhere in the unamended Constitution. Three important observations related to the notion of "systemic racism," regarding the 1787 "Three-Fifths Compromise," are discussed in Section 2, Chapter 9, "Woke Moral Subjectivity" & "The Abolition of Man."

171 Ibid.

Consequently, alongside of the "ideal of liberty," the Declaration of Independence's cornerstone, "*We hold these truths to be self-evident, that all men are created equal, that they are endowed by their Creator with certain unalienable Rights...*" (Gen. 1:27), and the three Constitutional "Reconstruction Amendments" the 13th, 14th, and 15th Amendments, were all subjected to the "Compromise."

The historical account above, and the following modern account under the subheading, "The Beloved Community or Black Led Segregation?" are founded on objective history. Our shameful history involving the grave compromise of Black dignity is distinguished from present-day compromise of human dignity, specifically founded on Marxist thought, and revisionist history, discussed below, under the heading: Critical Race Theory.

"THE BELOVED COMMUNITY" OR BLACK LED SEGREGATION?

> *"I have a dream that my four little children will one day live in a nation where they will not be judged by the color of their skin, but by the content of their character"*
> — Martin Luther King Jr.

Between WW1 and WW2, approximately six million African Americans moved into Northern urban cities in America. Liberal politicians quickly acted to put into effect racial segregation policies to prevent fighting and race riots. Liberals enacted their policies of racial discrimination by employing banks to design home loans that would result in the "redlining, block busting, and steering,"[172] of distinct races to specified districts in cities.[173] However, Liberal policies reaped vast economic and social gains for Blacks in the 1950s.

But a divide between African Americans in the North and the South created three distinct movements in response to white liberal society. Josephus H. Jackson, a Chicago Alderman, represented the "Black Bourgeoisie." Jackson contended for civil obedience in the fight against racial prejudice—That is, legal discrimination based on racial differences were to be pursued through "legal change to improve the economic and social situation of blacks through their own efforts rather than through an interracial movement."[174] Jackson urged segregation, emphasizing "the natural affinity different groups have for their own kind."[175] And further, Joseph Jackson's opposition to racial integration was then necessary to protect the Black Community from a "false consciousness," thus preserving Black genuineness.

Jackson accused Martin Luther King Jr. of colluding with "white elites" instead of directly working with the Black Community— In a word, Jackson accused King of being disingenuous towards Blacks. In response to Jackson, King contended for the assimilation of Blacks into White society— King's hope of a "Beloved Community" was a type of covenant among all human beings wherein the racial distinguishing of one another would no longer exist.

---

[172] Kevin Slack. Hillsdale College. "The American Left: From Liberalism to Despotism." Lecture 4: "Civil Rights and Black Power." https://online.hillsdale.edu/courses/american-left.

[173] In his *The Other America,* Michael Harrington argued for the need of a moral reformation of Blacks that would prepare them to assimilate into middle-class white America.

[174] Kevin Slack. Lecture 4: Civil Rights and Black Power." Page 2 of 5 pages.

[175] Ibid.

However, to achieve his ends, King advocated civil disobedience. Civil disobedience was warranted because America had failed to live up to the "higher law of the Declaration of Independence"— "We hold these truths to be self-evident, that all men are created equal, that they are endowed by their Creator with certain unalienable Rights, that among these are Life, Liberty, and the pursuit of Happiness." [176] And finally, King insisted, "Desegregation and integration were insufficient"; public and private "Affirmative Action" was needed for wealth redistribution—A $50 billion 'Marshall Plan' for the raising of Blacks' socio-economic status was proposed.[177]

Jackson's and King's relationship became contentious to the point that in 1960, during The National Baptist Convention, a faction of King's followers stormed the platform, and, in the chaos, Reverend A.G. Wright was pushed off the stage resulting in his broken neck. Jackson seized the moment, accusing King of waging violent protests, contrary to his claims of "nonviolent protests." Jackson charged that King's marches held no regard for the law and would become countermeasures against Black opportunities in society.

Malcolm X, the Black Nationalist Leader of the Nation of Islam, also opposed King's racial assimilation policies with white society, considering him to be a traitor to the Black Community. And, as well, in 1966 Stokely Carmichael, a leader in the Black Power Movement, opposed King and adopted an "Identity Politics-like" posture— Carmichael argued: "Racism is systemic; Racism is unconscious; White liberalism is a form of capitalistic

---

[176] Ibid. "The Higher Law" is founded on the Scripture: *"So, God created mankind in his own image, in the image of God he created them; male and female he created them"* — Genesis 1:27. Genesis 1:27 is implicated in "The Preamble of the Declaration of Independence."

[177] Martin Luther King Jr. *Where Do We Go From Here? Chaos or Community.* Boston, MA: Beacon Press, 1968, p.39. In Kevin Slack. *How Liberalism Became Despotism,* p.185.

oppression. The solution to racism is consciousness raising among Blacks to help them understand their need to unite in solidarity against Whites. Whites are the enemy; 'Radical Whites' can form an alliance with Blacks to help resist White tyranny and pursue greater Black awareness."[178]

King emerged as the Civil Rights Movement's leader, but throughout the decade of the 1960's, he moved farther to the left following his embracing of James Cone's Black Liberation Theology and the notion that "Whiteness" is a system of oppression— "Most Americans," asserted King, "are unconscious racists," and the only resolve is "a reconstruction of the entire society, a revolution of values."[179] King further adopted Cone's principal hermeneutic in his *Black Theology of Liberation*: Christianity ought to be interpreted in terms of systemic racism as a struggle against oppression, or "whiteness."[180] And additionally: "What we need is the destruction of whiteness, which is the source of human misery in the world."[181]

King influenced many Black Elites who "began to argue that blacks do not share white morality and should reject middle-class sexual restraint."[182] College attendance significantly increased, and unemployment decreased among Blacks. Additionally, poverty was reduced, income rose, making the earnings of Blacks more comparable to Whites. However, "illegitimacy rates increased, broken families increased, high school drop-out rates increased, and public assistance rates increased so that twenty to thirty percent of blacks became mired in dependency."[183]

---

178 Kevin Slack. "The American Left: From Liberalism To Despotism," Lecture 4: Civil Rights and Black Power," p. 3 of 5 pages.

179 Kevin Slack. *How Liberalism Became Despotism,* p.187.

180 Ibid.

181 Ibid.

182 Kevin Slack. "The American Left: From Liberalism To Despotism," Lecture 4: Civil Rights and Black Power," p. 4 of 5 pages.

183 Ibid.

CRITICAL RACE THEORY

"The only remedy to racist discrimination is antiracist discrimination. The only remedy to present discrimination is future discrimination"
— Ibram X. Kendi.[184]

Derrick Bell, the first tenured Black faculty member at the Harvard Law School, was the principal architect of the intellectual foundations of Critical Race Theory. Professor Bell's expertise was critical legal theory—The legal scholar's insertion of "race" in place of "legal" originates "Critical Race Theory." Critical Race Theory has transcended legal categories to include multi-disciplines under the heading of Social Justice.

"Critical race theory grew out of what its originators viewed as the failures of the civil rights movement to dismantle white supremacy," observes, Marina Bolotnikova.[185] Moreover, Critical Race Theory is an identity-based, reformulated Marxist phenomenon— Critical Race Theory stresses that "race" is a social construct[186] created by "White Privilege" for the purpose of maintaining "white supremacy."[187] On morally subjec-

---

184 Ibram X. Kendi. *How to Be an Antiracist.* One World—First Edition, 2019. P. 15.

185 Marina Bolotnikova. *Harvard Magazine.* "What is Critical Race Theory?" 03/22/2016. https://www.harvardmagazine.com/2016/03/bu-law-professor-khiara-bridges-teaches-critical-race-theory-at-harvardlaw#:~:text=Critical%20race%20theory%20grew%20out,by%20racist%20interests%20and %20assumptions. Downloaded: 10/26/2002.

186 By "a social construct," CRT is referring "to representations, messages and stories conveying the idea that behaviors and values associated with white people or 'whiteness' are automatically 'better' or more 'normal' than those associated with other racially defined groups." Advertising, film industry, history books, law, etc., are dominant conveyers of white inspired social constructs. RacialEquityTools.org, MP Associates, Center for Assessment and Policy Development, and World Trust Educational Services. https://www.racialequitytools.org/ Downloaded: 07/19/2023.

187 Helen Pluckrose & James Lindsay. *Cynical Theories. How Activist Scholarship Made Everything about Race, Gender, and Identity.* Durham, NC: Pitchstone Publishing, 2020.111.

tive grounds, CRT presumes the motives of an entire race— viz., White European —by defining racism as "prejudice plus power."[188]

Critical Race Theory therefore stresses that *only* white people are racists, and racism, by definition, is then systemic— *Critical Race Theory employs the classic Marxist binary of oppressor and oppressed but replaces "class" with "race," and thus reifies the notion that everyone within a particular race has shared the same experiences.*[189] CRT's contentions are sourced by the notion of "Structural Racism" —Though Structural Racism was briefly introduced above, CRT's emphases on its influence in America and Western Culture today warrants fuller understanding by conflating it with, "Interest Convergence," "Intersectionality," and "Standpoint Theory."

"STRUCTUAL RACISM" — "A WHITE SOCIAL CONSTRUCT"

Race is not 'biologically grounded and natural'; rather, it is a socially constructed category used to oppress and exploit people of color"
— Critical Race Theory.

"Structural Racism" legitimizes virtually *all* institutional and interpersonal discourse— *Structural Racism is a powerful, sweeping set of dynamics generated by the ultra-power of the Privileged hegemony and diffused throughout every sector and system of society to include history, culture, politics, economics, and academics.* Because Structural Racism is the cumulative effect of racism in "multiple institutions and cultural norms, past and present, continually

188 Ibid., 121.

189 My assertion is based on the insight of Victor Davis Hanson. American Citizenship and Its Decline. "The Rise of Tribal Politics." Notes, 2 of 3 pages. (The term "reify" is used in Section 2, primarily, Chapter 9. A brief definition here is: Reify refers to the transforming of abstract notions into empirically based reality).

reproducing old and producing new forms of racism,"[190] it is difficult to locate in a particular institution. Structural Racism is, according to CRT, the primary source of all forms of racism— CRT concludes that "racism is systemic."[191]

"INTEREST CONVERGENCE"

"All cultural norms, values and institutions in western society are structured to empower the white race and oppress minority races, particularly blacks"
— Derrick Bell.

Derrick Bell is well known for his thesis, "interest convergence." In his book, *Race, Racism, and American Law,* Professor Bell asserts that "interest convergence" stipulates that black people achieve civil rights victories only when white and black interests converge. [192]

Bell contested that "any amount of racial advancement signified temporary 'peaks of progress,' short-lived victories that slide into irrelevance

190 Keith Lawrence, Aspen Institute and Terry Keleher, Applied Research Center, for the Race and Public Policy Conference (2004). *Chronic Disparity: Strong and Pervasive Evidence of Racial Inequalities* And Maggie Potapchuk, Sally Leiderman, Donna Bivens, and Barbara Major *Flipping the Script: White Privilege and Community Building* (2005).

191 Ibid. Examples of this assertion are discussed by the authors quoted above: "... we can see structural racism in the many institutional, cultural, and structural factors that contribute to lower life expectancy for African American and Native American men, compared to white men. These include higher exposure to environmental toxins, dangerous jobs and unhealthy housing stock, higher exposure to and more lethal consequences for reacting to violence, stress, and racism, lower rates of health care coverage, access, and quality of care, and systematic refusal by the nation to fix these things."

192 Derrick A. Bell. *Race, Racism, and American Law.* Boston, MA: Little, Brown, and Co., 1984. In, Helen Pluckrose & James Lindsay, *Cynical Theories,* 115. *See the discussion of "revisionist history" below.*

as racial patterns adapt in ways that maintain white dominance."[193] Bell therefore urged his followers, especially his students, "to accept the reality that we live in a society in which racism has been internalized and institutionalized," a society that produced "a culture from whose inception racial discrimination has been a regulating force for maintaining stability and growth."[194]

Though racism is perpetual, in Bell's view, he nevertheless stressed that his followers "fight against it must be equally persistent." Regarding her teacher and mentor, Alexis Hoag asserts that Professor Bell "implored us to 'realize with our slave forbearers that the struggle for freedom is, at bottom, a manifestation of our humanity that survives and grows stronger through resistance to oppression even if that oppression is never overcome.'"[195]

Professor Bell originated and taught a course on civil-rights law at Harvard Law, providing his students the only sanctioned opportunity for left-of-liberal legal training on the interworking of race and power.[196] Kimberlé Crenshaw was a former student of Derrick Bell and cofounder with him of Critical Race Theory. Professor Crenshaw's concept, "Intersectionality," is a significant contribution to CRT.

---

[193] Alexis Hoag. Harvard Law Review, Blog. "Derrick Bell's Interest Convergence and the Permanence of Racism: A Reflection on Resistance." August 24, 2020. https://blog.harvardlawreview.org/derrick-bells-interest-convergence-and-the-permanence-of-racism-a-reflection-on-resistance/. Downloaded: 10/07/2022.

[194] Ibid.

[195] Ibid.

[196] As a civil rights attorney, Derrick Bell worked with Thurgood Marshall, at the N.A.A.C.P. Legal Defense Fund, creating legal strategies against school segregation in the South. Bell was also the deputy director of civil rights at the U.S. Department of Health, Education, and Welfare.

"INTERSECTIONALITY"

Kimberlé Crenshaw is a law professor at Columbia University and UCLA. She is the progenitor of "intersectionality." Professor Crenshaw first introduced intersectionality in a paper she delivered in 1989: "Demarginalizing the Intersection of Race and Sex: A Black Feminist Critique of Antidiscrimination Doctrine, Feminist Theory and Antiracist Politics."[197]

Professor Crenshaw provides an illustration of the layered concept of intersectionality— Crenshaw "… uses the metaphor of a roadway intersection to examine the ways in which different forms of prejudice can 'hit' an individual with two or more marginalized identities. She argues that— just as someone standing in the intersection of two streets could get hit by a car coming from any direction or even by more than one at a time— so a marginalized person could be unable to tell which of their identities is being discriminated against in each instance."[198]

Professor Crenshaw contends that legislation for the prevention of discrimination, on the grounds of race *or* gender, will not suffice for a black woman who may likely experience discrimination in unique forms apart from what white women or black men may experience.[199]

---

[197] Kimberlé Crenshaw, "Demarginalizing the Intersection of Race and Sex: A Black Feminist Critique of Antidiscrimination Doctrine, Feminist Theory, and Antiracist Politics," University of Chicago Legal Forum 1, no.8 (1989), chicagounbound.uchicago.edu/uclf/vol1989/iss1/8. In Helen Pluckrose & James Lindsay, *Cynical Theories, 5 Critical Race Theory and Intersectionality,* endnote, 31, 294.

[198] Helen Pluckrose & James Lindsay. *Cynical Theories.* 123.

[199] Ibid. Professor Crenshaw elaborated on intersectionality in 1991 in an essay entitled: "Mapping the Margins: Intersectionality, Identity Politics, and Violence against Women of Color," wherein she defines intersectionality as a "provisional concept linking contemporary politics and postmodern theory." Crenshaw's intention was to set forth a postmodern approach to intersectionality and critical race theory, as well as, feminism, to retain the understanding of race and gender as cultural constructs. Ibid. 123-124.

Professor Crenshaw's concept of intersectionality is framed in identity politics for the purpose of sustaining its foundational "social significance of identity categories"[200] relative to Social Justice categories. Crenshaw elucidates intersectionality's importance regarding Social Justice:

> We all can recognize the distinction between the claims "I am Black" and the claim "I am a person who happens to be Black." "I am Black" takes the socially imposed identity and empowers it as an anchor of subjectivity; "I am Black" becomes not simply a statement of resistance but also a positive discourse of self-identification, intimately linked to celebratory statements like the Black nationalist, "Black is beautiful." "I am a person who happens to be Black," on the other hand, achieves self-identification by straining for a certain universality (in effect, "I am first a person") and for a concomitant dismissal of the imposed category ("Black") as contingent, circumstantial, nondeterminate.[201]

In an interview in 2020, Professor Crenshaw was asked, "You introduced *intersectionality* more than 30 years ago, how do you explain what it means today?" Crenshaw responded: "These days, I start with what it's not, because there has been distortion. It's not identity politics on steroids. It is not a mechanism to turn white men into the new pariahs. It's basically a lens— a prism— for seeing the way in which various forms of inequality often operate together and exacerbate each other. We tend to talk about race inequality as separate from inequality based on gen-

---

200 Ibid. 124.

201 Crenshaw. "Mapping the Margins." 1297. In Pluckrose & Lindsay. Cynical Theories. 124.

der, class, sexuality, or immigrant status. What's often missing is how some people are subject to all of these, and the experience is not just the sum of its parts"[202] — that is, regarding social inequality, people's lives and existing power structures are understood to be shaped by multiple axes that work together and influence one another. Intersectionality is a heuristic— an analytic tool—that ostensibly gives people access to the complexities of life and themselves[203] —This is Intersectionality.

STANDPOINT THEORY—THE MANIPULATION OF "REALITY"

If the "Privileged" accept the definition of racism as "prejudice plus power," then they are bound to conclude that *only* white people are racist, and therefore, because "whiteness" is "hardwired" into every layer of Western Culture, to include America, racism in North America and Western Europe is systemic— It's not a matter of where racism is, in Western Civilization, it's a matter of what type of racism is present in any given location.

---

[202] Katy Steinmetz. TIME – INEQUALITY. Kimberlé Crenshaw. "She Coined the Term 'Intersectionality' Over 30 Years Ago. Here's What It Means to Her Today" February 20, 2020. https://Time.com/5786710/Kimberle-Crenshaw-Intersectionality/ Downloaded: 10/07/2022.

[203] Such contemporary applications of identity politics describe people of specific race, ethnicity, sex, gender identity, sexual orientation, age, economic class, disability status, education, religion, language, profession, political party, veteran status, recovery status, and geographic location. These identity labels are not mutually exclusive but are in many cases compounded into one when describing hyper-specific groups. An example is that of African-American, homosexual, women, who constitute a particular hyper-specific identity class. Those who take an intersectional perspective, such as Kimberlé Crenshaw, criticize narrower forms of identity politics which overemphasize inter-group differences and ignore intra-group differences and forms of oppression. Stanford Encyclopedia of Philosophy. "Identity Politics." *First published Tue Jul 16, 2002; substantive revision Sat Jul 11, 2020.* https://plato.stanford.edu/entries/identity-politics/. Downloaded: 11/12/2023.

The "Privileged" are told that only people of color can talk about racism; white people just need to listen because they lack the "racial stamina" to engage racism[204]— "Standpoint Theory is a socially constructed identity, occupying a particular location "within the privilege/oppression landscape."[205] Standpoint Theory is rooted in identity politics and pivots on two assumptions: "One is that people occupying the same social positions, that is, identities— race, gender, sex, sexuality, ability status, and so on, will have the same experiences of dominance and oppression and will, assuming they understand their own experiences correctly, interpret them in the same ways. From this follows the assumption that these experiences will provide them with a more authoritative and fuller picture."[206] And the "… other is that one's relative position within a social power dynamic dictates what one can and cannot know: thus, the privileged are blinded by their privilege and the oppressed possess a kind of double sight, in that they understand both the dominant position and the experience of being oppressed by it"[207] — This is Standpoint Theory.

And so, according to Critical Theorists, Whites should listen to and believe the accounts of those identified as Underprivileged/Oppressed relative to race, gender, sex, sexuality, and ability status and dismiss those identified as Privileged/Oppressors (especially white males) because they lack "racial stamina" —*Critical Theorists assume, vis-à-vis Standpoint Theory, the right to manipulate reality, and therefore, any accounts of truth regarding the experience of the privileged are simply dismissed.*

---

[204] Helen Pluckrose & James Lindsay. *Cynical Theories, How Activist Scholarship Made Everything about Race, Gender, and Identity— and Why This Harms Everybody.* Durham, NC: Pitchstone Publishing, 2020, 121.

[205] Ibid. 118.

[206] Ibid. 194.

[207] Christopher F. Rufo. *Imprimis.* "Critical Race Theory: What It Is and How to Fight." Page 3 of 7 pages.

A RADICAL REINTERPRETATION OF CIVIL RIGHTS

Identity Politics exchanges the presumption of innocence for the presumption of prejudice.

The altering of the 1964 Civil Rights Act by "a handful of Supreme Court decisions, Executive Orders, and agency regulations," [208] resulted in a Marxist makeover: *Legislated law promising to ban discrimination, is now used to justify discrimination.* Racial discrimination would no longer be against minorities and women, but in their favor— *That is, the law proactively discriminates in favor of "protected identity groups" (e.g., the "Oppressed").*

An example of Woke "Justice" and its perspective on juris prudence involves video evidence of government-financed Planned Parenthood's barbarous act of harvesting the internal organs of aborted babies and illegally trafficking them. But it was the producers of the video, David Daleiden and Sandra Merritt, who were indicted and charged with a felony rather than any one from the "protected identity group," Planned Parenthood— *"Justice" is bent to conform to the extreme subjectivity of Woke Marxist Critical Theory.*[209]

Critical Theory, Social Justice scholarship, advocates that a guilty verdict "… should include the lived experiences, emotions, and cultural

---

208 David Azerrad, Hillsdale College. "Civil Rights in American History," Lecture 9, "Identity Politics Today." Professor Azerrad acknowledged his colleague, Paul Moreno for this insight. https://online.hillsdale.edu/courses/civil-rights-in-american-history. Downloaded: 07/26/2023.

209 Interestingly, evolutionary theory views human nature as changing and progressing instead of the biblical view of the *Imago Dei*— human beings are created in the image of God (cf. Genesis 1:27) and because of the Fall (Genesis 3:1-21) our nature regresses until we are redeemed and made "new creations" in Christ. Evolution provides no objective basis for distinguishing male and female. Therefore, it is hard to see how Dr. Maroja can contend for the "bedrock insight" that distinguishes male and female.

traditions of minority groups, consider them 'knowledges,' and privilege them over reason and evidence-based knowledge, which is unfairly dominant."[210] Such a radically subjective argument for justice is able to command conformity because, today's powerful ideologies claiming the mantle of Civil Rights are obsessed with the color of people's skin, the perceived oppression of protected identity groups, and one's politics, not the content of one's character, evidence based arguments, or objective truth claims.

In everyday life, Americans are subject to "cancel culture," social media censorship, and political correctness— *Americans live under the shadow of the most dominant ideology in Western Culture today, "Identity Politics."*[211] And therefore, the one unforgivable sin in America today is to deviate from the Identity Politics script and regardless of intentionality, say something offensive regarding a protected identity group; and although you may not be a celebrity, you are still vulnerable to a lawsuit or at least, the loss of your job.

Reflecting on the dominant influence of Identity Politics, Vivek Ramaswamy's observation is not surprising: "A good measure of the health of any democracy, especially American democracy, is the percentage of people who feel free to say what they actually think in public" — "And," continues Ramaswamy, "we are doing abysmally on that metric."[212] Today the majority of Americans do not feel safe regarding their freedom of speech— A Cato Institute survey concluded that over 62% of Americans

---

[210] P. 187.

[211] David Azerrad, Hillsdale College. "Civil Rights in American History," Lecture 9, "Identity Politics Today."

[212] Vivek Ramaswamy. Interview: "DOJ To Crack Down on 'Threats' To School Boards." America's Newsroom, FOX News. October 10, 2021. https://twitter.com/VivekGRamaswamy/status/1447352486914891777. Downloaded: 07/27/2023.

(77% among Republicans), say that they are afraid to openly say what they believe because of the current political environment.[213]

CRT PLUS IDENTITY POLITICS

"This focusing upon our own oppression is embodied in the concept of identity politics. We believe that the most profound and potentially most radical politics come directly out of our own identity, as opposed to working to end somebody else's oppression."

The Combahee River Collective Statement, quoted above, is perhaps the origin of the term: "Identity Politics." It was authored in 1977 by Black Feminists based in Boston, MA. Of note is the opening words, "This focusing upon our own oppression" informs us that "Identity Politics" are defined by "oppression" — "The statement focuses on identifying and denouncing the multiple interconnected systems of oppression in America."[214] Today, Identity Politics underwrites civil rights laws. Therefore, the United States Commission on Civil Rights informed us in 1985, that civil rights laws, "… were not passed to give civil rights protections to all Americans, as the majority of this commission, seems to believe. Instead, they were passed out of a recognition that some Americans already had protection because they belong to a favored group and others, including blacks, Hispanics, and women of all races, did not because they belonged to disfavored groups."

213 Emily Ekins. Cato Institute. 08/2020. "Most Americans Are Scared Stiff To Talk Politics. Why?" https://www.cato.org/commentary/most-americans-are-scared-stiff-talk-politics-why. Majorities of Democrats (52 percent), Independents (59 percent), and Republicans (77 percent) all agree they have political views they are afraid to share.

214 David Azerrad, Hillsdale College. "Civil Rights in American History," Lecture 9, "Identity Politics Today."

[215] Identity Politics, in keeping with Marxist binary politics, divides, in this case, Americans, into two groups, the "Favored," and the "Disfavored."

Based on purely subjective moral reasoning, Identity Politics elevates the moral condition of the "Disfavored" over the moral condition of the "Favored" — Whites, particularly males, must atone for the sins of their ancestors in perpetuity, while others, viz., African Americans, LGBTQ community members, etc., are celebrated for their moral superiority over White, straight males.

SYSTEMIC RACISM IS PERPETUAL

America is "irredeemably racist" and therefore, discrimination against the Privileged, White race, is justifiable on every front— *This ideology is foundational to Critical Race Theory's worldview.* Because of this worldview, Critical Race theorists refuse to acknowledge any progress in race relations since the mid-twentieth century. Derrick Bell, the chief architect of Critical Race Theory, announced in 1991 that Black People had made no progress in America since 1865. Bell was a tenured professor at Harvard Law for over two decades when he made this claim— In 1865, Harvard University did not admit Black students.

In the thinking of Identity Politics' advocates— to include Critical Race theorists, systemic racism is perpetual; it has not, and will not be diminished, it rather just morphs into different forms: from slavery to Jim Crow to the "New Jim Crow" racism will remain unchanged. Michelle Alexander's best seller, *The New Jim Crow: Mass Incarceration in an Age of Colorblindness,* 2010, asserts: "We have not ended racial caste in America.

---

[215] Ibid. "Statements of Commissioners Blandina Cardinas Ramirez and Mary Frances Berry."

We have merely redesigned it."[216] Ta-Nehisi Coates, a Black activist and intellectual, thinks that White Supremacy is so foundational to America that it will not be destroyed in our present generation, or the next, or probably, never. Coates ponders "... that it is difficult to even imagine the country without it."[217] In his best seller, *Between the World and Me,* Ta-Nehisi Coates writes an open letter to his son: "It only takes one person to make a change,' you are often told. This is also a myth. Perhaps one person can make a change, but not the kind of change that would raise your body to equality with your countrymen."[218]

In the spirit of Derrick Bell's "Interest Convergence," Coates encourages his son to fight against racism, but to do so with no hope of ever defeating it— This is the sobering stance taken by Identity Politics/Critical Race Theorists today. And as a result, the resolve of Ibram X. Kendi is seen by Social Justice activists as irrevocably justified — *"The only remedy to racist discrimination is antiracist discrimination. The only remedy to present discrimination is future discrimination."*[219]

"ADVANCING EQUITY FOR ALL"

Critical Race Theory has spread throughout the United States, to include military and government agencies. In 2021, President Biden signed an executive order "requiring all organizations in the military—as well as in the rest of the federal government—to create Diversity, Equity, and Inclusion offices, to produce strategic DEI plans, and to create bureaucratic

---

216 Ibid.

217 Ibid. Ta-Nehisi Coates. *We Were Eight Years in Power: An American Tragedy.* New York, NY: One World Publishing, 2017.

218 Ibid.

219 Ibram X. Kendi. *How to Be an Antiracist.* P. 15.

structures to report on progress towards DEI goals. The overall goal, Biden said, was 'advancing equity for all'—Again using the Left's euphemism for achieving desired outcomes through discriminatory policies." [220]

The US federal government is spending billions on "Woke readiness" while the Chinese are "outpacing us on hypersonic weapons, quantum computing, and other important military technologies."[221] Further, it's not surprising that recruiting has been gravely affected— Young white men and women from rural America are hardly interested in being informed about the infirmities of their "Whiteness."

In his outstanding article, "Critical Race Theory: What It Is and How to Fight It," Christopher F. Rufo provides examples of Critical Race Theory's infiltration of multiple layers of American government agencies: "The FBI was holding workshops on intersectionality theory. The Department of Homeland Security was telling white employees they were committing 'microinequities' and had been 'socialized into oppressor roles.' The Treasury Department held a training session telling staff members that 'virtually all white people contribute to racism' and that they must convert 'everyone in the federal government' to the ideology of 'antiracism.' And the Sandia National Laboratories, which designs America's nuclear arsenal, sent white male executives to a three-day reeducation camp, where they were told that 'white male culture' was analogous to the 'KKK,' 'white supremacists,' and 'mass killings.' The executives were then forced to renounce their 'white privilege' and write letters of apology to fictitious women and people of color."[222]

---

[220] Ibid. Diversity, Equity, and Inclusion are focused on in Chapter 5.

[221] Christopher F. Rufo. *Imprimis.* "Critical Race Theory: What It Is and How to Fight." Page 5 of 7 pages.

[222] Ibid.

Why do so-called "Privileged, White Supremacists," allow themselves to be subjected to CRT's indignities, i.e., reverse forms of "discrimination"? The guilt-source, latent in the consciences of a significant portion of decent white Americans, is cultivated and activated by CRT's tactics, e.g., historical revisionism; and fear associated with the repercussions of dissent—Freedom of speech is suspended as charges of the "irrefutable evidence of a dissenter's 'white fragility,' 'unconscious bias,' or 'internalized white supremacy'" are leveled against those who resist reverse forms of discrimination.[223] But still worse than the slanderous accusations, dissent can result in loss of employment and therefore, employees are made vulnerable. Under these conditions, group-think dominates the white conscience, and consequently, people (particularly, White groups) are easily manipulated. CRT's "higher law" — "Party Ideology" — *Re: Specifically, the "Party's interest is to be treated as a reality that ranks above reality itself"*[224] is CRT's justification for its retributive justice on behalf of the Oppressed, and the manipulation of facts involved with historical revisionism.

REVISIONIST HISTORY

Is racism America's "original sin"?

Historical revisionism is the *reinterpretation* of a historical account. It usually involves challenging the orthodox (established, accepted or traditional) views held by professional scholars about a historical event, timespan or

---

[223] Ibid. 4 of 7 pages.

[224] Angelo M. Codevilla. "The Rise of Political Correctness." November 28, 2016. Originally published in *Claremont Review of Books* on November 8, 2015. p. 1 of 12 pages. https://claremontreviewofbooks.com/the-rise-of-political-correctness/ Downloaded: 06/16/2023.

phenomenon, introducing contrary evidence, or reinterpreting the motivations and decisions of the people involved.

Revisionism is sometimes legitimately employed to account for new facts and interpretations of historical events, and/or negligence involving evidence and accounts that would make known the "whole story." However, Critical Theory Social Justice activists intentionally make their case for systemic racism based on only half of the American story; viz., the half that supports *their* definition of racism as "prejudice plus power," and their presumptive indictment of the whole of white America as racists.[225]

The moral subjectivity of Critical Equity's "access versus outcomes" metric is instrumental *vis-à-vis* Woke Marxist ideology's historical revisionism.[226]

CRITICAL EQUITY—ACCESS VERSES OUTCOMES

The equitable principle of "Access Versus Outcomes" stresses equal access, but evaluation of this idea is done by measuring the "equality of access" in terms of "outcomes." And if the outcomes reveal a problem, access must be the source of the problem, or the whole structure has racism built into it;

225 The revision of the historical record can reflect new discoveries of fact, evidence, and interpretation, which then results in revised history. In dramatic cases, revisionism involves a reversal of older moral judgments. It is noteworthy to mention that Derrick Bell, best known for "interest convergence" was an advocate of historical revisionism, re: Bell's *Race, Racism, and American Law.* Source: Helen Pluckrose and James Lindsay. *Cynical Theories.* 115.

226 Chapter 9, Page 139 ff, develops an argument against Systemic Racism under several Subheadings, leading up to the Subheading, THE WOKE OPIATE. Add: Additionally, a self-evident argument against Systemic Racism is developed in Chapter 10, Page 157, under the Subheadings THE TRANSFORMING POWER OF THE GOSPEL AND TRUTH, Page 163, and AMERICA'S SUPERSTRUCTURE, Page 165.

the *only* solution is antiracism— *In the case of America's founding, no other variables are considered. If "prejudice is 'privilege plus power,'" then systemic racism is "legitimately" assumed with nothing further to prove.*

The reader will observe in the following chapter that CRT is the theoretical scaffolding for Diversity, Equity, and Inclusion— DEI.

CHAPTER 7

"DEI": DIVERSITY—EQUITY—INCLUSION

"The way to stop discrimination on the basis of race is to stop discriminating on the basis of race" — John Roberts, Chief Justice, The United States Supreme Court.

The National Football League is committed to "support programs and initiatives that reduce barriers to opportunity in four priority areas:" [227] Criminal Justice Reform, Education, Economic Advancement, and Community-Police Relations. The mission of each of the four pillars are as follows:

Criminal Justice Reform: "Contribute to changing local and state legislation and policies through advocacy around criminal justice reform legislation. Increase awareness around social justice and racial equality

[227] NFL Football Operations. Four Pillars of Inspire Change. https://operations.nfl.com/inside-football-ops/social- justice/socialjustice/#:~:text=OUR%20Mission,public%20in%20working%20towards%20solutions.&text=This%20opens%20in%20a%20new%20window. Downloaded: 01/05/2023.

issues that directly impact communities and engage the public in working towards solutions."

Education: "Support and promote efforts to provide equal access to education opportunities for low-income communities and help formerly incarcerated juveniles and adults with reentry services, programs and resources."

Economic Advancement: "Contribute to efforts to level the playing field and close the wealth gap for economically disadvantaged communities."

Community-Police Relations: "Support efforts to end racial disparity and the criminalization of poverty in policing and criminal justice. Establish greater trust between police and community and reduce instances of police brutality."[228]

The "NFL Football Operations, Four Pillars of Inspire Change," lists several player-led achievements to include: "changes in voter laws, juvenile justice, criminal justice reform," and "improved funding for educational opportunities across the country."[229]

Every Sunday morning and evening, and Thursday and Monday night, NFL coaching staffs wear sweatshirts, and shirts with large print reflecting the proactive commitment of the NFL to Social-Justice— "Diversity," "Equity," "Inclusion" and "Opportunity." Between 2020-21, Players' helmets displayed "Inspire Change," "Black Lives Matter," and "Stop Racism" on the border of the helmet's white leather coating over its insulation. And (between 2020-21) each of the end-zone borders featured the League's commitment— "It Takes All of Us," and "End Racism."

The "virtues" of DEI are coveted by a seemingly countless number of organizations (to include the NFL) for their ability "to respond to

[228] Ibid.

[229] Ibid.

challenges, win top talent, and meet the needs of different customer bases."[230] But the true nature of DEI is something very different from the perceptions of its corporate ferriages— *DEI is the primary channel for Marxist Socialism's access to the Corporate World.*[231]

WOKE CRITICAL THEORY

Woke ideology frames several culturally transforming (counter-hegemonic), identity-based instruments of Critical Theory, e.g., Social Justice Critical Race Theory, Intersectionality and Standpoint Theories, Queer Theory, Pedagogy (Education) Theory, and Gender Theory. Critical Theory's counter-hegemonic properties— "Diversity," "Equity," and "Inclusion" — act as organs for Woke Marxist's exquisitely fine-tuned insurgent "instruments" employed for the transformation of *all* "dimensions of the domination of human beings in modern societies."[232] The operational mode of DEI is determined by the detection and evaluation of "invisible identity-based systems."

---

230 McKinsey & Company. "What is Diversity, Equity, and Inclusion?" August 17, 2022. Page 1 of 9 pages. https://www.mckinsey.com/featured-insights/mckinsey-explainers/what-is-diversity-equity-and-inclusion. Downloaded: 03/27/2023.

231 James Lindsay. The Marxist Roots of DEI— Season 1: Equity. https://www.youtube.com/watch?v=xbby7yFrIxM. Downloaded: 03/25/2023. The term "Marxist Socialist State" is widely used by Marxist–Leninist parties, theorists, and governments to mean a state under the control of a vanguard party that is organizing the economic, social, and political affairs of said state toward the construction of socialism. *Marxists often refer to socialism as the first, necessary phase on the way from capitalism to communism.*

232 In the context of the discussion in this book, "all dimensions … of modern societies" include religion, family, education, law, and media.

"INVISIBLE IDENTITY BASED SYSTEMS"

"Social Justice scholarship presupposes that social inequalities are generated by 'invisible identity-based systems' of power and privilege."[233]

Invisible identity-based systems of power and privilege are maintained by dominant discourses and perpetuated by the social construction of knowledge "in the service of power."[234]

The Privileged are then presumed guilty of perpetuating power imbalances for the purpose of oppressing the Underprivileged. Therefore, Woke Social Justice activists conclude, with absolute certainty, (though apart from any evidence-based knowledge), that the Privileged are *all* racist "White Supremacists," and "all men are sexist; racism and sexism are systems that can exist and oppress absent even a single person with racist or sexist intentions or beliefs (in the usual sense of the terms); sex is not biological and exists on a spectrum, language can be literal violence, denial of gender identity is killing people, the wish to remedy disability and obesity is hateful, and everything needs to be decolonized."[235]

DEI's purported "decolonizing" involves the exposing of "invisible identity-based systems of power and privilege" and the dismantling and rebuilding of these systems of institutional racism and oppression. The Privileged are blind to their racist "white supremacy" and colonizing inclinations, but the inherent "standpoint"[236] of the Underprivileged is their source of awareness of "invisible identity-based systems." Diversity and

---

[233] Helen Pluckrose & James Lindsay. *Cynical Theories.* P.182.

[234] Ibid.

[235] Ibid., 183.

[236] CRT's version of diversity is based on cultural relativism and standpoint theory which stresses that truth is accessible only to minority groups.

Inclusion[237] effectively disrupt and dismantle the racist, and sexist power-dynamics, towards the rebuilding and re-envisioning of a corporation's equitable future.

CRT's version of diversity is based on cultural relativism and standpoint theory which stresses that truth is accessible only to minority groups, i.e., the Underprivileged. Men and maleness are "socially enforced by hegemonic, dominant and powerful, discourses"[238] and therefore, men, particularly white men, are "toxic." Consequently, standpoint theory assumes the politically correct right to place limitations on reality, and therefore, any accounts of truth regarding the experience of the privileged are summarily dismissed.

As inferred in Chapter 6, there are dissenters *vis-à-vis* the assumptions of Standpoint Theory. Inclusion then becomes a justification for the "firing" of "problematic" individuals. An old communist strategy, designed for the taking over of institutions, referred to as "entryism," is then employed.[239] The Human Resources Department puts in place a "Diversity Hiring Policy" and the new hires, the replacements of the dissenters, are then "friendlies," that is, they are fully supportive practitioners of Diversity, Equity, and Inclusion[240]— Once in place, "entryism" becomes a vital, spontaneous practice in the culture of a corporation.[241]

Diversity, Equity, and Inclusion simultaneously work together: Critical Diversity and Critical Inclusion are the means, and Critical Equity is the

237 "Inclusion," is seen as "irrefutable evidence of a dissenter's 'white fragility,' 'unconscious bias,' or 'internalized white supremacy.'"

238 Helen Pluckrose & James Lindsay. *Cynical Theories*. Page 155.

239 James Lindsay. The Marxist Roots of DEI— Season 1: Equity.

240 Ibid.

241 Ibid.

end[242]— *Re*: DEI's operational mode, "Diversity," and "Inclusion" will precede "Equity" below.

"CRITICAL DIVERSITY"

Critical theorists stress that Critical Race Theory's inherent "virtues" are diversity, equity, and inclusion.

The traditional (or common) understanding of diversity is centered in difference— Each individual possesses a different point of view, background, and experience from the rest of the group. Some individual traits, e.g., race, and gender, are seen, and some are unseen. A person is not diverse; a person is a unique member of a group, organization, neighborhood, or family that exists in relationship to one another— This is a common (normative) understanding of diversity.

Contrarily, "Critical Diversity," framed in Critical Race Theory, is defined by identity politics. Therefore, it has nothing to do with differing points of view but is rather committed to respect for superficial differences (e.g., race, gender, and identity) among social and cultural groups— Critical Race Theory's version of diversity is based on cultural relativism and standpoint theory which stresses that truth is accessible only to minority groups, i.e., the Underprivileged (The Marxist binary— Privileged Oppressors and Underprivileged Oppressed— is the political scaffolding for Standpoint Theory).

In the Woke Critical Theory context of DEI in general, and "Diversity" in particular, the only relevant "reality" (i.e., "pseudo-reality") is "power dynamics." "Power dynamics," in relation to Identity Politics (or "Identity

---

242 Ibid.

Marxism"[243]), stresses that "identity" is the most important attribute involving an authentic perspective— Standpoint Theory (*re:* CRT) is a power dynamic that magnifies the woke identity differences related to racial and/or sexual identity.

However, regardless of race, one must have the correct politics, otherwise they do not possess authentic identity. The reason for this is because, "Identity Marxism" is the indispensable "construct for understanding relevant difference"[244] — "The conditions of power in the society, structurally, and materially determine who you are"[245] — *Only Critical Theory, and specifically, the combination of "Intersectionality" and "Standpoint Theory," can determine what is "diversity" and what isn't.*[246]

People viewing diversity through mainstream social lens do not see power dynamics proactively involved in social scenarios as do people using Social Justice lens. Robin DiAngelo introduces a distinct student/instructor scenario to elucidate this point: "The students, looking through the lens of individualism, see diversity in terms of personality. From this lens, everyone is first and foremost a unique individual and social groups

---

243 "Identity Marxism" is a distinction made by James Lindsay. "Identity Marxism" is so-called because it is defined and used in the context of the Marxist binary. ("Identity Marxism" will be referred to and developed in this discussion. "The Marxist Roots of DEI - Session 2: Diversity" | James Lindsay https://www.youtube.com/watch?v=C-aarD-dFm4. Downloaded: 04/13/2023.

244 Ibid.

245 Ibid.

246 Equity is implicated in this conclusion. James Lindsay explains that "equity refers to social equity which becomes a pillar of public administration in the 1960s— And then when you infuse that with the Woke Marxist approach it becomes Critical Social Equity which is the administered precursor to Critical Social Justice. Critical Diversity is the way of explaining this."

memberships are unimportant. The instructor, who is looking through a critical social justice lens, sees the room in terms of key social groups."[247]

From the perspective of Social Justice, "… many minoritized groups are absent, including peoples of color, people with visible disabilities, people from a range of socio-economic classes, people in nontraditional gender career tracks, and people with different linguistic and cultural capital."[248] What does "minoritized" mean? Standpoint Theory and Intersectionality are power dynamics used by Critical Diversity to resist the minoritizing of minorities by systemic White Supremacy— Whites are blinded by their privilege and are therefore often unaware of the harm they impose, *viz.*, the reducing of minorities to irrelevancy, or "minoritizing" them.

In his, "New Discourses" lecture, "The Marxist Roots of DEI,"[249] James Lindsay analogizes the roles of ancient pagan gods and Woke Critical Theory power dynamics. For example, among the Greek gods and goddesses are Zeus, the god of the sky and king of Olympus; Zeus was the most powerful Greek god. Zeus had a bad temper, and when he lost it, the weather became extremely threatening to the inhabitants of the earth. Poseidon, the god of the sea was the brother of Zeus. And like his brother, Poseidon's bad temper would throw the sea into uncontrollable turmoil. Therefore, sailors prayed to Poseidon for safety. And Aphrodite was worshipped as the goddess of love and beauty in many of the city-states of Ancient Greece.

Regarding the "Invisible Identity-Based Systems" discussed above— Marxian mythology works the same way as the mythological deities of

---

247 Robin DiAngelo and Özlem Sensoy. *Is Everyone Really Equal? An Introduction to Key Concepts in Social Justice Education.* 2nd Ed. (2012). PP. 218-220. Quoted by: James Lindsay. "The Marxist Roots of DEI - Session 2: Diversity."

248 Ibid.

249 "The Marxist Roots of DEI - Session 2: Diversity" | James Lindsay https://www.youtube.com/watch?v=C-aarD-dFm4. Downloaded: 04/13/2023.

ancient Greece: human beings are manipulated and controlled by invisible power dynamics, the invisible super-structures and systems are powers over society— *What the pantheon of gods were to ancient Greek mythology, the power dynamic domains are to Critical Theory and Identity Marxism.*

POSITIONALITY AND CRITICAL CONSCIOUSNESS

According to Critical Diversity, our lives are ordered by power dynamics (like the mythological gods ordered the lives of the ancients). And a hierarchy of racial oppression and dominance exists and at the top is whiteness and at the bottom is blackness.[250] A mechanism moves in a downward direction towards "anti-blackness" and an upward direction towards "white adjacency" — Where you stand, in relation to the hierarchy, is your positionality according to power dynamics. (The hierarchal mechanism is rooted in a "master/slave" dialectic, that is, Privileged/Oppressors and Underprivileged/Oppressed).

"Critical consciousness is the idea that when you see it, you can see it"[251] — If you have access to privilege, you have a false consciousness. You are narcissistic, you believe the world is ordered for you, and it ought to be, you earned it. But if you were to become intoxicated by Critical Theory, you would have a true understanding of the world; the nature of the power dynamics would become visible to you, and you would have an awakened, "critical consciousness."

You don't have authentic diversity unless you have a critical consciousness; your diversity is not authentic unless it is expressed through an awakened critical consciousness, that is, you must express your authenticity

250 Ibid.

251 Ibid.

through Critical Race Theory, Gender Theory, Queer Theory, or whatever Social Justice theory that you conform to.

COUNTER-CULTURAL HEGEMONY

Antonio Gramsci (*re:* Ch. 2) believed that cultures, particularly western cultures, created a "force field" that repelled communism.[252] Western cultures transmit their anti-communism from generation to generation through key cultural institutions— religion, family, education, law, and media. To transform a culturally robust civilization like America, according to Gramsci, you must infiltrate those key cultural pillars— the media must become a source of Marxist propaganda, education must be dedicated to Marxist indoctrination, the church is to become a Marxist propaganda outlet— and the family must be abolished and replaced by the institution of the communist state.

How is the dismantling of the West accomplished? By purging key cultural institutions of dissidents through demoralizing them and forcing them to leave; and then replacing them with Woke conformists. The demoralization process— i.e., "entryism," involves extortion, fear, threats of PR nightmares, and ruined reputations.

The dismantling of the institution's culture continues until an authentic Marxist Identity emerges in the form of DEI, CRT, or SEL (Social-Emotional-Learning)— Since DEI is primarily dedicated to "leveling the playing field for everyone" — "Equity work is everybody's work."[253]

---

[252] Ibid.

[253] APPENDIX E. Letter to Governor Jay Inslee (June 2020). State of Washington, Office of Equity Task Force (Final Proposal). June 12, 2020. Downloaded: 03/28/2023.

"CRITICAL INCLUSION"

"Liberating tolerance, then, would mean intolerance against movements from the Right, and toleration of movements from the Left"
— Herbert Marcuse.

Before discussing "inclusion" in relationship to DEI, we need to distinguish "inclusion" from "critical inclusion." Traditionally, inclusion is about the acceptance of, and accommodation of anyone with a disability, infirmity, or limitation. Traditionally, inclusion is prompted by compassion. But the socio-cultural shift in the late 1980s towards intersectional feminism, Queer Theory, and Critical Race Theory, resulted in "ability" and/or "disability" being viewed as a social construct— Inclusion "… has since become increasingly radical and in denial about reality."[254]

However, "Inclusion" is generally defined in unqualified terms of acceptance in Critical Theory contexts, and consequently, it is passively incorporated into social and governmental practices, policies, and actions. For example, the Final Proposal of the Washington State 2020 Office of Equity Task Force defines Inclusion: "Intentionally designed, active, and ongoing engagement with people that ensures opportunities and pathways for participation in all aspects of group, organization, or community, including decision making processes. Inclusion is not a natural consequence of diversity. There must be intentional and consistent efforts to create and sustain a participative environment. Inclusion refers to how groups show that people are valued as respected members of the group, team, organization,

[254] Helen Pluckrose & James Lindsay. *Cynical Theories.* P. 160. The phrase, "denial about reality" is fully explained by Pluckrose and Lindsay, in the context of this book, the emphases here is on "moral subjectivity" which has no correspondence to objective reality and therefore, it is founded on arbitrary applications of Critical Theory.

or community. Inclusion is often created through progressive, consistent, actions to expand, include, and share."[255]

The State of Washington *appears* to define "Inclusion" traditionally. But, Washington State's definition of "Inclusion" is not traditional, it not inclusive— Critical Inclusion empowers Diversity to act in *exclusionary* ways. Critical Inclusion is a "moral lever" that initiates the censorship and purging of those whose presence makes people in "protected classes" — the Underprivileged— feel like they "cannot bring their whole self to work."[256]

Critical Inclusion is therefore *always* about power dynamics and consequently, it is equally about exclusion— *Psychological safety is hyper-emphasized by Critical Inclusion.* If, for example, white supremacy is suspected, someone who is a member of a minority race may hesitate to speak up, or if heteronormativity is even assumed to be present, a gay person may feel psychologically unsafe— "Microaggressions"[257] must be detected and eradicated before a working environment is negatively impacted.

---

[255] 2020 Office of Equity Task Force, Final Proposal. "Equity, Diversity, and Inclusion." Downloaded: 04/25/2023. p. 2.

[256] James Lindsay. "The Marxist Roots of DEI— Session 3: Inclusion." https://www.youtube.com/watch?v=IsX8zPuSVRk. Downloaded: 04/25/2023.

[257] C.M. Pierce defines microaggressions: "One must not look for the gross and obvious. The subtle, cumulative mini assault is the substance of today's racism." *Offensive Mechanisms: The Vehicle for Micro-Aggression.* Porter Sargent Publisher: Boston, MA. 1970. C.M. Pierce was a Harvard professor, and he appears to have originated the term: "microaggressions." Sue D. Wing, "Microaggressions: More Than Just Race," *Psychology Today.* https://www.psychologytoday.com/us/blog/microaggressions-in-everyday-life/201011/microaggressions-more-just-race, provides a full definition: "The everyday verbal, nonverbal, and environmental slights, snubs, or insults, whether intentional or unintentional, which communicate hostile, derogatory, or negative messages to target persons based solely upon their marginalized group membership. In many cases, these hidden messages may invalidate the group identity or experiential reality of target persons, demean them on a personal or group level. Communicate they are lesser human beings, suggest they do not belong with the majority group, threaten and intimidate, or relegate them to inferior status and treatment." Quoted by: James Lindsay. "The Marxist Roots of DEI— Session 3: Inclusion."

"REPRESSIVE TOLERANCE"

Critical Inclusion is the "mechanism" through which *Repressive Tolerance* is inserted into the operations of organizations, corporations, and institutions. "Repressive Tolerance" originates in the thought of Herbert Marcuse. [258] According to Marcuse, "Repressive tolerance" is to be understood on two levels— The first level directly applies to Critical Inclusion and "... the unthinking acceptance of entrenched attitudes and ideas, even when these are obviously damaging to other people, or indeed the environment (the painfully slow response to warnings about climate change and environmental degradation might be seen as an example of this)." [259]

Relative to Critical Inclusion, Repressive Tolerance incorporates means of totalitarian control into the culture of learning and work environments, prompting corporations, organizations, and institutions to ask, "*What causes exclusion*?" over, "*How can we create inclusive environments*"? Critical Inclusion then begins to create hostile environments in which a person who feels "minoritized" by a "privileged" person is advantaged over the one they claim makes them uncomfortable— the Marxist binary is in place: *Privileged individuals are the victimizers and the Underprivileged are victims.*

---

[258] Herbert Marcuse. A Critique of Pure Tolerance. 1965. https://la.utexas.edu/users/hcleaver/330T/350kPEEMarcuseToleranceTable.pdf. Downloaded: 04/19/2023.

[259] Ian Buchanan. *A Dictionary of Critical Theory.* (1st Ed.) Oxford University Press. 2010. https://www.oxfordreference.com/display/10.1093/oi/authority.20110803100414515;jsessionid=51A066FFA2AB8782E85350295629B46B. Downloaded: 04/27/2023. And second level of Repressive Tolerance directly applies to Critical Social Justice: "... the vocal endorsement of actions that are manifestly aggressive towards other people (the popular support in the US and the UK in the aftermath of 9/11 and 7/7 for the respective government's attempts to override or limit *habeas corpus* is a clear example of this)." Marcuse concludes this thought in a typical Marxist manner: "Genuine tolerance can only exist in a situation of intolerance for these limits on real freedom." Re: Chapter 8, "The Progressive Left's 'Long March Through The Institutions.'"

Inclusion then becomes leverage for policy changes, control of how people talk, and interact with one another— "The rationale is to create a non-discriminatory environment but when you frame it in the critical perspective, you create a 'hyper-non-discriminatory environment on their terms."[260] And therefore, any opposition to Social Justice's applied "Diversity," "Equity," and/or "Inclusion," is seen as "irrefutable evidence of a dissenter's 'white fragility,' 'unconscious bias,' or 'internalized white supremacy'"[261] — Marcuse's comments regarding "Discriminating Tolerance" are here, illuminating regarding a Marxist mindset: "I suggested in 'Repressive Tolerance' the practice of discriminating tolerance in an inverse direction, as a means of shifting the balance between Right and Left by restraining the liberty of the Right, thus counteracting the pervasive inequality of freedom (unequal opportunity of access to the means of democratic persuasion) and strengthening the oppressed against the [oppressor]. Tolerance would be restricted with respect to movements of a demonstrably aggressive or destructive character (destructive of the prospects for peace, justice, and freedom for all)."[262]

Marcuse's contention is clear, anything that can be used to provide support for the "unjust" majority (i.e., the Privileged) has on its side an unjust balance of power and therefore, it must not be tolerated "if it can oppose liberation from oppression."[263] Repressive Tolerance's pseudo-realistic world creates a double-standard: Those who uncritically accept Critical Theory and its form of "Inclusion," experience unrestricted tolerance but for those

---

260 James Lindsay. "The Marxist Roots of DEI— Session 3: Inclusion."

261 Ibid.

262 Herbert Marcuse. "Critique of Pure Tolerance." Subheading: "Repressive Tolerance." 109.

263 James Lindsay. "Tolerance: Social Justice Usage." Under the subtitle: "New Discourses Commentary." https://newdiscourses.com/tftw-tolerance/. Downloaded: 04/27/2023.

who represent "dominant groups" and are therefore, inclined to resist the policies prescribed by Critical Inclusion, experience abject intolerance.

This "double-standard" is unequivocally Marxist: "The basis for this double-standard is that intolerance plus power causes more harm whereas intolerance plus oppression creates less and may effect liberation."[264] And therefore, the outcome of the double-standard is justified in the name of Social Justice Critical Theory: The suspected Oppressor and the Oppressed victim, exchange places— Injustice is justice—*"The Party's interest is to be treated as a reality that ranks above reality itself"*[265] — A thoroughly Marxist way of thinking.[266]

"CRITICAL EQUITY" CASE STUDY: WASHINGTON STATE OFFICE OF EQUITY TASK FORCE

Equality means each individual or group of people is given the same resources or opportunities. Equity recognizes that each person has different circumstances and allocates the exact resources and opportunities needed to reach an equal outcome.[267]

---

[264] Ibid." https://newdiscourses.com/tftw-tolerance/. Downloaded: 04/27/2023. Under the heading of "New Discourses Commentary," Lindsay further observes: "… expressing genuine intolerance against white people as an 'antiracist' project, genuine intolerance against men as feminist project, and genuine intolerance against straight and straight-passing homosexuals as 'anti-heteronormative' project are all considered perfectly acceptable and are, in fact, encouraged by critical race Theory and whiteness studies, feminism and gender studies, and queer theory, respectively."

[265] Angelo M. Codevilla. "The Rise of Political Correctness." 1 of 12 pages

[266] *Re:* Herbert Marcuse: "Liberating tolerance, then, would mean intolerance against movements from the Right and toleration from movements from the Left." *Repressive Tolerance.* 109.

[267] Marin Health and Human Services. https://www.marinhhs.org › files › boards › genera.

Esmael López, Community Engagement Coordinator for the Washington State Office of Equity Task Force reported: "Since the beginning of this project, Task Force members agreed that the most marginalized communities hold the key to understanding strategies for meaningful and authentic community engagement. We must recognize that we still have barriers to knock down in order to do this work in an equitable way. One of these barriers is how we engage with tribes in this state." [268] The Washington State Office of Equity Task Force initially engaged "the most marginalized communities" with a survey. Responses to the online survey are reflected in in the Final Proposal, Figure 10[269]: What's your greatest hope or dream for your community?

"That every parent's dreams for their children will have a fair opportunity to be fulfilled."
"I dream of a place with sincere, compassionate, and sensitive conversation between decision-makers and community members and laws that reflect this."
"That each individual can aspire to be what they want to be and will see themselves represented in Government, leadership and in all types of careers."
"That Latinx immigrant, Yakama indigenous, and AAPI voices would be centered in decision-making."
"That black and brown persons are no longer systematically disenfranchised."
"My greatest hope is to be a part of a truly inclusive community."

[268] Esmael López, Community Engagement Coordination for the Washington State Office of Equity Force.

[269] 2020 Office of Equity Task Force, Final Proposal. P. 28.

Equity appears to be caring, compassionate, and worthy of the overwhelming support of, in this case, the residents of the state of Washington. But the subtitle above is: "Critical Equity;" Equity, framed in Critical Theory, references The Marxist Socialist State, and the repressive tolerance of Critical Theory is as much about intolerance as it is tolerance: "tolerance" is extended *only* to the Woke [progressive] Left and "intolerance" is reserved *only* for the "Privileged [conservative] Right." [270] And whereas, as above mentioned, the Marxist binary is posited on grounds of moral subjectivity and therefore, it is based on the mere preference of Woke Critical Theory, one must always remember, "Party Ideology" (i.e., Woke Marxist Ideology) displaces objective reality in Critical Theory contexts. A bold example follows.

EQUITY TASK FORCE "BIRTH PANGS" —JUNE 10, 2020

"That's news to me, so I'll have to reserve any comment about it," said a seeming oblivious Governor after hearing from a reporter that the largest city in his state was under siege by anarchists. In an apparent attempt to impress upon the Governor the seriousness of the situation, the reporter announced that the anarchists were not allowing people to come and go freely. The Governor responded, somewhat indifferently, "I have not heard anything about that."[271] News of the pending birth of the Capitol Hill

---

[270] Herbert Marcuse, Robert Paul Wolff, and Barrington Moore, Jr. A Critique of Pure Tolerance. 1965. https://la.utexas.edu/users/hcleaver/330T/350kPEEMarcuseToleranceTable.pdf. P. 109. Downloaded: 05/02/2023.

[271] Twitter Feed. June 10, 2020. https://twitter.com/Rebecca_Perry/status/1270857416955981825?ref_src=twsrc%5Etfw%7Ctwcamp%5Etweetembed%7Ctwterm%5E1270857416955981825%7Ctwgr%5E05714231d9d89880b4537d607e9a2bcd1b1db65d%7Ctwcon%5Es1_&ref_url=https%3A%2F%2Fwww.foxnews.com%2Fpolitics%2Fdem-governor-mocked-for-pleading-ignorance-on-seattle-anarchist-takeover. Downloaded: 03/30/2023.

Organized Protest (CHOP) was delivered to Governor Jay Inslee on June 10, 2020.

Once riots broke out, activists forged chasmic civil/racial divisions in the city— "... the first days[272] of Black Lives Matter protests in Seattle, following the police killing of George Floyd, were days of anger and power as thousands took to the streets to protest and form a movement." [273] By Thursday, June 4th, 2020, just ten days after George Floyd's murder in Minneapolis, the battlelines between protesters and police had been drawn at 11th and Pine."[274]

On June 6th, Seattle City Council Members joined the Black Life Matters protesters. And on June 8, 2020, Seattle police officers removed sensitive equipment and documents from the Eighth Precinct at 12th and Pine following Mayor Durkan's order to remove police lines and barriers that had provided a protective perimeter around the precinct. The forming of CHOP— The Capitol Hill Organized Protest,[275] followed.

The occupation of five square blocks in the city-center of Seattle made worldwide headlines. And as lawlessness prevailed, Seattle's WOKE 2.0, Mayor Durkan, described CHOP as having a "block party atmosphere," that could turn into a "Summer of Love.[276]" But instead, CHAZ (Capitol

---

272 Protests in Seattle, WA. began on May 29, 2020.

273 "CHOP: One year later — The East Precinct is Abandoned and the Protest Zone Forms." Capitol Hill Seattle Blog— Community News for All the Hill." Posted: June 9, 2021. https://www.capitolhillseattle.com/2021/06/chop-one-year-later-the-east-precinct-is-abandoned-and-the-protest-zone-forms/. Downloaded: 10/21/2022.

274 Ibid.

275 "Who ordered the abandonment of the East Precinct?" — Update. Capitol Hill Seattle Blog. Posted 11/18/2020. https://www.capitolhillseattle.com/2020/11/who-ordered-the-abandonment-of-the-east-precinct/. Downloaded: 10/21/2022.

276 Ian Schwartz. "Seattle Mayor Durkan: CHAZ - "Block Party Atmosphere," Could Turn Into "Summer of Love." https://www.realclearpolitics.com/video/2020/06/12/seattle_mayor_durkan_chaz_has_a_block_party_atmosphere_could_turn_into_summer_of_love.html. 06/12/2020. Downloaded: 10/21/2022.

Hill Autonomous Zone) turned into a "Summer of Crime" including property damage and assaults, but most tragic, two homicides took place—Horace Lorenzo Anderson Jr., 19 years-old, was shot on June 20, and just over a week later, another teenager, 16-year-old Antonio Mays Jr., was shot multiple times while inside a Jeep Cherokee.[277]

THE CHOP "PROTESTERS" DEMANDS

Whereas numerous demands were debated, some expressed their belief that the protests were the beginning of a larger revolution, while others contested that police brutality should be the immediate focus. In the spirit of "Repressive Tolerance," Three principal demands were settled on:

1. **Cut Seattle's $409-million police budget by 50%.**

Seattle Mayor Jenny Durkan asked police and city staff to develop scenarios for cuts of 20%, 30%, and 50%, respectively, to the Seattle Police Department's budget for 2021. But "We're not getting real answers," complained Councilmember Kshama Sawant. Sawant continued, "I think at some point the Council has to say to the Seattle Police Department, your budget is no more than $200 million, which is already too much...It's your job to use those funds in a way that actually protects people."[278] The 2021

---

277 Associated Press. "Family of Teen Killed in CHOP Zone: Seattle Enabled Danger." https://www.usnews.com/news/best-states/washington/articles/2022-07-19/family-of-teen-killed-in-chop-zone-seattle-enabled-danger. 07'19/2022. Downloaded: 10/21/2022.

278 Sebastian Robertson. KING5 News. "Proposal Would Cut $49 Million from Seattle Police Budget as Officers Leave in Record Numbers." Published: 10/19/2020. Updated: 10/20/2020. https://www.king5.com/article/news/local/seattle/seattle-budget-committee-to-consider-proposed-police-budget-cuts/281-8fd1edd9-5fe8-41a3-92c6-3f01c-b6e6bc3. Downloaded: 05/05/2023.

Seattle police budget was cut 18% ($49 million) and officers began leaving the department in record numbers (police resignations were double the highest month on record).[279] One officer captured the mood; in a written exit interview obtained by King 5 News, the officer stated: "I refuse to work for this socialist city council."[280]

2. **Redistribute funding to community programs and services in historically black communities.**

In response to the second demand made by protesters, Mayor Durkan committed $100 million in funding for Black, Indigenous and People of Color communities in the 2021 budget.

3. **And assurance must be made that protesters will not be charged with crimes.**

The vast majority of citations and charges against George Floyd protesters were ultimately dropped, dismissed or otherwise not filed, according to a Guardian (A News Website) analysis of law enforcement records and media reports in a dozen jurisdictions around the nation to include, L.A., Philadelphia, Chicago, New York, and Seattle.[281] (A more developed—national analysis/explanation of the lawlessness advocated by Critical Theory Social Justice, to include Seattle, will be made in Chapter 8, "The Progressive Left's Long March Through The Institutions").

---

[279] Ibid.

[280] Ibid. SPD Chief Carmen Best resigned as the chief of police three days later, after the Seattle City Council voted to downsize the department by up to 100 out of its 1,400 officers.

[281] Tom Perkins. "The Guardian" (A News Website). "Most Charges Against George Floyd Protesters Dropped, Analysis Shows." April 2021. https://amp.theguardian.com/us-news/2021/apr/17/george-floyd-protesters-charges-citations-analysis. Downloaded: 05/05/2023.

THE BIRTH OF THE EQUITY TASK FORCE —JULY 1, 2020

"*Disrupt—Dismantle—Re-Envision & Rebuild*"
— Equity Office Task Force[282]

Following Governor Inslee's signing E2SHB 1783, the Washington State Office of Equity was established on July 1, 2020. Washington is the first state in the United States to commit to the Critical Social Justice practices of "Disruption" of systems of power, dominance, and oppression,[283] and "Dismantling" of "racism, sexism, homophobia and heteronormativity, transphobia and cisnormativity, ableism and dis-ableism, fatphobia and thin-normativity, patriarchy, misogyny, and white supremacy[284]— Critical Theorists see these "unjust systems" as not merely plagues in our societies, but they are "woven into the fabric of our societies."[285]

Therefore, Washington State's Equity Office Task Force's "re-envisioning" and "rebuilding" is a clarion call for social revolution on the scale of the replacing of the present liberal order with a new Critical Order[286]: A Marxist Socialist State. Washington State government must, therefore, be transformed along Critical Race Theory lines— And therein, "The

282 Washington State Office of Equity. Summary Proposal. https://healthequity.wa.gov/sites/default/files/2022-01/Equity%20Office%20TF_Final%20Proposal%20Summary%20%28ADA%20compatible%29.pdf. Downloaded: 3/23/2023. P. 1 of 5 pages.

283 James Lindsay. "Disrupt," Social Justice Usage. https://newdiscourses.com/tftw-disrupt/ Downloaded: 08/07/2023.

284 James Lindsay. "Dismantle," Social Justice Usage. https://newdiscourses.com/tftw-dismantle/ Downloaded: 08/07, 2023.

285 Ibid.

286 Ibid.

Office of Equity will model the use of an intersectional, multi-dimensional framework."[287]

Washington State's *Equity's "Birth Pangs,"* and *Equity's "Birth"* were preceded by a Marxist ideological tactic known as: "Demoralization."

SEATTLE'S DEMORALIZATION

As the COVID 19 pandemic created an environment of despair, throwing people into disorder and confusion; disrupting every level of day-to-day life— Fierce protests, endorsed by progressive political power, quickly turned into violent riots, following the death of George Floyd. News outlets were dominated with images of wide-spread devastation—Cities across the United States were burning and as they were being reduced to rubble, so was the livelihood of millions of Americans. And as families stressed over their financial future, they watched looters, featured on every major network nightly, freely walk out of stores with the spoils of their lawlessness.

Seattle was among American cities subjected to such demoralization and its traumatizing effects. Demoralization is a totalitarian tactic (e.g., communism, fascism, socialism) used for the purpose of creating dependency on the state by, primarily, penetrating basic anxieties people have

[287] 2020 Office of Equity Task Force, Final Proposal. Linh Phung Huynh, Project Manager, Esmael Lopez, Community Engagement Coordinator, Hannah Fernald, Administrative Coordinator. "Our Greatest Hopes for the Office of Equity." https://healthequity.wa.gov/sites/default/files/202201/EquityOfficeTF Final%20Proposal%20 %28final%29.pdf. Downloaded: 03/28/2023. P. 54. This statement is reinforced by the final proposal of the Office of Equity Task Force, page 78: **Intersectional:** Accounts for people's overlapping identities for understanding of the complexity of their life outcomes and experiences. Intersectionality deals with multiple forms of discrimination (e.g., ableism, racism, sexism, ageism, classism, discrimination based on sexual orientation and gender identity) that compound oppression. Also, see: Ch. 6, Kimberlé Crenshaw, "Critical Race Theory, Intersectionality."

about the future in times of cultural turmoil. The pandemic environment plus the politically sanctioned anarchy, as a direct fallout of the murder of George Floyd, created a nation-wide sense of loss of control; an ideal opportunity to demoralize the city of Seattle and with it, the whole of Washington State.

The rewarding of the lawless protesters by meeting their demands, and the absence of justice on behalf of the Police and the Citizenry of Seattle, is typical of Marxist's outcomes [288]— The extreme disruption to day-to-day life by the pandemic, the hopeless sense of loss of control, and the lack of clarity as to ways out of the dilemma significantly reduce a population's resistance to whatever is next. *This is the purpose of demoralization.*

THE OFFICE OF EQUITY TASK FORCE

The Washington State Office of Equity defines "Equity"— "Developing, strengthening, and supporting policies and procedures that distribute and prioritize resources to those who have been historically and currently marginalized, including tribes. It requires the elimination of systemic barriers that have been deeply entrenched in systems of inequality and oppression— Equity achieves procedural and outcome fairness, promoting dignity, honor, and respect for all people."[289]

The goal of the Equity Office Task Force is introduced in two words, "Systems Change" — Explanation follows: "Participants hoped the Office of Equity can be a catalyst for change at the policy and systems level. The Office would promote the recognition that systems work as intended, and

---

[288] Re: Critical Inclusion and "Repressive Toleration."

[289] Washington State Office of Equity. Summary Proposal. https://healthequity.wa.gov/sites/default/files/2022-01/Equity%20Office%20TF_Final%20Proposal%20Summary%20%28ADA%20compatible%29.pdf. Downloaded: 3/23/2023. P. 1 of 5 pages.

we need to dismantle and rebuild the current one. Many participants said that mentorship and training for agency leaders would be critical in this work, especially around recognizing white privilege and white culture, since leaders cannot dismantle structures, they cannot see."[290]

The goal of the Equity Office Task Force reflects Woke Critical Theory— Diversity informs the blindness of the privileged ("they cannot see") and therefore the Office of Equity's Systems Change "at the policy systems level" must be ordered by Critical Race Theory's Standpoint Theory. And under the heading: Guiding Statements For The Office of Equity, the Summary Proposal speaks of Washington's determination to be an "Anti-Racist Government"— "The Office of Equity should lead the state toward becoming a truly transformed Government enterprise— one that embeds equity and justice into every action, and where doing so is simply the default. We believe that such a system is achievable and that a critical step forward is to *declare and manifest WA State as an anti-racist government system.* Doing so will send a powerful message across the state and help communities hold the enterprise accountable to change that is neither incremental nor reactionary—but rather—*Change that is transformative.*"[291]

The Final Proposal quotes Ibram X. Kendi, the author of, *How to Be an Antiracist,* as an apparent source of inspiration: "The opposite of racist isn't 'not racist.' It is 'anti-racist.' What's the difference? One endorses either the idea of a racial hierarchy as a racist, or racial equality as an anti-racist. One either believes problems are rooted in groups of people, as a racist, or locates the roots of problems in power and policies, as an anti-racist.

[290] 2020 Office of Equity Task Force, Final Proposal. "Systems Change." Downloaded: 03/28/2023. P.35.

[291] Washington State Office of Equity. Summary Proposal. Page 1 of 6 pages. Downloaded 03/29/2023. (Bolded phraseology is in the summary proposal document).

One either allows racial inequities to persevere, as a racist, or confronts racial inequities, as an anti-racist. There is no in-between safe space of 'not racist.'"[292]

It is noteworthy that Ibram Kendi unqualifiedly asserts, "*In order to truly be antiracist, you also have to truly be anti-capitalist.*"[293] Capitalism and "whiteness" are foundational to privileged hegemony qua Woke Marxist ideology (*re*: Ch. 3)— *The priority regarding "change that is transformative" is directly related to Marxist Socialism.*

"OFFICE OF EQUITY TASK FORCE OPERATING PRINCIPLES"

The Washington State Task Force Operating Principles provide cameos of the over-all mood of the Final Proposal and therefore, they serve to deepen the reader's understanding of Washington state's pursuit of "Equity." Issues surfacing in the five Task Force Operating Principles listed below are critiqued in terms of the final proposal's collusion with Critical Race Theory.

OPERATING PRINCIPLE #1: "EMBRACE EQUITY"

"We are on a journey toward well-being, where everyone has the opportunity to reach their full potential, as defined by those impacted by inequity. Embracing equity requires us to identify, name, and dismantle institutional racism and oppression."[294]

---

292 2020 Office of Equity Task Force, Final Proposal. "Systems Transformation: Toward an Equitable, Just, and Sustainable Future." P.109. Downloaded 03/29/2023.

293 Quoted by Christopher F. Rufo, *Primus* Ibid. 3 of 7 pages.

294 Office of Equity Task Force Operating Principles. Adopted: August 19, 2019. Download: 08/15/2023.

"EMBRACE EQUITY" — INTERPRETATION

"**Embrace Equity**" — Major corporations rely on Environmental, Social, and Governance scores for sustainability. The "S" (Social) is "Equity" — ESG scores incorporate different factors such as "climate change, diversity, equity, and inclusion (DEI), and human rights."[295] "An ESG score is an objective measurement or evaluation of a given company, fund, or security's performance with respect to Environmental, Social, and Governance (ESG) issues"[296] — ESG scores are generated by "external and internal stakeholders."[297]

External stakeholders scrutinize company disclosures, public information, "and conduct primary research with company management about the organization's sustainability efforts."[298] And Internal ESG scores, among other tasks, "gauge performance within an organization."[299]

Noah Miller, Chief Strategy Officer, and Head of ESG Advisory Services, summarily states, "ESG scoring systems are created for different use cases and for different stakeholders (based on their associated needs); some are designed to support capital allocation decisions (like investments or assessing credit risk), while others may support human capital management and staffing decisions."[300]

Additionally, in the first entry, "**Embrace Equity**," note, as well, "Embracing equity requires us to identify, name, and dismantle institutional racism and oppression." "Dismantle" is central to Gramsci's

---

[295] Noah Miller. Updated 12/14/2022. Reviewed by Kyle Perterdy. https://corporatefinanceinstitute.com/resources/esg/esg-score/. Downloaded: 03/31/2023.

[296] Ibid.

[297] Ibid.

[298] Ibid.

[299] Ibid.

[300] Ibid.

structural/superstructural approach to cultural revolution—This is the language of Woke Critical Theory, "Counter-Hegemonic" cultural revolution.

OPERATING PRINCIPLE #2: "FOCUS ON RACISM"

"Racism, a construct of white supremacy, is used to oppress communities as the 'Other.' We are committed to promoting equity for all historically marginalized communities. We recognize that different forms of discrimination and oppression are related to each other, and we will take these relationships into account. We also recognize that racism is ingrained in our history and deeply embedded in our institutions today, leading to the inequities we see across all sectors. We seek to challenge and undo all forms of oppression, and we are committed to centering racism as our primary focus."

"**Focus On Racism**" — In Woke Marxist categories, "white supremacy" is identified with the "Privileged" and coupled with the revisionist history of CRT: "We also recognize that racism is ingrained in our history and deeply embedded in our institutions today, leading to the inequities we see across all sectors" — Is "racism" a product of "Whiteness"? And if so, will a counter-cultural hegemonic revolution sufficiently dismantle "systemic racism" to the degree necessary to eliminate racism from the state of Washington, and the United States and Western Culture?

On page 41 of the Final Proposal, Adam Serwer, a writer for *The Atlantic,* expresses a fatalistic point of view shaped by CRT's revisionist history: "All the racial inequities that were in the 'before world'—they are nationally being reproduced in the coronavirus world, because the structure of our society is built along those tracks… The train is going to go to the same destination... because that's where the tracks are built to go."[301] The Final Proposal possesses this fatalistic view in its subjective limitation of the scope of "racial inequities" assigned to the "Privileged," and consequently, victim status is extended to some select groups who themselves, appear to otherwise victimize large portions of the population, particularly in the state of Washington: "The unique convergence of events across the nation, the COVID pandemic coupled with the rise of the Black Lives Matter movement, has highlighted the cracks in the systems designed to create equity and inclusion for all. Too often, the work to create equity and inclusion is disconnected from both potential champions of our causes and the communities this work will benefit."[302]

OPERATING PRINCIPLE #3: "CENTER COMMUNITY"

"We recognize that we can only achieve equity if communities impacted by inequities are at the center of our work. We acknowledge that communities know best their assets, needs, and solutions. We recognize and share power and structure our meetings to foster meaningful engagement. Community engagement will be intentional and inclusive. We will create opportunities as a Task Force, individual members, and staff to listen, learn, and seek input to guide our work. We will incorporate stories of lived experiences into our reports and recommendations."

"Center Community"— "We recognize that we can only achieve equity if communities impacted by inequities are at the center of our

[301] Hamblin, James, Katherine Wells, and Adam Serwer. *The Atlantic.* May 13, 2020. Social Distance Podcast: The Racial Contract. https://www.theatlantic.com/health/archive/2020/05/the-racial-contract/611614/. Quoted in: 2020 Office of Equity Task Force, Final Proposal. P. 41.

[302] Figure 17. Statement from the Governor's Committee on Disability Issues and Employment (GCDE). 2020 Office of Equity Task Force, Final Proposal. P. 51.

work." Whereas it is sound wisdom to appeal to those directly affected by injustice, it is unwise for some state agencies to malign large portions of the state's population with arguments that are logically fallacious, and contradictory to State Law.

For example, on page 42 of the Final Proposal, Figure X. COVID-19 Update from the Department of Health (June 19,2020), under the heading: "Viruses don't discriminate, but we do," the public update from the WA State Department of Health states: "In Washington state, 37% of the people diagnosed with COVID-19 are white. But 68% of our population is white. If the virus causing COVID-19 affected people equally regardless of race, we would think that 68% of the people diagnosed with COVID-19 would be white. So why does COVID seem to be disproportionately avoiding white people? In a word, privilege...[303]— They are more likely to have been able to clearly understand the language their doctor was using."

The logically fallacious accusation (i.e., a *non-sequitur* fallacy) that a significant portion of the Washington State population is to be condemned because they understand their doctor, is clearly founded on subjective moral reasoning and further, it fails to account for Washington State Law. On page 45, under the subtitle— "Language Access" in the Office of Equity Task Force: "Title VI of the 1964 Civil Rights Acts and the Washington State Law Against Discrimination (Chapter 49.60 RCW) — All individuals are protected from discrimination based on national origin, which includes birthplace, ancestry, culture, and language: *Title VI requires all organizations receiving federal support to ensure meaningful access to information and provide language assistance.*

Washington state and local jurisdictions ramped up their efforts to provide multilingual resources during the pandemic. Governor Inslee issued

---

[303] When the stated conclusion does not follow from its premise, the logical fallacy of a *non sequitur* is the outcome.

a memo in April detailing a state language access plan to provide vital COVID-19 information to individuals with disabilities and individuals with limited English proficiency (LEP).[304]

OPERATING PRINCIPLE #4: "COMMIT TO BOLD ACTION"

"Eliminating racism and oppression requires revolutionary change. We commit to using the authority we have and our collective influence to propose changes that interrupt and dismantle historical systems of institutional racism and oppression. We will use our time in Task Force meetings to engage in discussions that lead to actionable recommendations. We will commit as individual Task Force members to be bold and serve as leaders for equity in our respective roles. We share a commitment to being comfortable with discomfort as a bold action."

"**Commit to Bold Action**" — Opens with a sentence that is the focus of the first two entries, and therefore, attention will be given to the last statement in this topic: "*We share a commitment to being comfortable with discomfort as a bold action.*"

Equity must be distinguished from equality— Whereas equality places an individual in a passive, receptor role, "Equity is not the same as equality, and it goes beyond reaching parity. Equity ensures everyone has full access to the opportunities, power, and resources they need to flourish and achieve their full potential."[305] How does "equity," as defined by the Equity

---

[304] Joint Information Center News Release. 4/30/2020. Retrieved at: http://www.cha.wa.gov/news/2020/4/30/inslee-announces-new-initiative-to-expand-language-access-to-covid-19-information).

[305] 2020 Office of Equity Task Force, Final Proposal. "Definition of Equity & Guiding Statements for the Office of Equity." Downloaded: 03/28/2023. P. 56

Office Task Force of Washington State ensure everyone's flourishing and achievement?

Equity makes unelected minorities (the "Underprivileged") "stakeholders;" in this case, they are administrators of governmental policy. Therefore, stakeholders have "a place at the table" — They participate in decision-making, and policy-making that shape the lives of the citizenry of the State of Washington.

Stakeholders directly participate in the distribution of funds, training, and the prioritizing of "resources to those who have been historically and currently marginalized." An "Equity Statement" prepared by the Equity Office Task Force discloses its impetus for "bold action":

> Equity requires a commitment to bold action. It begins with the acknowledgement of historical systems of institutional racism and oppression that have led to the uneven distribution of benefits and burdens in our communities. Racism is ingrained in our history and deeply embedded in our institutions, affecting all sectors. An equitable decision-making process prioritizes community-led solutions, driven by those most affected. Generational healing takes time and requires us to embrace discomfort and practice humility. Equity ensures everyone has full access to the opportunities, power, and resources they need to flourish and achieve their full potential.[306]

How is the "uneven distribution of benefits" reversed in Washington State? If the role of "stakeholder" is interpreted in the framework of Critical Theory, then, the presence of Critical Race Theory's revisionist history in

306 Ibid. Downloaded: 03/29/2023.

the "Equity Statement" is apparent and its justification of the stakeholders' reversing of the "uneven distribution of benefits" by means of inserting socialism (in place of capitalism) into the administration of the state of Washington's Equity Task Force is logically anticipated. [307] This is typical of a communist/socialist redistribution scheme— *The bold, uncomfortable, conclusion is, equity is Woke Marxist Socialism.*

OPERATING PRINCIPLE #5: "BE VIGILANT FOR ADVERSE CONSEQUENCES AND IMPACTS"

"We commit to using an equity lens in the development of recommendations as a Task Force and in our decisions as individual members. Policy, program, and budget decisions can have adverse consequences and impacts if equity is not intentionally and systematically considered. We honor the Seven Generation Principle as standing in the present, while looking back three generations to the wisdom and experience of our ancestors, thinking about issues in the current context, and planning forward for three generations for the protection of our children and the generations to come."

"Be Vigilant for Adverse Consequences and Impacts," *is a refreshing departure from progressivism.* The Office of Equity Task Force provides a footnote acknowledging The American Indian Health Commission for Washington State as the source of the "Seven Generation Principle." In an American Indian tribal context, because of the honoring tribal traditions by Native Americans, this principle would, no doubt, remain a consistent source of wisdom for generations to come. However, in a [Progressive] Critical Theory framework, "the Seven Generation Principle

[307] Communism is, essentially, "the abolition of private property" (Karl Marx), and Socialism is, essentially, suspending free-market enterprise.

will undoubtably yield "Animal Farm" like outcomes (*re*: The Introduction to this book — Sub-topic: "Animal Farm: All Animals Are Equal But Some Are More Equal"). The "Repressive Tolerance" practice of "Access verses Outcomes" concludes that "equality of access" is to be evaluated in terms of "outcomes" — *But this way of thinking encourages subjective moral reasoning that oftentimes produces incoherent outcomes characteristic of Marxist's thinking.*

EQUITY—ACCESS VERSES OUTCOMES

Under the heading: "Principles for Success" the first entry is entitled: "Disrupt and Dismantle Systems of Institutional Racism and Oppression": Eliminating racism and oppression requires revolutionary change. The Office of Equity's work must be transformative. It must disrupt and dismantle historical systems of institutional racism and oppression throughout every sector and layer of government. Agencies must systematically identify the harm and exclusions built into our current systems and take immediate action to undo these inequities.[308]

The equitable principle of "Access Versus Outcomes" stresses equal access, but evaluation of this idea is done by measuring the "equality of access" in terms of "outcomes." And if the outcomes reveal a problem, access must be the source of the problem, or the whole structure has racism built into it; the only solution is antiracism. Such a counterproductive solution is what equity is about— *CRT's racial metrics (re: "Access Versus Outcomes") are irresolvable*— If "historical" systems of racism and oppression are being eliminated, when are they no longer "historical"? You cannot

[308] 2020 Office of Equity Task Force, Final Proposal. "Principles for Success." Downloaded: 03/29/2023. P. 60.

eliminate "historical racism" any more than you can eliminate bad memories—*Critical Race Theory places reconciliation and redemption out of reach and therein CRT opts for no real "transformative change."*

It is necessary to stress the importance of *access* as commonly understood. We all must acknowledge people with disabilities and the responsibility to build ramps in place of stairs, install sensors that serve the automatic opening of doors, place beeps that sound like bird's chirping on light poles that are located on either-side of crosswalks for the blind, and reserved parking spots for disabled people, among many other access aids. And it is virtuous to be forgiving, to seek reconciliation and seek forms of redemption for people who need to be freed from the cares and burdens of life common to everyone, regardless of their race or ethnicity.

EQUITY— SEEING REALITY AS AN UNEVEN PLAYING FIELD

Disciples of Diversity, Equity, and Inclusion see the world as an uneven playing field—The Privileged and the Underprivileged, the Oppressors and the Oppressed, the "haves" and the "have nots." And therefore, "Equity" is *not* committed to equality, it is committed to disrupting, and dismantling all systems of oppression— Dominant discourses are viewed as advantage for Whites and disadvantage for all others. White people, especially males, are "white supremacists," and capitalism sustains white dominance as a system of oppression rooted in America's "class order" — And America's class order is rooted in, and stabilized, by [traditional] Christian values, therefore, "... *unless and until Western Culture is dechristianized, Western society will never be decapitalized.*"[309]

Woke Marxist Socialism then appears to be the means to an equity-based government. Socialism addresses the economic imbalance by disrupting and dismantling the means of capitalism's production. Capitalism concisely involves the production of goods and services produced for profit in a free market. And as capital is accumulated, it is reinvested for further production. In the "marketplace" of free enterprise, the means of production are mostly privately owned.

Marxist Socialism's dismantling of capitalism results in the end of private property ownership, and individual rights associated with self-governance founded on Christian values or religious values in general that espouse the notion that "your rights end where my nose begins" (Harold Lindsell/*et. al.,* Mt. 7:12). Additional individual rights lost to socialism include equality under the law, freedom of speech, and federalism— Socialism, like communism and fascism, is totalitarian by nature. Professor Cheryl Harris, UCLA Law, and Critical Theorist clearly states, *"Equity is ... suspending private property rights, seizing land and wealth and redistributing them along racial lines."*[310]

---

[309] John Fulton, "Religion and Politics in Gramsci: An Introduction," *Sociological Analysis* 48 (1987): 197-216. Quoted in: Robert S. Smith, "Cultural Marxism: Imaginary Conspiracy or Revolutionary Reality?" 442.

[310] *Imprimus.* "Critical Race Theory: What It Is and How to Fight It." Christopher F. Rufo. 2 of 7 pages. https://imprimus.hillsdale.edu/critical-race-theory-flight/. Downloaded: 10/25/2022.

CHAPTER 8

THE PROGRESSIVE LEFT'S 'LONG MARCH THROUGH THE INSTITUTIONS'

"If destruction be our lot, we must ourselves be its author and finisher. As a nation of freemen, we must live through all time, or die by suicide"
— Abraham Lincoln.

In the Fall of 1964, the "Free Speech Movement" was born on the campus of the University of California, Berkeley. In its beginning, the Free Speech Movement was intended to give students an opportunity to engage in political activism. There was diversity, in the pre-Woke Marxist sense of the term, among political perspectives; there was no hardline identity between "left" and "right."

And parallel with the Free Speech Movement, the "Hippie Movement" emerged as part of America's 1960s socially disoriented milieu. The hedonistic driven Hippie Movement was thoroughly "antiestablishment," which means, they were all about unrestrained moral freedom— absolute autonomy. Whether they were aware of it, or not, they were knockoffs of Rousseau's "Bohemian man." The Hippies were societal dropouts —they were rebellious for the sake of being rebellious— they had no real cause. Hippie life consisted of "drugs, sex, and rock and roll;" "making love, not war,' and singing, "let us dance in the sun, wearing flowers in our hair." And anyone who attempted to restrain their "freedom" — e.g., their radical speech and/or out-of-control hedonism— were called out and labeled "fascists."

Both the Free Speech and Hippie movements were channeled through four widely influential intellectuals: Allen Ginsberg, described as a poet, and Zin-Rabbinic Sadhu, Alan Watts, former Harvard sociologist, Gary Snyder, also referred to as a poet, and Timothy Leary, the "psychedelic psychologist" from Harvard, known for his "turn on, tune in, or drop out" mantra, together anticipated a futuristic drug-inspired utopia dominated by unbridled freedom— Everyone would be free from all restraints to enjoy a blissful, hedonistic existence in a drug-induced "reality."

But Ginsberg suddenly interrupted everyone's "trip" by sounding-off to Leary, "But, Tim, somebody must make the posters"—Translation: "freedom without form produces nothing."[311] Societies free from all restraints (i.e., societies "without posters"), and left to themselves, are vulnerable to one of two extremes: (1) A totalitarian regime ruled by elites who, through intimidation and coercion, control people's lives or (2) A society turned-over to itself and controlled by its own narcissistic impulses; distracted from critical, evaluative thinking by constantly changing technology that thinks for them.[312] Both extremes were remarkably predicted in detail in

---

311 Francis Schaeffer. *The Church at the End of the Twentieth Century.* The Complete Works of Francis A Schaeffer, A Christian Worldview. Vol. 4. *A View of the Church. Second Edition.* Westchester, IL.: Crossway Books, 1982. 25.

312 Jefrey Breshears. *American Crisis. Cultural Marxism and the Culture War: A Christian Response.* 134. (Paraphrase).

two classics: The first extreme was thematic of George Orwell's *Nineteen Eighty-Four* (1949),[313] and the second extreme over-flowed from the imagination of Aldous Huxley's *Brave New World* (1932).[314] Jefrey Breshears summarily observes: "While Orwell warned of an oppressive regime that controlled the media and utilized propaganda to spread lies and suppress the truth, Huxley depicted a self-absorbed, complacent and entertainment-obsessed society in which no one *cared* about the truth."[315]

THE WOKE MARXIST 'MATRIX'[316] — THE "A.I." OF "REPRESSIVE TOLERANCE"

Changing a person's thinking about communism is much more permanent than attempting to beat them into submission to the communist vision
— Antonio Gramsci.

The second level of "Repressive Tolerance"[317] directly applies to "Critical Social Justice." Repressive Tolerance's author, Herbert Marcuse stresses, "… the vocal endorsement of actions that are manifestly aggressive towards other people (the popular support in the US and the UK in the aftermath

313 George Orwell. *1984.* Berkley, Penguin Random House, LLC. 1949.

314 Aldous Huxley. *Brave New World.* New York: Harper &Brothers, Publishers, 1932.

315 Jefrey Breshears. *American Crisis. Cultural Marxism and the Culture War: A Christian Response.* 134.

316 'MATRIX' is a reference to "The Matrix" released in 1999, starring Keanu Reeves. The Matrix is a computer simulation of the "realty" that Neo (Reeves character) is living in. The Matrix was created by an evil Artificial Intelligence (A.I.).

317 Recall, the first level of "Repressive Tolerance," Chapter 6, Critical Inclusion: The first level directly applies to Critical Inclusion and "… the unthinking acceptance of entrenched attitudes and ideas, even when these are obviously damaging to other people, or indeed the environment (the painfully slow response to warnings about climate change and environmental degradation might be seen as an example of this," Ch. 7 — Marcuse.)

of 9/11 and 7/7 for the respective government's attempts to override or limit *habeas corpus* [318] is a clear example of this)." Marcuse concludes this thought in a typical Marxist spirit: "Genuine tolerance can only exist in a situation of intolerance for these limits on real freedom"[319] — "Real Freedom" in a *Repressive Tolerant* context means: *"Something that was nearly universally condemned is now, nearly universally celebrated."* And *"That which was celebrated is condemned."* And *"Those who refuse to celebrate are condemned."*[320]

The task of equity is to artificially take control, that is, to create "a situation of intolerance." An opportune time for taking control was the summer of 2020. The pandemic coupled with protests turned into riots, released the process of leveling through demoralization, disrupting and dismantling of "systemic oppression" — That is, the "dominant hegemony"/ the "false consciousness" associated with the "Privileged/Oppressors."

The Progressive Left, in the spirit of repressive tolerance, seeks to centralize socio/economical control in the form of Marxist Socialism. The

---

318 *Habeas corpus*: "The name given to a variety of writs … having for their object to bring a party before a court or judge. … The primary function of the writ is to release from unlawful imprisonment." Henry Campbell Black. *Black's Law Dictionary.* Fifth Edition. St. Paul, MN.: West Publishing CO. 1979. 638.

319 Ian Buchanan. *A Dictionary of Critical Theory.* (1st Ed.) Oxford University Press. 2010. https://www.oxfordreference.com/display/10.1093/oi/authority.20110803100414515;jsessionid=51A066FFA2AB8782E85350295629B46B. Downloaded: 04/27/2023. Again, (re: footnote #309 above) — Recall, the first level of Repressive Tolerance applies to Critical Inclusion, Chapter 7).

320 Theo Hobson, British Theologian. British Church Ministry Network. Copywrite: 2012-2024. https://baptistcmn.com/three-things-must-happen-for-a-moral-revolution-to-occur/. (NOTE: The conclusion here is the author's, not Theo Hobson's).

"A.I." of American and Western culture eerily sounds like Marcuse —viz., "Repressive Tolerance":

> Withdrawal of tolerance from regressive movements *before* they can become active; intolerance even toward thought, opinion, and word, and finally, intolerance in the opposite direction, that is, toward the self-styled conservatives, to the political Right—these anti-democratic notions respond to the actual development of the democratic society which has destroyed the basis for universal tolerance. The conditions under which tolerance can again, become a liberating and humanizing force have still to be created....
>
> And when this perversion starts in the mind of the individual, in his consciousness, his needs, when heteronomous[321] interests occupy him before he can experience his servitude, then the efforts to counteract his dehumanization must begin at the place of entrance, there where the false consciousness takes form (or rather: is systematically formed) —it must begin with stopping the words and images which feed this consciousness. To be sure, this is censorship, even pre-censorship, but openly directed against the more or less hidden censorship that permeates the free media.

---

[321] Heteronomous refers to an individual acting in accordance with one's desires rather than reason or moral duty. Dictionary.Com: For example, "The law says don't steal. If you don't steal because you believe it's wrong, that's autonomy at work. But if the only reason you don't steal is because you're afraid of being caught, that's an external force pressuring you, or heteronomy," https://www.dictionary.com/browse/heteronomous. Downloaded: 05/04/2024.

> Where the false consciousness has become prevalent in national and popular behavior, it translates itself almost immediately into practice: the safe distance between ideology and reality, repressive thought and repressive action, between the word of destruction and the deed of destruction is dangerously shortened. Thus, the breakthrough the false consciousness may provide the Archimedean point for a larger emancipation—at an infinitesimally small spot, to be sure, but it is on the enlargement of such small spots that the chance of change depends.[322]

Marcuse's "*Repressive Tolerance*" anticipates the "withdrawal of tolerance from regressive movements," namely, the unalienable right of "freedom of consciousness" —the First Amendment's establishment of Religious Liberty. Such unprecedented "censorship," or "even pre-censorship" is justified based on "Anti-democratic notions," that is, the ideas of the Founding Fathers, e.g., Madison's, Hamilton's, and Jefferson's understanding of Representative or Republican Democracy contrary to Critical Theory's totalitarian "direct democracy" (Horkheimer) and the classless, binary society of the Marxist Socialist State.[323]

The "anti-democratic notions" that foster the control of industrial society by white capitalists, in the thinking of Woke Marxists, sustains the "actual development of the democratic society" — that is, the "false

---

[322] Herbert Marcuse. "Critique of Pure Tolerance." p. 110-111.

[323] Please recall from the Introduction: The term "socialist state" is widely used by Marxist–Leninist parties, theorists, and governments to mean a state under the control of a vanguard party that is organizing the economic, social, and political affairs of said state toward the construction of socialism. *Marxists often refer to socialism as the first, necessary phase on the way from capitalism to communism.*

consciousness" of the "Privileged Hegemony" — "which has destroyed the basis for universal tolerance." "The conditions under which tolerance can again become a liberating and humanizing force have still to be created" — *The conditions "under which tolerance can again become a liberating and humanizing force" is the total leveling of Western culture by means of critical equity and the emergence, and celebration, of the Marxist Socialist/Communist State.*

In the West's *repressive-tolerant* culture, the Orwellian/Huxleyan prognoses coexist in paradox: "… an Huxleyan society can so weaken the social and moral fabric as to set the stage for the ultimate Orwellian nightmare"[324] — The destabilizing of Western Civilization, through the initial uprooting of Judeo-Christian values and faith, renders the institutions of civil society vulnerable to, as Gramsci's revolutionary pathology was/is referred to, "the long march through the institutions of power." "In the new order," wrote Gramsci, "Socialism will triumph by first capturing the culture via infiltration of schools, universities, churches, and the media by transforming the consciousness of society."[325]

The summer of 2020 signaled the effectiveness of the Progressive Left's march through the institutions and the metastasizing of "repressive tolerance" throughout the civil culture, that is, Gramsci's so-called "superstructure," e.g., religion, family, education, law, and media. The "posters have all been burned"[326] — i.e., *The "systemic oppression" of the Privileged hegemony*

---

324 Jefrey Breshears. *American Crisis, Cultural Marxism and The Culture War: A Christian Response.* 135.

325 Damien Tudehope. "What's left of Western Culture? Just about Everything," *The Spectator,* 9 October 2017, https://tinyurl.com/y4jdlbhg.

326 See Kevin Slack. *How Liberalism Became Despotism. The War on the American Republic.* New York: Encounter Books. 2023. And Francis A. Schaeffer, The Complete Works of— A Christian Worldview, Vol. 4, "A Christian View of the Church." Westchester, ILL.: Crossway Books, 1982. Especially Chapter 1, "The Roots of the Student Revolution."

is being dislodged by the Repressive Tolerance of Woke Marxist Ideology[327] — Demoralization, in the Summer of 2020, was a defiant demonstration of the Left's near completion of the "First Stage" of Gramsci's destabilization of America's civil culture (See Chapter 2, Antonio Gramsci and the destabilization of the Chinese culture under the subheading of: "The Long March Through The Institutions").

THE PROGRESSIVE LEFT'S CULTURE WAR OF ATTRITION

Following the negligent homicide of George Floyd, Minneapolis Police Officer, Derek Chauvin was charged with (and later convicted of) murder.[328] Protests turned into violent riots, churches were desecrated, historical monuments were toppled, police were injured, some were killed, and multiplied cities across America burned, e.g., Atlanta, St. Louis, New York City, Chicago, Philadelphia, Detroit, Los Angeles, San Francisco, Seattle, Portland, and Minneapolis.329

In the Summer of 2020 Americans witnessed unrelenting attacks on many of their Constitutional rights— The First Amendment: Religious Liberty, Freedom of Speech, the right to peacefully assemble, and The Second Amendment: The "Right to Bear Arms" — Our rights are under

---

[327] Woke Marxist Ideology majors in the philosophical force of Repressive Tolerance and the rhetorical persuasive power of Political Correctness.

[328] Molly Hennessy-Fiske. "George Floyd died a week ago, rocking Minneapolis and its mayor." https://www.latimes.com/world-nation/story/2020-05-31/george-floyd-died-a-week-ago-rocking-minneapolis-and-its-mayor. May 31, 2020. Downloaded: 10/21/2022. NOTE: My example does not call into question the charge of murder regarding Officer Chauvin. I fully support Chauvin's conviction. My illustration does question the deaths, destruction, and looting of businesses, owned by multiple different races in cities throughout the United States.

[329] Jim Geraghty. Senior Political Correspondent, National Review. "Burning Cities." https://www.nationalreview.com/the-morning-jolt/burning-cities/. August 2020. Downloaded: 10/21/2022.

assault by those who capriciously wield "the sword" (Rom. 13:4), "the Party," that is, the Progressive Left. Additionally, many unelected bureaucrats, using the pandemic as a cover, claimed authority under exception to the law and to be acting under emergency powers for the occasion to undermine the freedoms of Americans in 2020— The "Archimedean point for a larger emancipation" that is, power centralized in the "Ruling Elite" (The Party) was "front and center."

In the aftermath of the "protests," damages to property in American cities was estimated to be $2 billion.[330] Critical Theory's Social Justice "justifies" anarchy, destruction, looting, and even death— The American public was simply informed that the rioters had a right to destroy property, and with it, people's livelihoods.[331] And therefore, whereas it was reported by the Washington Post that 14,000 BLM protesters were arrested, and by The Hill that over 17,000 arrests were made, most of those protesters were not booked for violent crimes, but for violating curfews, obstructing roadways, carrying open containers, and failure to disperse.[332]

According to an analysis of a dozen jurisdictions across the country by *The Guardian*, a significant majority of citations and charges against "protesters" were dropped, dismissed, or simply not filed. For example, in Dallas and Philadelphia, approximately 95% of citations were dropped; in Houston and Los Angeles, as many as 93% of citations were not prosecuted and in San Francisco, the prosecutor's office "dismissed all 127 cases involved with 'peaceful protest-related charges,' though data for

---

[330] World Economic Forum's website. February 2021. Quoted in: USA Today: https://www.usatoday.com/story/news/factcheck/2022/02/22/fact-check-thousands-black-lives-matter-protesters-arrested-2020/6816074001/. Downloaded: 02/23/2023.

[331] Kevin Slack. *How Liberalism became Despotism. War On The American Republic.* New York: Encounter Books, 2023. pp. 1-2.

[332] World Economic Forum's Website.

more serious citations was not available."[333] And in Minneapolis, where the George Floyd homicide took place, over 90% of criminal cases were dropped. In Portland, only 15% of cases have been filed and the Multnomah County Prosecutor has dismissed 82% of criminal cases. And in New York City, Brooklyn's prosecutor vacated 83% of 136 serious criminal cases, and the Manhattan prosecutor "dropped about 64% of nearly 1,000 cases." Astoundingly, "… some prosecutors and law enforcement observers charge that departments carried out mass arrests as a crowd control tactic, as a means to silence peaceful protesters, and as a public relations strategy designed to turn the public against demonstrators by making them appear more violent than they were."[334]

Black Lives Matter and Antifa suffered no serious charges or convictions, but police departments were defunded and betrayed by those who "bear the sword" nation-wide—police officers were either laid-off or resigned. "Marxist Social Justice," and, Marcuse's "Repressive Tolerance" — and especially, revised Civil Rights Law[335]— was in full view in its destructive rage as it *increased levels of demoralization throughout American and Western Culture.*

---

[333] Tom Perkins. "Most charges against George Floyd protesters dropped, analysis shows." April 2021. https://amp.theguardian.com/us-news/2021/apr/17/george-floyd-protesters-charges-citations-analysis. Downloaded: 05/24/2023.

[334] Ibid.

[335] PLEASE RECALL: **Chapter 6, Critical Race Theory—A Tale of Two Histories**; Sub-heading: **A Radical Reinterpretation of Civil Rights:** "*Legislated law promising to ban discrimination, is now used to justify discrimination.*" Plainly stated, following this "Marxist Makeover," the revised Civil Rights law proactively discriminates in favor of "protected identity groups," that is, the "Oppressed." The reinterpretation of Civil Rights laws is the power behind Political Correctness and Repressive Tolerance— *The twisted outcome in the courts was that which appeared as lawlessness to many, was otherwise treated as though it was within the bounds of the law.*

THE PSYCHOSIS OF DEMORALIZATION

Julia Frank, MD, posits: "… demoralization is the state of mind of a person deprived of spirit or courage, disheartened, bewildered, and thrown into disorder or confusion."[336] The "pathological condition" induced by demoralization, "always takes place within the context of a past, present, anticipated or imagined stressful situation."[337] This "pathological condition" is described as "subjective incompetence" (SI).[338] Symptoms associated with SI include "distress, such as depression, anxiety, resentment, anger, or combinations thereof."[339] SI further results in a sense of diminished capacity to "perform tasks and express feelings deemed appropriate in a stressful situation, resulting in pervasive uncertainty and doubts about the future."[340] People with the condition of SI find themselves at an impasse in which they are confronted with the dilemma of an inability to see ways out of the situation they have been thrown into— Both cults and totalitarian ideologies (e.g., socialism, communism, fascism) utilize such techniques for the purpose of manipulation and control.

DM Clarke and DW Kissane propose six criteria for the diagnosis of demoralization:

---

336 John M. de Figueiredo, MD, ScD. Yale University School of Medicine. "Distress, Demoralization and Psychopathology." *The European Journal of Psychiatry*. Vol.27 no.1 Zaragozaene. March 2013 https://scielo.isciii.es/scielo.php?script=sci_arttext&pid=S0213-61632013000100008. Downloaded: 05/06/2023.

337 Ibid.

338 Ibid.

339 See: de Figueiredo JM, Frank JD. Subjective incompetence, the clinical hallmark of demoralization. Compr Psychiatry 1982; 23(4): 353-363. And Dr. Figueiredo's, "Deconstructing demoralization: Subjective incompetence and distress in the face of adversity." In: Alarcon RD, Frank JB, editors. The Psychotherapy of Hope: The Legacy of Persuasion and Healing. Baltimore, MD: The Johns Hopkins University Press; 2012. p. 107-124.

340 John M. de Figueiredo, MD, ScD. "Distress, Demoralization and Psychopathology."

(1) "... existential distress" and "... hopelessness or loss of meaning and purpose in life;"
(2) "cognitive attitudes of pessimism, helplessness, sense of being trapped, personal failure, or lacking a worthwhile future;"
(3) An "... absence of drive or motivation to cope differently;"
(4) A sense of "... social alienation or isolation and lack of support."
(5) "... fluctuation in emotional intensity."
(6) "... feelings of helplessness, or hopelessness, or giving up."[341]

In the context of Critical Theory Social Justice, increasing levels of demoralization throughout American and Western Culture eventually results in "helplessness" wherein the personal resolve of a mass number of the population is surrendered and societal breakdown occurs.

GRAMSCI'S HISTORIC BLOC— THE END OF THE CULTURE WAR?

The Woke Marxist objective: "... *unless and until Western Culture is dechristianized, Western society will never be decapitalized.*"[342]

The destabilizing of Western Civilization, through the perpetual uprooting of Judeo-Christian values, renders the institutions of civil society vulnerable to Antonio Gramsci's culturally transforming pathology— "the long

[341] Kissane D, Clarke D, Street A. "Demoralization syndrome, a relevant psychiatric diagnosis for palliative care." J Palliative Care 2001; 17: 12-21. And Clarke DM and Kissane DW. "Demoralization: its Phenomenology and Importance." Aust N Z J Psychiatry 2002; 36: 733-742. Quoted in: John M. de Figueiredo. "Distress, Demoralization and Psychopathology."

[342] John Fulton, "Religion and Politics in Gramsci: An Introduction," *Sociological Analysis* 48 (1987): 197-216. Quoted in: Robert S. Smith, "Cultural Marxism: Imaginary Conspiracy or Revolutionary Reality?" 442.

march through the institutions of power." The reader is reminded that, "In the new order," proclaimed Gramsci, "Socialism will triumph by first capturing the culture via infiltration of schools, universities, churches and the media by transforming the consciousness of society."[343]

The Progressive Left's "long march through the institutions" has netted a "near monopoly of America's cultural institutions"[344]— The counter-cultural hegemony of the Woke Marxist inspired Progressive Left is "… molded, and opinionated, a uniform class now presides over nearly all federal, and state, government bureaucracies, over the media, the educational establishment, and major corporations,"[345] they all speak the same language, that is, political correctness, and anyone who dissents regarding Marxist means of transforming the workplace, is swiftly confronted with their "unconscious bias," or "internalized white supremacy" and forced out.

If a "near monopoly" alchemizes into the dominant cultural hegemony, then the Progressive Left's "long march through the institutions" is either finished, or near its end. And Antonio Gramsci's "historic bloc," that is, the transforming of America's Democratic Republic into a Marxist Socialist State, will soon begin to emerge.[346] Does this signal the near end of the "Culture War" in the West? ***NO!*** — given the "repressive tolerant/politically correct" intoxicated Marxist "clown world" in which we live, would

---

343 Damien Tudehope. "What's left of Western Culture? Just about Everything," *The Spectator,* 9 October 2017, https://tinyurl.com/y4jdlbhg. (Gramsci, an Italian Communis[[t, is referring to the Marxist Socialist State, the precursor to Communism).

344 Angelo M. Codevilla. "The Rise of Political Correctness." 9 of 12 pages.

345 Ibid.

346 The term "socialist state" is widely used by Marxist–Leninist parties, theorists, and governments to mean a state under the control of a vanguard party that is organizing the economic, social, and political affairs of said state toward the construction of socialism. *Marxists often refer to socialism as the first, necessary phase on the way from capitalism to communism.*

it not be extremely naive for anyone to believe that the "Critical Woke Revolution" would end with the transference of power to the Oppressed?

POLITICAL CORRECTNESS AND '*UN*REALITY'

A "Grand Canyon" like gap between what is *politically correct* and what is *reality,* is the cause of vexing paranoia in the psyche of the Progressive Left. Consequently, "Leftist Elites" are continually driven to force people to speak and act as though what is politically correct, and therefore, serves the party's interest, is *actual* reality.[347] Because of their fear of losing control, the Progressive Left often overreacts to situations that may result in people perceiving the *gap* that separates political correctness from reality.

For example, President Biden closed out 2022 by signing into law the "Respect For Marriage Act" (H.R. 8404).[348] H.R. 8404 "... establishes statutory authority for same-sex and interracial marriages and repeals provisions of law that once prevented any State or territory from being required to give effect to a same-sex marriage from another State or territory."[349]

Since the Supreme Court made Same-Sex Marriage the law of the land in 2015, why was the "Respect For Marriage Act" necessary? Before the Court overturned Roe V. Wade as federal law, passing the legality or illegality regarding abortion down to the individual states, President Biden warned that same-sex marriage would be next.[350] The point is, the "Respect For Marriage Act" is not about same-sex marriage or marriage between one

---

[347] Angelo M. Codevilla. "The Rise of Political Correctness." 1 of 12 pages.

[348] Danielle Jarvis. "Joe Biden Signs Respect For Marriage Act Into Law, Jeopardizing Religious Liberty." December 14, 2022. https://soulpurposemag.com/joe-biden-signs-respect-for-marriage-act-into-law-jeopardizing-religious-liberty/. Downloaded: 02/24/2023.

[349] Ibid.

[350] Ibid.

man and one woman, rather, it's a vindicative, deceptive political tactic, asserts Ryan Bagert, Senior Vice President of Strategic, Alliance Defending Freedom, "… that intentionally jeopardizes the First Amendment freedoms of millions of Americans who have sincerely held beliefs about marriage."[351]

The millions of Americans who believe the Bible defines marriage are considered racist, sexist, and above all, stupid[352]— These Americans are made "vulnerable to legal attack" by the President's signing of this bill into law (Franklin Graham).[353] Senator Mike Lee (R-UT) agrees, "What we can expect should this bill become law is more litigation against those institutions [and] individuals trying to live according to their sincerely held religious beliefs [and] moral convictions."[354]

Americans made vulnerable to more litigation are those whom President Barack Obama opined: "It's not surprising then that they get bitter, they cling to guns or religion or antipathy toward people who aren't like them or anti-immigrant sentiment or anti-trade sentiment as a way to explain their frustrations."[355] Or perhaps those targeted by the 2016 Democratic Presidential Nominee, Hillary Clinton: "You could put half of Trump's supporters into what I call the basket of deplorables. Right? The racist, sexist, homophobic, xenophobic, Islamophobic — you name it. And unfortunately, there are people like that… Now, some of those folks—they are irre-

---

351 Ibid.

352 Angelo M. Codevilla. "The Rise of Political Correctness." 9 of 12 pages.

353 Quoted in, Danielle Jarvis. "Joe Biden Signs Respect For Marriage Act Into Law, Jeopardizing Religious Liberty." December 14, 2022. Danielle Jarvis comments: "It is very disappointing that 12 Republican senators sided with ultra-liberal Senator Schumer and voted for the Respect for Marriage Act which strikes a blow against millions of Americans who believe in and support traditional marriage."

354 Ibid.

355 Victor Davis Hanson. Hillsdale College, Lecture 3, "American Citizenship And Its Decline." 3 of 4 pages.
https://online.hillsdale.edu/courses/american-citizenship-and-its-decline. Downloaded: 02/24/2024.

deemable."[356] Or President Joe Biden: "These forces of intolerance remain determined to undermine and roll back the progress you all have made .... They're a small percentage of the American people, virulent people, some of them the dregs of society"[357] —The Progressive Left will continue, with no end in sight, to react with insult, slander and intimidation against any confrontation, challenge, or threat, to their power, and ideological hope of transforming the American Democratic Republic into a Marxist Socialist State.

SECTION 2— TRANSITION

A Christian polemic involves the art of engaging in a controversial debate. Christian polemics counter insidious intentions and/or suppositions (e.g., Woke Identity Marxism). A Christian writer should refrain from contentious rhetoric; however, a critical (polemical) examination of the origins, structure, and claims of Woke Identity Marxism is biblically warranted.[358]

---

[356] Ibid.

[357] Ibid.

[358] *Sincerely, my (the author's) intention is to "snatch [Woke devotees] from the fire and save them (Jude 23a);" just as God snatched me from the fire and saved me by his unbounding grace, through faith in Jesus Christ's name.*

PART— 2

'THE WOKE OPIATE'

CHAPTER 9

WOKE MORAL SUBJECTIVISM & THE DEHUMANIZING OF THE HUMAN RACE

"The Law of Human Nature, or of Right and Wrong, must be something above and beyond the actual facts of human behaviour. In this case, besides the actual facts, you have something else— a real law which we did not invent and which we know we ought to obey"

— C.S. Lewis.[359]

C.S. Lewis argues that morality is not only objective, but, as well, its objectivity is both historically and universally acknowledged. Lewis explains that the awareness of these axiomatic moral absolutes is what makes us human, and thus our very humanity is threatened by the rise of moral subjectivism in the West. [360] Contrary to moral subjectivism's dehumanization, Lewis contends:

---

[359] C.S. Lewis. *Mere Christianity.* San Francisco, CA: Harper, 1952. Bk. I, Chap. 4, p. 21.

[360] Michael Ward. C.S. Lewis On Christianity. Lecture 2: "Good and Evil." https://online.hillsdale.edu/courses/c-s-lewis-on-christianity. Downloaded: 12/19/2022.

(1) *Moral value is objective* —Moral value is a self-evident axiom, which is to say, if nothing is morally self-evident; nothing can be proved to be moral or immoral.[361]

(2) *Moral value is universally held to be objective*— In the Appendix of *The Abolition of Man,* Lewis provides 116 examples of the universality of moral objectivity.[362] The following are merely a sample of Lewis' examples (please read the footnotes for a brief explanation of each example): "The Law of General Beneficence;"[363] "The Law of Special Beneficence;"[364] "Duties to Parents, Elders, Ancestors;"[365]"Duties to Children and Posterity;" [366] "The Law of Justice;"[367] "The Law of Good Faith and Veracity;"[368] "The Law of Mercy,"[369] and "The Law of Magnanimity."[370]

---

361 Ibid.

362 C.S. Lewis. *The Abolition of Man.* "Appendix, Illustrations of the Tao." New York: Collier Books, Macmillan Publishing Company, 1947, 95-121. (The examples provided here in footnotes 339-346 are merely a sampling of those Lewis lists in his work).

363 Ibid. For example, an ancient Egyptian text, "The Confession of the Righteous Soul, 'Book of the Dead,'": "I have not slain men." "Do not murder," — An ancient Jewish text (Exodus 20:13). "Slander not," — Babylonian, *Hymn to Samas.*

364 Ibid. "It is upon the trunk that a gentleman works. When that is firmly set up, the Way grows. And surely proper behaviour to parents and elder brothers is the trunk of goodness" (Ancient Chinese, *Analects,* i.2.). "Natural affection is a thing right and according to Nature," (Greek. Epictetus, 3:24). "Nothing can ever change the claims of kinship for a right-thinking man," (Anglo-Saxon, *Beowulf,* 2600).

365 Ibid. "Your father is an image of the Lord of Creation, your mother an image of the Earth. For him who fails to honour them, every work of piety is in vain. This is the first duty," (Hindu, Janet, i.9).

366 Ibid. "The Master said, Respect the young," (Ancient Chinese. *Analects,* ix. 22).

367 Ibid. "Has he approached his neighbour's wife?" (Babylonian. "List of Sins." *ERE* v. 446).

368 Ibid. "I have not spoken falsehood," (Ancient Egyptian. "Confession of Righteous Soul." *ERE* v.478).

369 Ibid. "Has he failed to set a prisoner free?" (Babylonian. "List of Sins." *ERE* v. 446).

370 Ibid. "There are two kinds of injustice: the first is found in those who do an injury, the second in those who fail to protect another from injury when they can," (Roman. Cicero, *De Off.* I, vii.).

The examples of moral objectivity provided by Lewis in the Appendix of *The Abolition of Man* are more than sufficient for him to make his point— Originating among ten civilizations/ethnicities, e.g., Anglo-Saxons, Australian Aborigines, Babylonians, Ancient Chinese, Ancient Christians, Ancient Egyptians, English (Locke, Hooker), Greek (Epictetus, Stoics), Hindu, Indian (ethnic, India), and Ancient Jewish— Lewis' "Illustrations Of The *Tao*," (i.e., the Natural Law)[371] serve to establish the case that Woke Critical Theory's *moral subjectivism* is a dehumanizing descent into the depths of human depravity.[372]

Lewis continues by providing a convincing (biblically conforming) argument against the notion of the "progressive changing of human nature": "The idea of collecting *independent* testimonies presuppose that 'civilizations' have arisen in the world independently of one another; or even that humanity has had several independent emergences on this planet. The biology and anthropology involved in such an assumption are extremely doubtful. It is by no means certain that there has ever (in the sense required) been more than one civilization in all history"[373] — *Arguably, every civilization has derived from a former civilization: originating from single beginnings.*[374]

(3) *Moral value is learned by practice*— The realization of moral value is something humans discover. "Recognition of objective moral values," acknowledges Lewis Scholar, Michael Ward, "is part of what defines us as human beings."[375]

---

[371] Ibid. 95.

[372] Ibid.

[373] Ibid.95-96.

[374] The significance of this conclusion to Lewis' argument is twofold: (1) This conclusion supports the Biblical doctrine of "original sin," and (2) this conclusion supports the Biblical teaching of the unity of the human race (presupposed in the Preamble of The Declaration of Independence).

[375] Michael Ward. "C.S. Lewis On Christianity." Lecture 2: "Good and Evil." 2 of 4 pages.

Lewis concisely summarizes these three moral axioms: "First, … human beings, all over the earth, have this curious idea that they ought to behave in a certain way, and cannot really get rid of it. Secondly, … they do not in fact behave in that way. They know the Law of Nature; they break it. These two facts are the foundation of all clear thinking about ourselves and the universe we live in."[376]

But politically correct Woke Marxism considers moral (objective) value to be "bourgeois morality." In the Western Woke context, "bourgeois morality," or Christian (Traditional) morality, is regarded as a negation of Woke Marxist identity and authority.[377] Christian morality contends that the acknowledgement of human beings' "… objective moral value is part of what defines us as human beings"[378] and the "… denial of our objective value rejects humanity's moral inheritance and negates one's humanity"[379] — *Contrary to objective human dignity and value, the whole of Woke Marxist identity and authority is founded on the moral subjectivity of the Party's Ruling Elites and Social Justice theorists as follows.*

STRUCTUAL RACISM — 'A WHITE SOCIAL CONSTRUCT'

Race is not 'biologically grounded and natural'; rather, it is a socially constructed category used to oppress and exploit people of color"
— Critical Race Theory.

---

[376] C.S. Lewis. *Mere Christianity.* Bk. I, Chap. 1, para. 11, p. 21.

[377] Angelo M. Codevilla. "The Rise of Political Correctness." Page 3 of 12 pages.

[378] Michael Ward. "C.S. Lewis On Christianity." 2 of 4 pages.

[379] Ibid. Please observe, a human being's objective moral value is based on the image of God (*the imago Dei*) within us (Gen. 1:27)— *God sees us as objective moral beings created in His image* (Psalm 8:4).

Structural Racism, according to Critical Race Theory, legitimizes virtually *all* institutional and interpersonal discourse— *Structural Racism is a powerful, sweeping set of invisible identity dynamics generated by the ultra-power of the Privileged hegemony and diffused throughout every sector and system of society to include history, culture, politics, economics, and academics.*

Because the [alleged] White "social construct" [380] of Structural Racism is the cumulative effect of racism in "multiple institutions and cultural norms, past and present, continually reproducing old and producing new forms of racism,"[381] racism is difficult to locate in a particular institution. Never-the-less, Social Justice scholarship, apart from any evidence, subjectively concludes that racism exists, and oppression is present even when no one with racist intentions or beliefs is present[382]— And, hence, concludes Critical Race Theorists, "racism is systemic." [383]

---

380 Re: The Coalition for Racial Equalities and Rights, examples of structural racism are seen: "… in the many institutional, cultural, and structural factors that contribute to lower life expectancy for African American and Native American men, compared to white men. These include higher exposure to environmental toxins, dangerous jobs and unhealthy housing stock, higher exposure to and more lethal consequences for reacting to violence, stress, and racism, lower rates of health care coverage, access, and quality of care, and systematic refusal by the nation to fix these things."

381 Keith Lawrence, Aspen Institute and Terry Keleher, Applied Research Center, for the Race and Public Policy Conference (2004). *Chronic Disparity: Strong and Pervasive Evidence of Racial Inequalities* And Maggie Potapchuk, Sally Leiderman, Donna Bivens, and Barbara Major *Flipping the Script: White Privilege and Community Building* (2005).

382 Helen Pluckrose & James Lindsay. *Cynical Theories.* 183.

383 Examples of this assertion are observed in Keith Lawrence, Aspen Institute and Terry Keleher, *Chronic Disparity: Strong and Pervasive Evidence of Racial Inequalities* And Maggie Potapchuk, Sally Leiderman, Donna Bivens, and Barbara Major *Flipping the Script: White Privilege and Community Building*: "… we can see structural racism in the many institutional, cultural, and structural factors that contribute to lower life expectancy for African American and Native American men, compared to white men. These include higher exposure to environmental toxins, dangerous jobs and unhealthy housing stock, higher exposure to and more lethal consequences for reacting to violence, stress, and racism, lower rates of health care coverage, access, and quality of care, and systematic refusal by the nation to fix these things."

THE POLITICALLY CORRECT 'REIFYING' OF SYSTEMIC RACISM

"What we need is the destruction of whiteness, which is the source of human misery in the world"
— James Cone.[384]

The "reifying" of systemic racism begins with the politically correct manipulation of reality by making something abstract, i.e., something not real; real, by expressing it through Woke Marxist verbal constructs as though it is real.[385] An example of the calculus of reification (politically correct pseudo-realities) is the redefining of racism as "privilege plus power" and consequently the "Privileged" are made the architects of Structural Racism and thus, the originators of "systemic racism" —*But the evidence supports the truth that the interests of Progressive Left Elites are served by such a reification, and not the interests of the so-called "Privileged."*[386]

THE PROGRESSIVE LEFT'S 'EMANICIPATION'

Power and betrayal are simply the nature of Progressive Left regimes, for whom "emancipation" is the perpetual celebration

[384] Ibid.

[385] Another definition of "refry" is the social alchemizing of the abstract (unreality) into reality. Please see "essentialism" for further development. See the Oxford Dictionary. https://www.oxfordreference.com.

[386] The Heritage Foundation. "How to Identify Critical Race Theory." (See footnote #418).

> *and empowerment of the Party— The Party's emancipation justifies their perpetual drive for power and betrayal.*[387]

"Systemic Racism" is the centerpiece of the Progressive Left's betrayal of both the "Underprivileged" and Western Culture— *If racism in America, and the West, is systemic, then reconciliation between the Privileged and the Underprivileged, the White majority and minority peoples, is beyond hope.* The "American Experiment," and its Western democratic counterparts, must be socially and politically "flattened" (equity's outcome) and replaced by a new nation constitutionally created in the image of a Marxist Socialist State— *The emancipation of the Progressive Left's Elite's ambitions are then celebrated, but there is **NO** emancipation for the Underprivileged* (This adverse assertion is addressed below under the subheading: "The Progressive Left's Betrayal of The Underprivileged").

WOKE MARXIST IDEOLOGY: 'A REALITY ABOVE REALITY ITSELF'

> *Political Correctness creates "new realities" conformed to the dictates of the Party.*

387 R.J. Rummel, Center for National Security Law, Charlottesville, Virginia, and author of *Death by Government.* New Brunswick, NJ: Transaction Publishers,1994 states: "Collecting data on democide was a horrendous task. I soon was overwhelmed by the unbelievable repetitiveness of regime after regime, ruler after ruler, murdering people under their control or rule by shooting, burial alive, burning, hanging, knifing, starvation, flaying, beating, torture, and so on and on. Year after year. Not hundreds, not thousands, not tens of thousands of these people, but millions and millions. Almost 170,000,000 of them, and this is only what appears a reasonable middle estimate. The awful toll may even reach above 300,000,000, the equivalent in dead of a nuclear war stretched out over decades." "Statistics on Democide," Genocide and Mass Murder Since 1900. https://www.hawaii.edu/powerkills/NOTE5.HTM. Downloaded: 09/13/2023.

Voltaire's pithy remark penetrates the depths of human depravity: "If God has made us in his image, we have returned him the favor."[388] "God" is fallen man's autobiography— "... our created nature enables us to reflect the glory of God in a dependent and finite form, but our fallen nature impels us to appropriate the glory of God in an autonomous and infinite form"[389]— *The Woke Marxist Ruling Elites enthrone the Party (themselves) in the place of God; and in their conquest for power, they strain to illicitly reach for a "lesser good."*[390]

In the world of Woke Marxism, nothing exists behind the visible reality, the material world is all there is, and ever will be. But to the contrary, if "... *there is any value that does have value, it must lie outside the whole sphere of what happens and is the case .... Ethics is transcendental."*[391] If an ideology, or revolutionary cause, *does not* have a transcendent, unchanging, and therefore, objective moral/ethical point of reference, how does the revolutionary cause know if it's progressing or digressing, evolving, or devolving, serving good, or serving evil?

'THINGS GONE WRONG'?

"First, ... human beings, all over the earth, have the curious idea that they ought to behave in a certain way, and cannot really get rid of it. Secondly,

---

[388] Voltaire [Francois Marie Arouet]. 1880. *Le Sottisier.* Paris: Librairie des bibliophiles. Quoted in: Kilner, *Dignity and Destiny, Humanity in the Image of God,* 28.

[389] Alexander, "Occult Philosophy and Mystical Experience," 17.

[390] Reminder: Throughout Chapter 9, (and this book in general), "The Woke Opiate" references to: "*The Progressive Left,*" "*The Party,*" and "*The Ruling Elites*" as synonymous. Further, the "lesser good" is a reference to Augustine's hierarchical scale relative to good and evil; and additionally, the transgression of God's commandment by Eve (and Adam) to not eat from the Tree of Knowledge and Evil.

[391] Ludwig Wittgenstein. *Tractatus Logico-Philosophicus.* Translated by: D.F. Pears and B.F. McGuinness. London: Routledge, reprinted, 1994. 6.41; 421, 71.

... they do not in fact behave in that way. They know the Law of Nature; they break it. These two facts are the foundation of all clear thinking about ourselves and the universe we live in"

— C.S. Lewis.[392]

"In the beginning" of evolutionary theory, materialists, e.g., atheists, secular humanists, and Marxists believed: "The cosmos is all that is, or ever was, or ever will be."[393] Oxford scholar, and atheist, Richard Dawkins is profoundly clear in his assessment:

> In a universe of blind physical forces and genetic replication, some people are going to get hurt, and other people are going to get lucky; and you won't find any rhyme or reason to it, nor any justice. The universe we observe has precisely the properties we should expect if there is at the bottom, no design, no purpose, no evil and no good. Nothing but blind pitiless indifference.[394]

Dawkins' observation incriminates a Marxist worldview, for it has "no design, no purpose, no evil and no good" — A materialist (atheist) world view has no basis for human dignity, human purpose, and "the problem

---

[392] C.S. Lewis. *Mere Christianity.* Book 1, Chapter 1, p. 21.

[393] Ludwig Wittgenstein. *Tractatus Logico-Philosophicus*, p. 53. Greg Koukl comments, ***Chapter 8: Matter-Ism***, endnote #1, p. 181: "These words launch what is probably the most famous science documentary of all time, PBS's The Cosmos, hosted by the late astronomer Carl Sagen." Koukl points out that this "science documentary" is not at all scientific. "No empirical analysis can ever tell us all that ever was, or is, or will be, even in principle."

[394] Richard Dawkins' quote appears in *River Out of Eden.* New York: Basic Books, 1996. P. 133. Quoted in: Gregory Koukl. *The Story of Reality, How the World began, How It Ends, and Everything important that Happens in Between.* P. 54.

of evil."[395] A significant portion of the population of the United States and Western Culture acknowledges that something is severely wrong with America, and Western Culture— "But that can only be so if there is a right way for things to be," asserts Gregory Koukl.[396] If there is no design, no purpose, no evil, and no good, "… it's extremely unlikely one is able to distinguish between a 'right way for things to be,' and 'things gone wrong'…."[397]

'THE WOKE OPIATE'

"Die Religion ist das Opium des Volkesis"— "*Religion is the opiate of the masses,*" Karl Marx.

In the 1930s, political correctness was employed by Communists as a reminder that "*… the Party's interest is to be treated as a reality that ranks above reality itself.*"[398] Woke Marxist Ideology is exclusively framed in the *interests* of the Ruling Elites— *Thus, for Marxists, both classic and contemporary, the Party's "interest" is "objective truth."* And therein, the Ruling Elites (the Party) are, *themselves*, "a crisis of legitimation" for Woke Marxist Ideology.[399]

A "crisis of legitimation" is best understood by the query, *"Does Woke Marxist Ideology possess the resources to legitimate 'their truth' on its own?"*

---

395 Please see Appendix #2: "The Problem of Evil" for an explanation of what appears to be a philosophical dilemma used often to confront Christian faith.

396 Gregory Koukl. *The Story of Reality, How the World began, How It Ends, and Everything important that Happens in Between.* P. 55.

397 Ibid.

398 Angelo M. Codevilla. "The Rise of Political Correctness." Page 1 of 12 pages.

399 "The crisis of legitimation" involves Jean-Francois Lyotard's "metaphysical search for a first proof" or "a transcendental authority" which places his thinking beyond the secular, empirical world, to whatever is behind the "truth claims" of Woke Marxist Ideology. *The Postmodern Condition: A Report on Knowledge.* Minneapolis, MN: University of Minnesota Press, 1979. 29.

[400] The prolific postmodernist philosopher, Jean-Francois Lyotard observes two problems regarding "the problematic of legitimation," that is, who or what can speak for these people?[401] To begin, (1), Lyotard insists on the need of a "transcendental authority;"[402] but, of course, Woke Marxist Ruling Elites are "on their own," there is no transcendental authority—*there is literally nothing behind Woke Identity Marxism to "legitimate," i.e., to "speak for," any of its ideological claims.*[403] And thus, (2) "… the conditions of truth,"[404] i.e., the conditions that legitimate (literally, "speak for") Woke Marxist's ideological constructs, "are immanent" [405] within "the bonds of debate that is already," Woke Marxist "in nature" [406]—*Woke Marxism's "truth" or "reality" is insulated within the politically correct, moral subjectivis-*

---

400 Ibid. xxiv. Lyotard is speaking of science's inability to legitimate its truth-claims on its own. I am applying Lyotard's "legitimation of truth" to Woke Marxist Ideological claims. Please see my: *A Letter from Christ, Apologetics in Cultural Transition,* 20-21, for the full context of "science's inability to legitimate its truth-claims on its own" *vis-à-vis* Lyotard's examination of the claims of "scientific knowledge."

401 Jean Francois Lyotard. *The Postmodern Condition: A Report on Knowledge.* 29. "The problematic of legitimation" essentially asks the question: "Who can speak for these people?" Repeatedly, it has been asserted in this book: *Political Correctness creates "new realities" conformed to the dictates of the Party.* The Party is "self-legitimating;" Political Correctness' pseudo reality is Woke Marxist Ideology's "truth."

402 Ibid. Please recall and reflect on the significance of the C.S. Lewis quote under the subheading immediately before this segment of the polemic: *"First, … human beings, all over the earth, have the curious idea that they ought to behave in a certain way, and cannot really get rid of it. Secondly, … they do not in fact behave in that way. They know the Law of Nature; they break it. These two facts are the foundation of all clear thinking about ourselves and the universe we live in."*

403 Re: C.S. Lewis. *Mere Christianity.* San Francisco, CA: Harper, 1952. Bk. I, Chap. 4, p. 21.

404 Jean Francois Lyotard. *The Postmodern Condition: A Report on Knowledge.* 29.

405 Lyotard's words, following "immanent in…" are "that game…" Lyotard wrote in the prior paragraph, "the language game of science desires it statements to be true but does not have the resources to legitimate their truth on its own…" "that game" is related to Wittgenstein's "language games." Ibid.,28.

406 The phrase, "the bonds of debate that is already," are Lyotard's words regarding science's inability to legitimate "its truth" on its own. Ibid., 29.

tic interests" of the Ruling Elites. It is thus plainly evident that Woke Identity Marxism does not have the resources to legitimate "its truth" on its own.[407]

In its anxious attempt to reify (create out of nothing) its own reality, Woke Marxism's inane worldview disregards any law of human nature, or of right and wrong above and beyond the actual facts of human behavior.[408] *Woke Marxism conforms to its own politically correct creation of pseudo realities; and therefore, it "has no relevance for judging what is true or just" — Consequently, universal human rights, human dignity and human moral/ethical actions have no value; they are meaningless relative to the interests of the Ruling Elites.*[409] Thus Woke Marxist Ideology, ranging from Political Correctness, and Repressive Tolerance, to Diversity/Identity, and/or Gender Politics, and from Critical Theory, e.g., Critical Race Theory, Queer Theory, Social Justice Theory, e.g., Diversity, Inclusion, and Equity, etc., is a "self-legitimating" and thus, unfalsifiable, philosophical absurdity—*Die Woke ist das Opium des Volkesis* ("*Woke is the opiate of the masses"*).

---

[407] Ibid. 28 (Again, Lyotard references "truth" or "truth claims").

[408] C.S. Lewis. *The C.S. Lewis Signature Classics. Mere Christianity.* "What Lies Behind The Law." Harper One. (1952)/2017. 28.

[409] Reification is the politically correct morphing (manipulation) of the abstract (unreality) into reality. The phrase set off in quotes is Lyotard's wording (although he, Lyotard, is referring to "technological" knowledge, and I am referring to Woke Marxist's Ideology). See: Jean Francois Lyotard. *The Postmodern Condition: A Report on Knowledge.* Introduction, xxv.

BUT WHAT ABOUT THE EMANCIPATION OF THE UNDERPRIVILEGED?

> *A scorpion and a frog meet on the bank of a stream and the scorpion asks the frog to carry him across on its back. The frog asks, "How do I know you won't sting me?" The scorpion says, "Because if I do, I will die too." The frog is satisfied, and they set out, but in midstream, the scorpion stings the frog. The frog feels the onset of paralysis and starts to sink, knowing they both will drown, but has just enough time to gasp "Why?" Replies the scorpion: "It's my nature…"*[410]

Social Justice scholarship presupposes that social inequalities are generated by "invisible identity-based systems" of power and privilege.[411] And therefore, it is not surprising that the Marxist reification of "Systemic Racism" casts the "Privileged" in the role of the "Scorpion" (the "victimizer") and the "Underprivileged" in the role of the "Frog" (the "victim").

Woke Marxist ideological propaganda portrays the Privileged as "white supremacists" committed to the systemic domination and oppression of the Underprivileged, to include, by implication, their vision of "emancipation"— *The emancipation of the Underprivileged will take place when the "conditions under which tolerance can again become a liberating and humanizing force."*[412] The "conditions" referred to by Marcuse relate to the emergence of the Socialist/Communist Marxist State and the transferring of

---

410 This illustration is astutely used by Alasdair Elder. *The Red Trojan Horse. A Concise Analysis of Cultural Marxism.* 138. (Alasdair Elder applies this illustration to the nature of radical Islam in his excellent analysis of Cultural Marxism).

411 Helen Pluckrose & James Lindsay. *Cynical Theories.* P.182.

412 Herbert Marcuse. "Critique of Pure Tolerance." p. 110-111.

the Progressive Left Elites' power to the Underprivileged/Oppressed, thus extending to them rule over the new classless utopia.[413]

But, Work Marxist Ideology is a deceptive illusion, as argued above— *It is, in truth, a politically correct construct (i.e., a pseudo-reality) used to "exploit and betray people of color."* (Allow me to expand the meaning of this conclusion under the next subheading: "The Progressive Left's Betrayal of the Underprivileged").

THE PROGRESSIVE LEFT'S BETRAYAL OF THE UNDERPRIVILEGED

Paulo Freire's *The Pedagogy of the Oppressed*, reflects on an inviolable law of Progressive Left Movements: "*For a revolution to be authentic it must be perpetual for the second it stops, it becomes the status quo.*"[414] The "perpet-

---

[413] Please recall, Paulo Freire's "The Pedagogy of the Oppressed," and its reflection on an inviolable law of Progressive Left Movements: "*For a revolution to be authentic it must be perpetual for the second it stops, it becomes the status quo.*" The "perpetual" nature of Progressive Left Movements makes explicit that like the pigs in Orwell's *Animal Farm*, the "Elites" do not intend to disinherit their power for the sake of the Underprivileged— *This point, as founded on the consistent nature of Progressive Left Movements, the historical evidence of no true a purely Communist regime has ever emerged, principally because Progressive Left Movements have never disinherited their power to the "Proletariats" or the "Underprivileged."*

[414] Albert Mohler. Podcast: "Thinking In Public." Subject: "Critical Theory and the Cynical Transformation of Society." Interview: James Lindsay. https://www.youtube.com/watch?v=de7j0npQu-4. Downloaded: 06/26/2023.

Please do not deflect my assertions assuming they come from a "Privileged" mind intent on being right; my assertions are founded on the writing of an extremely devoted Marxist who, in his work, *The Pedagogy of the Oppressed,* calls "*repeatedly,* dozens upon dozens of times, for an outright *and perpetual* cultural revolution by which all "dehumanizing structures" will be thrown down in a perpetual cycle of destruction. This society will be cast down, as will the society that replaces it, and the society that replaces that, and so on and so forth ... until Utopia." James Lindsay is quoting Paulo Freire in his, *The Marxification of Education, Paul Freier's Critical Marxism and the Theft of Education.* New Discourses. 2022. 13-14.

ual" nature of Progressive Left Movements makes explicit that the "Ruling Elites" do not intend to disinherit their power to the Underprivileged— The author's conclusion here, is self-evident. Progressive Left Movements are pre-Socialist-States, and Socialist States are pre-Communist[415]— *There has never been a successful Communist State, that is, a leveled, classless utopia, because the Elites, "the dictatorship of the Proletariat" (i.e., Underprivileged) have never disinherited their power on behalf of the Oppressed."*[416] Instead, if Progressive Left ambitions succeed, the alleged "Scorpion" (the Privileged) and the "Frog" (the Underprivileged) will together "die" ("drown") in vain— Perhaps "death" equates to the loss of our Republic following a civil war between the Underprivileged and the Privileged. (Such a discomforting notion is not far removed from the demoralization and destruction of the Summer of 2020 orchestrated by the Progressive Left).

Social Critic, Os Guinness observes: "If the founders were correct, contemporary America's pursuit of political leadership without character, economic enterprise without ethics and trust, scientific progress without human values, freedom without virtue and negative freedom without

---

415 Re: **From footnote #307 above**: The term "socialist state" is widely used by Marxist–Leninist parties, theorists, and governments to mean a state under the control of a vanguard party that is organizing the economic, social, and political affairs of said state toward the construction of socialism. *Marxists often refer to socialism as the first, necessary phase on the way from capitalism to communism.*

416 Admittedly, it is very doubtful that Freire would himself concede to what I have referred to as "self-evident" because of his radical Marxist's convictions. *But he is an invaluable "hostile witness" regarding the point to be made regarding the Ruling Elites on the "Progressive Left" consistent record on not relinquishing their power.*

positive freedom can end only in disaster.[417] It rings the death knell of sustainable freedom, and as it works itself out socially and politically on multiplied levels, it makes the decline of America only a matter of time."[418]

The many books written that expose Woke Marxism's treachery will not, on their own, slow down the Progressive Left's "Long March Through The Institutions" (Antonio Gramsci's "historic bloc"). What we urgently DO about Woke Identity Marxism is most important. *How should the Church respond to Woke Identity Marxism? In Section 3, the Church is exhorted to follow through with a missional response (i.e., "The Priesthood of All Believers") to the ideological invasion of the Woke Opiate.*

---

[417] Guinness' distinction between "negative freedom" and "positive freedom" is striking. Philosopher, Isaiah Berlin spoke of "Two Concepts of Liberty": "Negative freedom … is freedom *from*— in essence, freedom from interference and constraint. Positive freedom is freedom *for*— in essence, freedom for excellence according to whatever vision and ideals define that excellence. The framers' position here is also clear and balanced, but contemporary Americans have abandoned it. They have voted unambiguously for negative freedom rather than positive and have therefore exalted freedom as an essentially private matter, for where else can a person be truly free *from* all outside interference?" Os Guinness. *A Free People's Suicide, Sustainable Freedom And The American Future.* Downers Grove, IL: Inter-Varsity Press, 2012. 61.

[418] Ibid., 34.

PART— 3

A MISSIONAL RESPONSE: 'THE PRIESTHOOD OF ALL BELIEVERS'

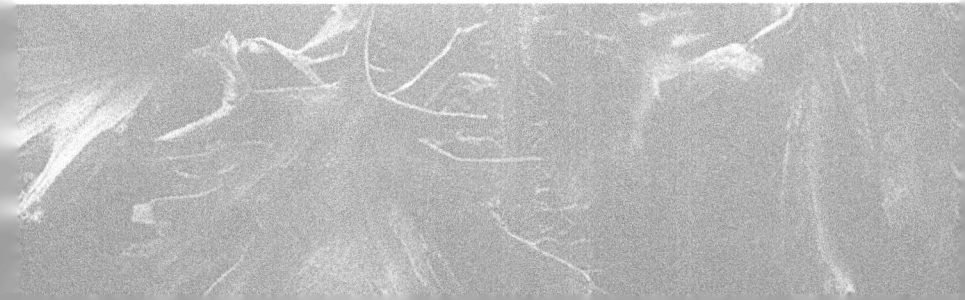

CHAPTER 10

THE MEANING OF TRUTH

"… the Party's interest is to be treated as a reality that ranks above reality itself."[419]

"Why have elite colleges gone bad?" Hillsdale College President, Larry Arnn unequivocally responds: "The cause of these colleges going bad is very deep, but it is mostly this: they no longer understand their purpose as the pursuit of truth. Instead, they see it as training their students to be revolutionaries."[420]

Arnn observes, "Being trained to be a revolutionary requires different virtues — First, the student must think he can perfect the world and think

---

[419] Angelo M. Codevilla. "The Rise of Political Correctness." Page 1 of 12 pages. *The author has used this quote multiple times throughout this book. This is because Woke Identity Marxism's "truth" is expressed in this quote, and this book is, essentially, about "Truth" — What it is not (Woke Identity Marxism's "truth,") and what it is: Truth is objective as developed in this chapter.*

[420] Larry P. Arnn. "The Life of Hillsdale College: Why Have Elite Colleges Gone Bad?" Gmail-The Life of Hillsdale College Why Have Elite Colleges Gone Bad. pdf. Page 2 of 4 pages. Downloaded: 04/06/2024.

he knows how. And Second, he must learn to comply."[421] Do these "virtues" appear to conflict with one another? The law of non-contradiction does not apply to those infected with the Woke Marxist virus and consequently, these two "virtues" are seen as "in-sync."[422] Arnn expands: "The law of contradiction would mean that a governor could not simultaneously hold that the COVID pandemic renders church services too dangerous to allow, and that massive protest marches are fine. It would preclude a man from declaring himself a woman, or a woman declaring herself a man, as if one's sex is simply a matter of what one wills it to be."[423] Larry Arnn concludes: "Revolution today is made easy by the view that the standards of perfect and imperfect, of good and bad, are completely subjective."[424]

FAITH & VIRTUE— OBJECTIVE TRUTH

"If anything does now exist, either something must be eternal, or something not eternal must have come from nothing"
— J. Oliver Buswell.[425]

"In the beginning" — both Genesis 1:1 and John 1:1— confronts human reason with ultimate reality: The *something* "that caused the universe was

---

421 Ibid.

422 The author has added the "third virtue" mentioned by Larry Arnn in a different Hillsdale College publication from the one I quoted him in above. Please see: Larry P. Arnn. *Imprimis.* "Orwell's *1984* and Today." December 2020. Vol. 49. Number 12. Page 4 of 6 pages.

423 Ibid.

424 Larry P. Arnn. "The Life of Hillsdale College: Why Have Elite Colleges Gone Bad?" Page 2 of 4 pages.

425 J. Oliver Buswell, Jr. *A Systematic Theology of the Christian Religion.* Grand Rapids, MI.: Zondervan, 1962. Vol. 1, p.72. (An axiom of physics is that "nothing comes from nothng").

actually some *One*...."[426] And the *Some One* spoke— *"Let there be* ... and *there was*" (Gen. 1:3). "By the word of the Lord were the heavens made .... He spoke, and it came to be" (Ps. 33:6,9) — "The Word of God is thus God at work;"[427] the Word is the Creator of all things visible and invisible (Jn. 1:3). And "In him was *life"* (Jn.1:4) — "There is no physical life in the realm of created things except in and through him."[428] He is the One who formed the "crown of his creation," man, from the clay of the earth (Gen. 2:7a[429]; Ps. 8:5). And the Creator then breathed life into the nostrils of man (Gen. 2:7b)[430]— "And that life was the *light of men*; man became a 'living soul'" (Ps. 2:7c; Jn. 1:4).[431]

And "The Word *became flesh"* (Jn. 1:14) — Through the womb of "the virgin" (Isa. 7:14), Incarnate Deity entered human history. As image bearers of God (Gen. 1:27),[432] we relate to "Truth" (Ultimate Reality) in per-

---

426 Gregory Koukl. *The Story of Reality.* 51-52.

427 J.I Packer. *Knowing God.* Ch. 5: "God Incarnate." Downers Grove, IL.: Inter-Varsity Press, 56.

428 Ibid.

429 The first clause of Genesis 2:7: "*... the Lord God formed the man from the dust of the ground...*" reveals "that man is part 'dust,' a better word is, 'clay,' personally fashioned by God." Our origins are from the earth (Genesis 2:7a), and upon death, we return to the earth (Ecclesiastes 3:20). Bruce Waltke. "Reflections From The Old Testament On Abortion." Delivered as the presidential address at the 27th annual meeting of the Evangelical Theological Society, December 29, 1975.

430 The second clause of Genesis 2:7 continues, "*... and breathed into his nostrils the breath of life....*" Human life is animated by God's breath— our origin is not only from the earth but also from heaven. Ibid.

431 The third clause—Genesis 2:7c, follows, "*... and the man became a living being...*" or a "living soul" (Heb. *nephesh*). Genesis 2:7c informs us that rather than "soul" being a distinct part of a person's being (as though we contained a soul), a person is a "living soul," a wholly integrated being— body, spirit/soul. *Therefore, if any part of the body is formed, so also is the spirit/soul.* Ibid.

432 The "likeness-image" of God "involves humanity's special *creation relationship* with God, which makes it possible for humanity to be a meaningful *reflection* of God." John F. Kilner, *Dignity and Destiny. Humanity in the Image of God.* Grand Rapids, MI: William B. Eerdmans, 2015. 114.

sonal terms— Truth is our constant pursuit. But "… if anyone does not have the Spirit of Christ, they do not belong to Christ" (Rom. 8:9) and they, the "natural man" (1 Cor. 2:14) relates to, and understands truth as *correspondence* with the created order, that is, *empirical reality* (Rom. 1:19-20)—This is "public truth." That is, the facts inherent in empirical reality are objective, and therefore they are open to all people's testing regarding the claims made (*et. al.,* Acts 2:22).

Truth, for the unregenerate person, is *indirect* through the created order. But if the image of God is fully restored, through regeneration (Titus 3:5b) as is true of the believer in Christ— or in the case of the Jew, who is thoroughly familiar with the scriptures— truth is then *direct*; godly Jews and Gentiles understand "heavenly things" (i.e., *metaphysical reality)* by hearing the words of the Word Himself— *"Everyone on the side of truth listens to me;" ultimately, truth is about some One, the Creator himself* (18:37b).

The Apostle Paul's delivery of truth, first to Jews, and then to pagan Gentiles in Acts 17 is a practical illustration/demonstration of what we have just discussed:

ACTS 17— A VIVID MODEL OF DELIVERING TRUTH

"Truth is always about something, but reality is that about which truth is"
—C.S. Lewis.[433]

Acts 17 begins with Paul in Thessalonica reasoning with the Jews about the identity of the Messiah and how he was to suffer and rise from the dead (Acts 17:3a): *"The Jesus I am proclaiming to you is the Messiah"* (Acts 17:3b). As above-mentioned, a Jewish audience had sufficient understanding of who God was because of their knowledge of the Scriptures; and

[433] C.S. Lewis. "Myth Became Fact." 66.

they were anticipating the coming of Israel's Messiah. But when proclaiming the Gospel to a Gentile audience (as alluded to above), who had no understanding of Israel's history or the Scriptures, it was necessary for "the Apostle to the Gentiles" to begin at the Bible's starting point: *"In the beginning, God created the heavens and the earth"* (Genesis 1:1) —God is ultimate Reality— He is the Creator of the *visible, empirical world,* that is, the *created order* and the *metaphysical (invisible) world.*

Paul's delivery of truth to Jewish and Gentile audiences was distinct, but regarding both audiences, truth is transcendent; it is *always* anchored in reality as it is, both *visible* reality (i.e., the created order) and *invisible* reality (metaphysics) — *Truth is then that which corresponds with empirical reality, that is, facts open to verification; and invisible* reality (Paul begins with the metaphysical world, that is, the understanding of who God is, as known by Jews). Paul's understanding of reality as both *visible* and *invisible* was critical to a dialogue Jesus had with a learned Jewish teacher: "I have spoken to you of earthly things, and you do not believe; how then will you believe if I speak of heavenly things?" (Jn. 3:12).[434]

Acts 17 continues with Paul in Athens. While Paul was waiting for his companions, Silas, and Timothy to join him, he became greatly distressed

---

[434] Re: "... reality as it is," is "coupled": "In the beginning God created the heavens and the earth" (Gen. 1:1). Creation is a series of binary relationships in Genesis 1— "the heavens and the earth" (1:1), "light and darkness" (1:4), "land and seas" (1:10), "evening and morning" (1:13), "day and night" (1:14), male and female (1:27). All these relationships are intended by God to work together— *The nature of creation, and how God has designed the cosmos to work, relates to these couplets.* The idea that these couplets would become uncoupled or separated results, for example, in the eighteenth-century Enlightenment wherein the couplet of "the heavens and the earth" was broken into the secular world, and the sacred world. Reality did not change, but the thinking of people in Western culture changed because of the philosophical rift created by French Enlightenment philosophers. For a more detailed explanation of the effects of the uncoupling of the created order in the minds of the West, please see my: *Living Missionally Beyond Sunday, ... and all peoples will be blessed through you...* (12:3). Chapter 2, "Challenging 'Nest-Bound' Believers," pages 17-22. Ark House Press, 2023.

by the overwhelming abundance of idols he saw in Athens (Acts 17:16). The Apostle then began reasoning with both Gentiles ("God-fearing Greeks") and Jews (Acts 17:17). Soon, Paul attracted a "group of Epicurean and Stoic philosophers" who began to debate with him (Acts 17:18). Following his initial encounter with these philosophers, the Apostle was summoned to appear before the world renown high council of Athens, the Areopagus, where he was asked: "*May we know what this new teaching is that you are presenting? You are bringing some strange ideas to our ears; we would like to know what they mean*" (Acts 17:20-21).

Paul begins his defense by observing the religious nature of his pagan audience, and their ignorance concerning the many gods they worship (Acts 17:22-23). Paul then informs them about the one true God: *24 "The God who made the world and everything in it is the Lord of heaven and earth and does not live in temples built by human hands. 25 And he is not served by human hands, as if he needed anything. Rather, he himself gives everyone life and breath and everything else"* (Acts 17:24-25). Paul makes it very clear that he is not merely talking about another idol, like all the idols scattered throughout Athens[435] — The God whom Paul is proclaiming is the Sovereign, Self-Existent, Creator of "heaven and earth."

With his extraordinary gift for knowing how to address every crowd he faced, Paul extends his thought by quoting the sixth-century BC Cretan poet Epimenides of Cnossos to help illustrate his teaching to the highly sophisticated philosophers at the Areopagus: "'For in him we live and move and have our being.' As some of your own poets have said, 'We are his offspring'" (17:28). Nancy Pearcey's insight is timely: "Logically, if humans are God's 'offspring,' the implication is that God must be a personal being,

---

[435] Nancy Pearcey. Forward: Gregory Koukl. *The Story Of Reality, How The World Began, How It Ends, And Everything Important That Happens In Between.* Grand Rapids, MI: Zondervan. 2017. P. 14.

as we are… If a personal God created us as personal beings, then it is logical to conclude that we stand in a personal relationship with him."[436] *Truth is that which corresponds to the created order, as it is* (Romans 1:18-20); *and ultimately, truth is that which corresponds to ultimate Reality— "Everyone on the side of truth listens to me"* (John 18:37c); *ultimately, truth is about some One, the Creator himself* (Gen. 1:1/John 1:1).[437]

THE TRANSFORMING POWER OF THE GOSPEL AND TRUTH

"American schoolchildren today learn two things about Thomas Jefferson: that he wrote the Declaration of Independence and that he was a slaveholder"
— Larry Arnn, Hillsdale College.

"The astounding thing, after all," asserts Larry Arnn, "is not that some of our Founders were slaveholders. There was a lot of slavery back then, as there had been for all recorded time. The astounding thing— the miracle, even, one might say— is that these slaveholders founded a republic based on principles designed to abnegate slavery."[438]

The most outstanding example of the principles our Republic is founded on is The Prologue of the Declaration of Independence. Thomas Jefferson

[436] Ibid. P. 15.

[437] Now, of course, in relation to the practicalities of daily life, the Christian constantly relates to truth in a composite manner, we understand truth as correspondence with the created order, as it is, and we understand "heavenly things" through our relationship with ultimate Reality, Jesus Christ— For the believer, God's Word is always, in every situation in life, immutable Truth.

[438] Larry P. Arnn. President, Hillsdale College. IMPRIMUS— Orwell's *1984* and Today. December 2020 |VOLUME 49, ISSUE 12. https://imprimis.hillsdales.edu/orwells-1984-today/. 05/12/2024.

was the author of the Declaration of Independence.[439] Our nation's 3rd President regretted his sin of having owned slaves and in his repentance, he committed himself to fighting against slavery— *Jefferson acknowledged in the Declaration of the Independence's Prologue, and throughout, that the personal dignity of every human being was founded on their special creation in the image of God; every human being is therefore, equal on that basis* (*et. al.*, Gen. 1:27).

Indeed, Jefferson explicitly condemned the injustice of the slave-trade in the original Declaration; however, the reader will recall from the former discussion regarding political expediency *vis-a-vis* representation in the House to be apportioned on the state's free population plus three-fifths of its enslaved population (*et. al.* Chapter 6). The Three-Fifths Compromise resolved that the Continental Congress would conveniently remove Thomas Jefferson's statement regarding the injustice of the Slave Trade (and, by implication, slavery) from the final version of the Declaration of Independence."[440]

---

[439] Thomas Jefferson's draft of the Declaration of Independence was written in June 1776. John Adams (1735-1826) later made eighty-six changes to Jefferson's draft. Benjamin Franklin 1706–1790), and other members of the committee were appointed to finalize the draft of the original Declaration by Congress. Library of Congress, https://www.loc.gov/exhibits/jefferson/jeffdec.html#:~:text=Written%20in%20June%201776%2C%20Thomas,the%20document%2C%20and%20by%20Congress. Downloaded: 04/18/2024.

[440] Please recall this discussion in Chapter 6, "Critical Race Theory— An Historical Introduction." Three-Fifths Compromise. United States History. Re: The "Three Fifths Compromise": The Editors of *Encyclopedia Britannica*. (The most recent edition of my source was revised and updated by Adam Augustyn). https://www.britannica.com/topic/three-fifths-compromise. Downloaded: 08/14/2023.

AMERICA'S "SUPERSTRUCTURE"[441]

Every major cultural institution in the United States of America was founded on the Gospel. Civil religion is symbolic of the Gospel's influence in America.

Our nation's most foundational documents, especially the Declaration of Independence, point to our Creator as our source of rights: "We hold these truths to be self-evident, that all men are created equal; that they are endowed by their Creator with certain unalienable rights; that among them are life, liberty, and the pursuit of happiness"— *Our unalienable rights are founded on divine absolutes and our special creation in God's image.*

Christians courageously stand for unalienable human rights, dignity, and equality throughout the earth. Driven by her Christian roots, America is the greatest nation-building, world relief and benevolent nation in the history of the world.

Following the founding of the church itself, as an extension of Christ's resurrection, William Wilberforce led Great Britain in freeing slaves in all her colonies and England itself. Sierra Leone was created a slave-free state on the African continent through Wilberforce's original efforts to free slaves. Wilberforce was a great influence on many nations, to include Abraham Lincoln and the United States.

Roger Williams was heroic in his fighting for religious freedom for all; Elizabeth Fry reformed prisons, Dietrich Bonhoeffer resisted the evils of Nazism, Gary Haugen freed prisoners from modern sex trafficking and bonded slavery; and dared to believe that a better world was possible. And Martin Luther King Jr., a pastor from Atlanta, embodied kingdom virtues in the nonviolent African American Civil Rights Movement in the 1960s.

---

[441] "Superstructure" is a reference to Antonio Gramsci, Chapter 2, 'The Long March Through The Institutions.'

And today, countless nations are served, in humanitarian, benevolent and compassionate ways, by Christian missionaries who although this world is unworthy of them, they will never be featured on any news outlet.

Further, Christian faith is the source for modern science and technology. Sir Francis Bacon, a devout believer in the Bible and Lord Chancellor of England, founded and established the "scientific method" by reference to the reality of the created order of the systems of the universe. Following in the footsteps of Sir Francis Bacon, consider some of the great scientific discoveries and developments in science by men, who as Christians, interpreted their observations in accord with a Christian world view: Isaac Newton (dynamics); Johann Kepler (astronomy); Robert Boyle (chemistry); Lord Kelvin (thermodynamics); Louis Pasteur (bacteriology); Matthew Maury (electrodynamics); John Ray (biology); and Carolus Linnacus (taxonomy).

These scientific discoveries and developments were possible because of three basic axioms of science: "The first of the unprovable [self-evident] premises on which science has been based is the belief that the world is real and the human mind is capable of knowing its real nature; the second and best known postulate underlying the structure of scientific knowledge is that of cause and effect; and the third basic scientific premise is that nature is unified."[442] These three axioms are basically Christian in origin and nature, concludes Dr. Stanley D. Beck.[443]

The major divisions of science reflect the creation of the universe by the personal God of the Bible. The biblical commandment of God to man to take "dominion" over the earth (Genesis 1:28) is explained by Henry Morris: "There are only three specific acts of 'ex nihilo' creation recorded in

---

[442] Stanley D. Beck, "Natural Science and Creationist Theology," *Bioscience* 32 (Oct. 1982), 739. Quoted in: Henry Morris, *The Biblical Basis for Modern Science*, 30-31.

[443] Ibid.

Genesis, indicating three fundamentally different entities in God's universe. These acts are indicated by the use of the verb 'create' (Hebrew: *'bara')*:

1. In the beginning God 'created' the heaven and the earth (Genesis 1:1).
2. God 'created' … every living creature that moves (Genesis 2:21).
3. God 'created' man in his own image (Genesis 1:27)."[444]

Genesis 1:1 refers to the creation of the world; and Genesis 2:21 relates to all living creatures except God's special creation in his own image as recorded in Genesis 1:27. These three major categories of God's creation provide a basis for the physical sciences, the life sciences, and the social sciences (inclusive of the humanities).[445]

The concept of the "dominion" mandate in Genesis (2:15;19-20) is the basis for many of the great scientific discoveries that benefit the Western world. Medical advancements, hospitals, the American Red Cross, and scores of national and international relief agencies and efforts are founded upon the Christian ethic and worldview.

And finally, the unified field of knowledge— the physical sciences, the life sciences, and the social sciences, to include the humanities (cf. Genesis 1:1,2:21,1:27), inherit in God's creation is the source for the great institutions of education in America. The IVY League Schools, owe their existence to the Judeo-Christian faith: every school, except one (Cornell), began as a training center, a Bible College/Seminary, for ministers.

The Puritans founded Harvard; and John Harvard, a Baptist Minister, donated his library to the new college in Massachusetts. Jonathan Edwards, the brilliant Reformed Theologian, was the first president of The New

---

444 Henry Morris, *The Biblical Basis for Modern Science*, 42.

445 Ibid.

Jersey State College (Princeton University); Roger Williams founded Brown University; Brown's motto is: "In God we hope."

Columbia was a training center for Episcopal clergy. Columbia's founder, Samuel Johnson wrote (1754): "The chief thing that is aimed at in this college is to teach and engage the children to know God and Jesus Christ, and to love and serve him in all sobriety, godliness and righteousness of life with a perfect heart and a willing mind."

Penn's seal says: "Laws without morals are useless." The "Public Academy of Philadelphia" originated on property owned by George Whitefield. There, Benjamin Franklin oversaw the construction of a great preaching hall as the first building of what would become the University of Pennsylvania (the first graduating class was 7 people, 4 of which went into full time ministry).

Dartmouth's motto is: "A voice of one crying in the wilderness" and one of the Yale founding presidents penned to his incoming students: "Above all, have an eye to the great end of all your studies which is to obtain the clearest conception of divine things and to lead you to a saving knowledge of God in His Son Jesus Christ." [446]

Although traditional assessments of what it means to be human have been banished from the public square, especially in the modern university, the different schools in the university system depend on some notion, or ideal, of what it means to be human. For example, the School of Business is concerned with creating well-being, or "wealth" and The School of Psychology is concerned with notions of human sanity or insanity. The School of Anthropology is concerned with human origins and The Law School presupposes human morality. The School of Fine Arts is concerned

---

[446] Although some today attempt to trace the origin of universities back to Plato's Academy or the madrasa at Cairo's Al-Azhar Mosque, there is no doubt that the source behind the first universities in Bologna, the Sorbonne, Oxford, and Cambridge was the rise of the cathedral schools in the late medieval world. Oxford's motto is founded on Psalm 27, *Dominus Illuminatio Mea* - "The Lord is my Light."

with human creativity and until recently, Medical School graduates affirmed the words of the Hippocratic Oath, "I will not give a woman a pessary[447] to produce an abortion."[448]

The United States is the wealthiest, most productive, best educated system in the world. America has the greatest agricultural output, the U.S. has 17 of the top rated 20 universities in the world; it has the best, most advanced technology on earth because it is a meritocratic system.[449] The "cultural melting pot" of the American Republic, founded on the idea that under the auspices of the Constitution, people surrender their innate ethnic or racial identities and assimilate into a shared idea of citizenship, is very rare in human history— Americans give up something of themselves for the gift of citizenship in the United States.[450]

Although America's history has been tainted by slavery, it is self-evident that the United States was founded on a transcendent, virtuous Freedom.[451] *Before we discuss America's completed restoration (Chapter 12, Racial Reconciliation),*

---

[447] A "pessary" is a small soluble block inserted into the vagina. Re: Kaiser Jr., *What Does The Lord Require?"*, 105.

[448] I am here paraphrasing Sommerville's introduction to: "Trouble Defining The Human," *The Decline of the Secular University*, 23.

[449] Victor Davis Hans Hanson, Hillsdale College. The Rise of Tribal Politics," Lecture 5, "American Citizenship and its Decline."

[450] Ibid.

[451] To ensure clarity, my argument involving CRT's historical revisionism is, precisely: The roots of America's founding as a free Democratic Republic are traced to Plymouth, Massachusetts, and the signing of the Mayflower Compact (See: Peter W. Wood. *1620, A Critical Response to the 1619 Project.* New York: Encounter Books, 2022).

Following the Mayflower Compact, America's freedom is founded, and lived, on the bedrock foundations of the Declaration of Independence, The U.S. Constitution, and the Bill of Rights. American social and cultural institutions— Our shared beliefs, values, and patterns of social order are formed by freedom themes woven throughout our founding documents and through which serve religious, family, governmental, legal, economic, educational, healthcare, the arts— music, film industry, art galleries, museums— archives, and monuments, most of which are ostensibly rooted in traditional Judeo-Christian values.

we will discuss how the Church can lead in turning back the influence of Woke Identity Marxism; and the saving of the Republic and Western Civilization (Chapter 11).

CHAPTER 11

THE PRIESTHOOD OF ALL BELIEVERS

LIVING MISSIONALLY BEYOND SUNDAY

To live missionally is to daily join Jesus Christ on His mission, and for Him to work through missional-driven disciples so that "all peoples on earth will be blessed through you" (Gen. 12:3b). *Every believer "from every nation, tribe, people and language"* (Rev. 7:9), *is called to join God on His mission and live missionally beyond Sunday!* (Cf. Mt. 28:18-20).

Acts, chapter 8, begins by describing Saul's consenting to Stephen's martyrdom. A "great persecution" of the primitive church in Jerusalem then results in the scattering of Jesus' "witnesses" throughout "Judea and Samaria" (Acts 8:1).

The widespread persecution began with the Sadducees, but Stephen's death was directly at the hands of the Pharisees— Both parties then united in the "great persecution." And Saul soon becomes the leader of the widespread persecution (Acts 8:3).

Although it is a mystery why the Apostles were not directly attacked, nevertheless, God's missional ends prevail over the rage-driven persecution of Saul and the two parties of the Sanhedrin— The Lord uses the persecution of his church to *send* (the Greek term translated, "scatter" means *disperse,* "to sow in separate or scattered places"[452]) his disciples from Jerusalem to specific people groups, particularly, Samaria (Acts 8:4).[453] Jesus' disciples are to be "witnesses" (Acts 1:8)[454] of God's grace in Christ to a people who have been the objects of their racial hatred for centuries![455]

It is noteworthy that although Acts 1:5 speaks of Philip going "to a city in Samaria" and proclaiming, "the Messiah there," this is not a reference to the apostle, named Philip (Mk. 3:18), but rather a deacon (et.al., Acts 6:5).

Jesus' earlier ministry in Samaria was modeled for the disciples (John 4), though the disciples had been forbidden to go to Samaria. But the time is now right—The promise of the Father has clothed the church in power (Lk. 24:49/Acts 1:4-5; 2:1-4). And Jesus' disciples are sent (beginning with

---

[452] A.T. Robertson. *Word Pictures of the New Testament.* Vol. III, Acts. Grand Rapids, MI. Baker Book House, 1930. 102.

[453] Jesus told his disciples to remain in Jerusalem until after the "promise of the Father" came upon them (Acts 1:4; cf. Luke 24:49). But the disciples continued to remain in Jerusalem, after receiving the promise of the Father, instead of proclaiming the Gospel to other peoples (cf. Acts 1:8).

[454] The Greek term translated "witnesses" is *martures* from which comes our word, martyrs.

[455] The acrimony between Jews and Samaritans originated centuries before, during the disruption of the Hebrew monarchy following Solomon's death in 930 B.C. The Judeans regarded the Samaritans to be "racial and religious half-breeds" because these foreign settlers were planted in Samaria by the Assyrians to take the place of the upper classes of the land who were deported at the time of the fall of the northern kingdom of Israel (Cf. 2 Kings 17:24ff.; Ezra 4:2, 9f.). This period was from 721 – 705 B.C. during the reign of Sargon II, the Assyrian king). Despite the Samaritans turning from their pagan roots and embracing Judaism, the Jews continued to refuse to have anything to do with them, their hatred ran deep in their souls.

a deacon, not an apostle, and perhaps his daughters, Acts 21:8) to missionally engage Samaria.

Philip's proclamation of the Gospel was followed by two signs that point to the now present kingdom of God, the deliverance of people bound by malignant spirits and the healing of many who were "paralyzed" or "lame."[456] The awe-struck Samaritans "paid close attention" to Philip[457] (Acts 8:6-7).

The Samaritans had come under the spell of the occult power of a sorcerer, but the power working through Philip was greater than Simon Magus' power. And the Samaritans believed the Good News proclaimed by Philip and they were baptized (Acts 8:12).

Simon, the sorcerer, was "astonished by the great signs and miracles he saw," and he, "himself believed and was baptized" (Acts 8:13). But it is apparent that Simon's motives were self-serving, he wanted the power Philip had so that he could regain his power over the Samaritan people— "He was probably half victim of self-delusion, half conscious imposter" (Furneaux).[458]

Philip is joined by Peter and John (Acts 8:14)— Since "the apostles in Jerusalem heard that Samaria had accepted the word of God," they sensed a need to go to Samaria, perhaps they felt the need to sanction Philip's ministry among the Samaritans, particularly for the sake of the acceptance of Jewish Christians.

Because "the Holy Spirit had not yet come on any" of the Samaritans, Peter, and John "prayed for the new believers," so that they "might receive the Holy Spirit" (Acts 8:15-16). When Simon "saw that the Spirit was

---

456 Setting people free from torment by demonic spirits is a sign pointing to God's willingness to set all repentant people free from bondage to sin and healing points to God's ultimate intention to "make all things new" (Rev. 21:1-7).

457 A.T. Robertson. *Word Pictures in the New Testament.* 103.

458 Ibid. 105.

given at the laying on of the apostles' hands, he offered them money" (Acts 8:18). "When Simon saw," grammatically implies "that those who received the gift of the Holy Spirit spoke with tongues."[459] Simon *saw* power given to others, and he is determined to purchase this authority for himself.

Peter confronts Simon's evil motives (Acts 8:20) but he still leaves room for the sorcerer to repent (Acts 8:22). As Peter and John returned to Jerusalem, they preached the Gospel in many Samaritan towns (Acts 8:25).

Acts 8:1-25 is a *missional text,* that is, it is a divinely inspired model of the *Missio Dei* and the corresponding missional practices of the Lord's earliest disciples on a liminally-ladened mission. *A missional reading/interpretation of Acts 8:1-25 is applied to biblically based practices essential for the formulation of a missional theology in the following:*

PRACTICES OF MISSIONAL CONGREGATIONS

"… *you are a chosen people, a royal priesthood*"
— 1 Peter 2:9

The restoration of the full thrust of the Abrahamic Covenant to the Gentile world has made *all* believers, Jew, and Gentile, male and female, a "kingdom of priests." And the Priesthood of *all* Believers is called to join God on his mission— *"and all peoples on earth will be blessed through you"* (Gen. 12:3b/Mt. 28:18-20).

Towards the fulfillment of the Great Commission, Jesus' restoration of the full thrust of the Abrahamic Covenant includes God's original missional intention for Israel— *"Although the whole earth is mine, you will be for me a kingdom of priests and a holy nation"* (Ex. 19:5-6; cf. Gen. 12:3).

---

[459] Ibid. 107. "When Simon saw" — participle, second aorist active of *horáō.*

The "priesthood of all believers" was one of three dynamic motivations for the Protestant Reformation. Two of the three motivations, *Sola Scriptura,* the sole authority of holy Scripture, and *Sola Fide*, justification by "faith alone," are universally known among Protestant Christians.

But the third preeminent doctrine behind the Reformation, the "priesthood of all believers," has been virtually ignored and consequently, disobeyed by the church universal.

THE PRIESTHOOD OF ALL BELIEVERS

"The only answer we should give to the question of the secret of the church's cultural power is that the Christian faith is true, and that its power is the power of God himself"
— Os Guinness.

Exodus 19:5-6, quoted above, clearly tells us that Israel, as a nation, was to be "a priestly kingdom," "a royal priesthood." Exodus 19:5-6 provides theological foundation for 1 Pet 2:5, 9 and Rev 1:6 and 5:10— The New Testament doctrine of "the priesthood of all believers."[460]

The kingdom of God is "a priestly kingdom" — 1 Peter 2:5 says to *all* believers that "you also, like living stones, are being built into a spiritual house to be a holy priesthood, offering spiritual sacrifices acceptable to God through Jesus Christ." And 1 Peter 2:9 continues, "… you are a chosen people, a royal priesthood" called to intercede between God and sinful humanity.

460 Walter Kaiser. "The Great Commission in the Old Testament," 4.

MISSIONAL THEOLGY

"As the Father has sent me, I am sending you"
— John 20:21

A missional reading of the Bible, to include Acts 8:1-25, serves as basis for the formulation of a missional theology— *Missional theology defines missional congregations.* And therefore, a missional theology properly frames the practices of both missional congregations and individual missional practitioners. The *Missio Dei* —The Mission of God— is the nucleus of a missional theology and consequently, it is the primary *cause* of missional congregations.

THE MISSIO DEI

"Our mission flows from and participates in the mission of God"
— Christopher Wright.[461]

The *Missio Dei* originates with God— The *Missio Dei* is a divine reality from which flows the space-time missions by which God engages and transforms the world through his covenant people. *The biblical view of the divine origins of the Missio Dei calls 21st Century disciples to observe that God created the church for mission, instead of mission for the church* (*et. al.* John 20:21b).

And consequently, God's Mission— *Missio Dei*— providentially preceded and sovereignly presided over the "great persecution" in ordinary space-time and history in Acts 8:1-3. That is, the "great persecution" of God's church was in the flow of the mission of God— *The "great*

[461] Christopher J.H. Wright. *The Mission of God.* 23.

persecution" was used by God towards his missional ends, the reign of Christ in the lives of a specific people group, the Samaritans (Acts 8:4-5).

God's grand narrative (Biblical revelation) places redeemed humanity— from the beginning of creation and time until the return of Christ and a new heaven and a new earth— in the flow of the eternal reality of his mission. And thus, God's covenant people glorify God through their obedience to the *Missio Dei*— "Fundamentally, our mission (if it is biblically informed and validated) means our committed participation as God's people, at God's invitation and command, in God's own mission within the history of God's world for the redemption of God's creation."[462]

Towards the formulation of a missional theology, the *Missio Dei* is the nucleus around which space-time mission orbits— *Biblically based practices of missional congregations and individual missional entrepreneurs flow from God's mission.* The following practices of missional congregations are outstanding in a missional reading of the Bible, to include, Acts 8:1-25.

THE MISSIO DEI AND ITS MISSIONAL ORBIT

Mission… "arises from the heart of God himself and is communicated from his heart to ours. Mission is the global outreach of the global people of a global God"
— John Stott.[463]

---

[462] Ibid., 22-23.

[463] John Stott. *The Contemporary Christian: Applying God's Word To Today's World.* Downers Grove, Ill.: InterVarsity Press, 1992. 335.

MISSION

"And what does the Lord require of you?
To act justly and love mercy and to walk humbly with your God"
— Micah 6:8.

Mission, in the context of a missional theology, "means the committed *participation* of God's people in the purposes of God for the redemption of the whole creation."[464] Mission is divinely distinguished as follows:

- Mission does not begin with God's elect, e.g., the patriarchs, the prophets, the apostles, the primitive, or the modern church— *Mission is not in the flow of church tradition, but rather, its origins are divine, mission flows from the holy Trinity, the Father, the Son, and the Holy Spirit into world history and particular events* (e.g., Lk. 24:49/Acts 1:4-5; Acts 1:8/2:1-4).
- The church (and individual believers) is therefore called to obediently join God on His mission— The *Missio Dei* is at the heart of the Great Commission: *"All authority in heaven and on earth has been given to me. 19 Therefore go and make disciples…."* (Mt. 28:18-20/Acts 8:1).
- Mission requires the mindset of believers to pivot from a centripe -tal— "church-centric" perspective, to a centrifugal view, that is, mission is centered in the identity, nature, and purposes of God— Mission is Christo-centric and therefore, it is culminated in the transforming power of the Gospel (e.g., Acts 8:4; 5-8).
- Missional entrepreneurs are always on mission (Mt. 28:20b).

---

464 Ibid. 67.

- Mission is for the purpose of making the present kingdom of God tangible (reality) for defined people-groups in spiritual exile (e.g., Acts 8:5).
- Mission (plus liminal) is the catalytic "factor" in disciplemaking and cultural transformation (e.g., Acts 8:12, *et. al.* Lk. 10:1-24).
- The ultimate vision of mission is God's redemption of his creation— God is "making everything new!" (Rev. 21:5; 2 Cor. 5:17; Acts 8:25). And God invites us to join him in bringing into reality a new heaven and a new earth (Mt. 28:19/Rev. 21:1-7)!

How do we accept God's invitation and participate in the mission of God?

In his exposition of Psalm 147, Martin Luther spoke of the coupling of "the Priesthood of all Believers," and the "masks of God" to describe how God works through believers in their vocation and their everyday life (*et. al.,* Chapter 5, "Incarnational Mission").

INCARNATIONAL MISSION

When "followers of Jesus live out the gospel in
the world, as we are called to do, we become an incarnation
of the truth of the gospel and an expression of the character and shape of its
truth. It is living-in-truth that proves culturally powerful"
— Os Guinness.

The Spirit *sends* the church to a particular people group, district or location in a city or a geographical [ethnic] area in a state, province or nation to perform in a priestly role (1 Pet. 2:9)— *The missional congregation (or individual missional entrepreneur) occupies the space between humanity's alienation and the reality of the present kingdom of God— Ministers of reconciliation (priests) are making the reality of the kingdom of God tangible [real] for unbelievers by creating spaces or environments for the power of the Gospel to bring new creation* (2 Cor. 5:17-20).

Michael Frost and Alan Hirsch stress: "For us the Incarnation is an absolutely fundamental doctrine, not just as an irreducible part of the Christian confession, but also as a theological prism through which we view our entire missional task in the world."[465] Luther asserted, "God is the giver of all good gifts; but you must fall to, and take the bull by the horns, which means you must work to give God an occasion and a mask."[466] The "offering of spiritual sacrifices" focuses on Spirit-empowered priests (1 Peter 2:5) doing the works God has prepared in advance for us to do (Eph. 2:10) as "masks of God."

Luther's theological nuance, "masks of God," coupled with the Priesthood of all Believers, is what we refer to as incarnational mission, that is, missional practitioners perform as priests by creating spaces for God to work through them as his "mask," primarily their vocation; but one's vocation is not limited to where they work, it includes where "they do life" (any role God calls a believer to fill).[467]

Wherever a missionally driven disciple does life, incarnational mission is at the center of their activities. Incarnational mission calls the missionally driven disciple to incarnate the Word and Spirit of the Lord. Micah 6:8 introduces a concise (three-fold) biblical theology of incarnational mission:

---

[465] Michael Frost & Alan Hirsch. *The Shaping of Things To Come.* Peabody, MA.: Hendrickson Publishers, 2003. 35.

[466] Luther on God's 'Masks,' Martin Luther's exposition of Psalm 147._Posted August 29, 2012, The Rev 2011 in Church History, Providence, Reformed Piety & Christian Nurture. https://christcovenantopc.wordpress.com/2012/08/29/luther-on-gods-masks/. Downloaded: 12/12/2019.

[467] See the outstanding book: Samuel Wells. *Incarnational Mission, Being With the World.* Grand Rapids, MI.: William B. Eerdmans Publishing Company, 2018.

MICAH 6:8c— "ACT JUSTLY"

"To act justly … "

Missional entrepreneurs engaging in incarnational mission are "*to act justly*;" or "do justice;" "act" or "do" are verbs. We are required to obediently engage justice. The Hebrew term translated "act justly" (*mispat*) finds "its source in God himself and therefore carrying with it his demand."[468]

In the Old Testament, this term (*mispat*) is connected to widows, orphans, the poor, the needy, the oppressed, the stranger, the prisoner, and the fatherless (Isa. 1:17; Isa. 61:1-2, cf. Lk. 4:18-19; Isa. 58:6-7).[469] To "act justly" connects the believer to people living on the extreme margins of culture (that is, people in the greatest need)— *Our relationship with God directly relates to how we care for these people.*

"In the study of the history of missions," Alan Hirsch observes, "one can even be formulaic about asserting that *all great missionary movements begin at the fringes of the church,* among the poor and the marginalized, and seldom, if ever, at the center."[470] Mission focused on the extreme margins of culture is consistently liminal and therefore, catalytic in the life of "masked priests," i.e., missional practitioners on incarnational mission. And through obedience to the modeling of her Lord "*… when the church engages at the fringes, it almost always brings life to the center.*"[471]

The disciples' obedience (cf. Acts 8:1-25) leads them into a liminal situation in which they are confronted by spiritual strongholds— malignant spirits, and racial prejudice—their own, and the Samaritans'— Jesus'

---

468 Harris, Archer, Jr., and Waltke, *Theological Wordbook of the Old Testament,* Vol. II (Chicago, IL.: Moody Press, 1980), 948-49.

469 Brown, Driver, and Briggs, *Hebrew and English Lexicon*, (490), 48; (3490), 450, (1800), 195, (34), 2, (7533), 954, (1616), 158, (615/16), 64, (3490), 450.

470 Alan Hirsch, *The Forgotten Ways,* 30.

471 Ibid. 30.

disciples have no idea how the Lord's divinely ordered mission is going to turn out, but they are, never-the-less, obedient (Acts 8:6-11).

MICAH 6:8c— "LOVE MERCY"

"... and to love mercy..."

"Christ in us" compels us to "love mercy." The Hebrew term (*hesed*) is related to our understanding of "compassion." The Latin understanding is more precise however: we are to *"co-suffer, to come alongside of"* the hurting, the weak, the vulnerable and the poor.

God's love means many things in Scripture. But God's "delivering love" is consistent throughout the Bible— *God's love is consistently demonstrated in Scripture as a delivering action.* The Parable of the Good Samaritan is a vivid example of God's delivering love. The parable is Jesus' answer to the lawyer's question, "Who is my neighbor?" The point of the parable is to teach us *how* and *whom* we should love.[472]

A Samaritan man sees a Jewish man, who after having been attacked by robbers, was stripped of his clothing, beaten and left half dead on the side of the road (Lk. 10:30). The Samaritan is described as having pity on this man. The Greek term translated "pity" or "compassion" refers to a "gut-feeling."[473] The Samaritan's response is intense, it is a strong emotional response followed by a delivering act of love— *Drawn by compassion, the Samaritan enters the situation of the helpless, wounded Jewish man.* By contrast, the priest and the Levite are described in strong terms as "moving

---

472 John Dominic Crossan. *In Parables.* New York: Harper & Row, 1973, 57. Quoted in: Glen H. Stassen & David P. Gushee. *Kingdom Ethics,* 334.

473 Glenn Stassen & David Gushee, *Kingdom Ethics,* 335.

away." Jesus tells this story in a way that emphasizes that compassion moves toward need and identifies with the need, to include our enemies.[474]

To love mercy, you must be where the pain is, because God is hidden in the pain. By throwing yourself into a place of pain, you discover the joy of Jesus. All ministry in the history of the church is built on a vision of *holistic redemption,* that is, ministry is committed to the common good of the culture by its unashamed, single-minded commitment to the Cross, and the dynamic power of the Holy Spirit's presence in the lives of believers (Acts 8:12).

Mission (ministry) is for helping people discover that in the middle of pain there is hope and blessing. In our world, there is an enormous distinction between good and bad, sorrow and joy, but in God's eyes, they are never separated: where there is pain, there is healing; where there is mourning, there is dancing; and where there is poverty, there is the riches of the kingdom (Acts 8:14-17).

MICAH 6:8d— WALK HUMBLY

"... and to walk humbly with your God..."

And God requires us to: *"walk humbly."* The Hebrew term translated "walk humbly" literally means, "creating space."[475] We are to "create space" or environments for the kingdom of God to be made tangible in the lives of those living in exile, people without Christ, without life and without hope (Acts 8:25).

We are to see the staggering needs in our world and acknowledge that God is before all other things in our lives: ourselves, our family, our

---

474 Ibid.

475 Brown, Driver, and Briggs, *Hebrew, and English Lexicon*, 857a, 6800 (Hiph. *Inf.abs.*)

friends, our life's goals and aspirations, our personal security and comfort, *everything.* We are called to take the place of others and see the physical and spiritual needs in our community and the world and ask ourselves: *"What can I do for the person I see across the street, across my office space, on my work site, on the other side of my city, across the world?"*[476]

The missional congregation is to join God by identifying a specific group in exile—e.g., those enslaved in sex-trafficking, addicts, the homeless, those in multi-housing projects, prisoners, at-risk youth, etc., and create environments, e.g., low-income housing, trailer parks, coffee houses, training centers, etc.[477] Incarnational mission requires our obedience by way of making ourselves available for God, as mediators (priests) for His works to flow through us to those alienated from God (cf. Genesis 12:3b).

As they stand in the space between God and the Samaritans, the disciples took their place alongside of the Samaritans, and in obedience to Christ, they loved their enemies and proclaimed the Gospel to them with an acute awareness of the cultural expectations of the Samaritans—*They exchanged their racial prejudice for identification with the Samaritans in their exile* (Acts 8:1-25).

Following a missional reading of scripture, and a thorough parsing of principles and practices that flow from the *Missio Dei*, we are ready to formulate a missional theology.

---

[476] My thoughts are inspired by Paul Hurkman, *Venture Expeditions,* contained in a sermon delivered at Cedar Valley Church, Bloomington, MN., January 13, 2013.

[477] Consistent with the nature of the Incarnation is the Spirit's drawing of Jesus to those in the greatest need— the indigent, the disenfranchised and outcasts. Jesus' missional sights are consistently set on a *specific* group or individual (cf. Lk. 4:18-19; Mt. 11:4-6). And through God's delivering love, Jesus takes the place of those in spiritual, social, economic exile — *Consistently, Jesus' missional patterns primarily means that he works from the margins to the center, rather than the reverse.*

A MISSIONAL THEOLOGY

Every believer is to involve themselves "... in the eternal purposes of God in the world to redeem it to Himself, to sum up all things to Himself in Christ Jesus"[478]

The *Missio Dei* —The Mission of God— is the nucleus of a missional theology. And therefore, the *Missio Dei* is the primary *cause* of missional congregations.

Missional texts saturate both the Old Testament and the New Testament— The "... *whole Bible is itself a 'missional' phenomenon.*"[479] A missional reading of the biblical text (e.g., Acts 8:1-25) enables the believer to see that the Scripture itself is the result of and witness to the *Missio Dei*— A missional theology is formulated around the *Missio Dei* and the layers of missional praxis that flow from God's invitation to join Him on mission.

The eternal Trinity is the Author of mission: The Father *sent* the Son; the Father and the Son *sent* the Spirit, and the Spirit sends missional congregations— *God is a sending (Latin, missio) God. Believers are sent by God to join Him on His mission (the Missio Dei) — Mission was not made for the church; the church was made for mission.*

And therefore, any space-time missional enterprise flows from the prior reality of God's eternal mission (*Missio Dei*). Consequently, the Lord does not send his disciples ahead of himself, he is always waiting for us to come, and when we show up, he empowers us to join him, and witness the flow of his mission through us — *In their priestly role, missional practitioners stand in the space between people in exile and God; and as masks of God,*

---

[478] Allan Hirsch. "What is Missional Discipleship?" https://www.youtube.com/watch?v=WhEwxSQ5tqA. Downloaded: 02/28/2019.

[479] Christopher Wright. *The Mission of God.* 22.

practitioners engage in incarnational mission: God works through missional practitioners to make known the present reality of the kingdom of God.

The *Missio Dei* engages all of life, to include all legitimate vocations—all work, e.g., waiter, physician, construction, truck driver, logger, lawyer, grocery clerk, custodian, teacher, airman, sailor, soldier, marine, police officer, etc. These vocations are sacred callings, no less than a pastor, bishop, or missionary. *And therefore, all missional practitioners are always on mission with God, restoring the environment, renewing cultures, and rescuing people by offering healing and hope.*

Ultimately, a missional theology informs the redemptive purposes of God, climatically concluding in the ultimate achievement of "The Great Commission" — Revelation 7:9-10:

> *9 After this I looked, and there before me was a great multitude*
> *that no one could count, from every nation, tribe, people and*
> *language, standing before the throne and before the Lamb.*
>
> *They were wearing white robes and were holding palm branches*
> *in their hands. 10 And they cried out in a loud voice:*
>
> *"Salvation belongs to our God,*
> *who sits on the throne,*
> *and to the Lamb."*

MISSIONAL THEOLOGY: THE MISSIO DEI AND ITS MISSIONAL ORBIT

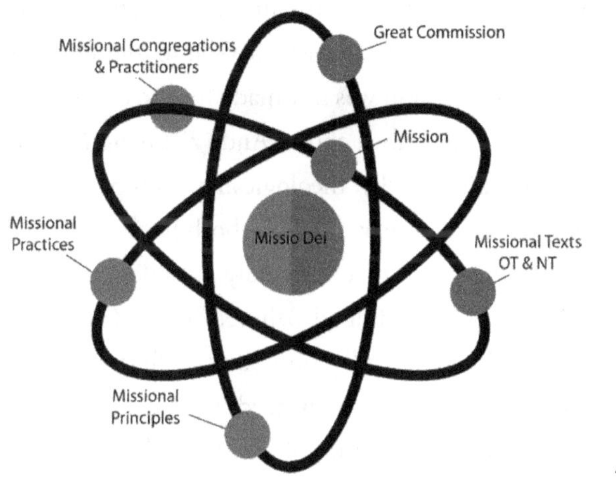

480

LIVING MISSIONALLY BEYOND SUNDAY

Chapter 11 is extracted from the author's book: *Living Missionally Beyond Sunday— "and all peoples on earth will be blessed through you"* (Gen. 12:3b). This book, *The Woke Opiate,* is designed to be coupled with *Living Missionally Beyond Sunday* because *Living Missionally Beyond Sunday* fully explains/illustrates what the church in each local community can do to turn back Woke Identity Marxism's total dismantling and recreation of Western Culture into a Marxist Socialist State— *The transforming power of the Gospel in each local church from 20 members to 20,000 members is*

[480] Neurons and Electrons Images: https://www.shutterstock.com/search/neutrons+and+electrons.

the bedrock on which Western Culture was founded. (Please see Chapter 10: "The Meaning of Truth," Subtitle: "America's Superstructure").

Three outstanding Biblical patterns (*et. al.,* Acts 8:1-25) through which the missional church transforms its cultural context: (1) God is a sending (Latin, missio) God. Believers are sent by God to join Him on His mission (the Missio Dei) — Mission was not made for the church; the church was made for mission, as described above. And (2) Living Missionally Beyond Sunday develops historically, theologically, and practically how disciple-making in the 21st Century should be both participated in by the whole of the body of Christ, and practiced daily by individual missional practitioners (i.e. "The Priesthood of all Believers"), and (3) from its beginning to its end, Living Missionally Beyond Sunday illustrates why our culture, at this time in its history, desperately needs the Church to be *missional*, that is, the Church needs to go to the culture, instead of expecting the culture to come to the church.

Chapters 8-16 in the author's book: *Living Missionally Beyond Sunday, "and all peoples on earth will be blessed through you"* (Gen. 12:3b), contains interviews the author conducted with pastors of missional congregations, directors of Christian organizations and managers of "third places." The reader of *Living Missionally Beyond Sunday* is encouraged to critically observe how these select missional congregations, organizations, and third places "live missionally beyond Sunday!" More specifically, please see how they transform the cultural rhythms of their host communities by uniquely modeling a missional theology in imaginative, creative, and nuanced ways through incarnational mission—A coherent missional theology is not prescriptive but rather, as viewed through the lens of Biblical Revelation, it is contextual, and therefore, it is *nuanced* in ways that serve the unique purposes of the *Missio Dei* in a particular location.

CHAPTER 12

RACIAL RECONCILIATION— AN INTRODUCTION

The delegitimizing of systemic racism abolishes the claim that racism is America's "original sin." But "covert racism" continues to be an evil presence in America and Western Civilization, making any hope of racial reconciliation an extremely difficult challenge.

The Oxford Dictionary defines racism as, "… prejudice, discrimination, or antagonism directed against someone of a different race based on the belief that one's own race is superior."[481] The notion of racial superiority is rooted in man's fallenness (Gen. 3:1-21) — *"We put ourselves where only God deserves to be, and we unjustly judge "others," ("image bearers of God") as though we are God* (cf. Rom. 3:9-18; 23). This leads to evil machinations, such as the categorizing of human beings into "racial groups."

[481] *The Oxford Dictionary* The Coalition for Racial Equalities and Rights. "Racism in Scotland."

The categorizing of racial groups originates from certain anthropological theories. These theories, developed in the late 19th and early 20th century in Western Europe, proposed that racial groups should be distinguished by physical and behavioral characteristics linked "to ethnicity, nationality, and related concepts like shared language."[482] Further, colonialism and imperialism shaped these theories in a manner that elevated white groups over non-white groups. This allowed for the justification of policies, norms, and exclusion of minorities in Western nations.

Racism possesses deeply infected beliefs, and behaviors in Western nations— colonialism and imperialism continue to influence all areas of life to varying degrees, "from social attitudes to the way organizations are run, making inequalities for Black and minority ethnic people continue over generations."[483] Even after the Civil War (1865), and the Reconstruction Amendments to the Constitution (The 13th, 14th, and 15th Amendments), Jim Crow Laws, and Black Codes[484] perpetuated in the form of overt racism in America from 1865–1968— America was definably racist for 103 years. *But following 103 years of overt racism, Civil Rights legislation has resulted in racism becoming covert.* (It should be clear to every conscientious American and/or citizen of Western Civilization that the abolition of racism *cannot* merely be legislated, it must be a daily priority of the Church, like-minded institutions, and conscientious individuals). *And such a daily priority must be "legitimate" — It must be led by a racial makeup of (objectively) moral/ethical individuals from a variety of walks of life.*[485]

482 The Coalition for Racial Equalities and Right. https://www.crer.org.uk/what-is-racism#:~:text=The%20term%20'racism'%20is%20often,explanation%20of%20a%20complex%20issue.

483 Ibid.

484 *re:* Ch. 5, Critical Race Theory.

485 The author is aware of his ambiguity here, but at this stage of "Introduction," my ambiguity is intentional.

OVERT/COVERT RACISM

George Yancey, professor of sociology, Baylor University, without using terms such as "overt" and "covert," [Yancey] informs my distinction between pre-Civil Rights legislation when racism was *overt*, and post-Civil Rights legislation where racism is now *covert*. The following discussion will concentrate on Professor Yancey's comments on the "historical effects" of overt racism and will serve as a segue to "Distinguishing Covert Racism from 'Systemic Racism.'" [486]

Discussing only a couple of historical effects of overt racism in the post-Civil Rights era will serve to illustrate what is meant by "covert racism." Before Civil Rights legislation, Jim Crow laws forced minorities, particularly African Americans, to live in segregated neighborhoods; Blacks were not allowed to live anywhere they desired. Residential segregation involved real estate agents "steering" minorities, particularly Blacks, away from White neighborhoods, and towards Black neighborhoods. This form of racism results in lower property value on the homes of racial minorities, higher interest rates, and "red lining" (i.e., discrimination regarding home loans).

In the post-Civil Rights era, laws have changed so that today, steering is illegal. Residential segregation is now the choice of the individual seeking to buy a home. But whereas people are free to live anywhere they desire, enough "cultural momentum" (Yancey) continues to exist resulting in many people choosing to segregate. "Choice" is then two-sided, European Americans are more likely to choose to live around white people, whereas people of color are inclined to choose to live around other people

[486] Dr. George Yancey. Christian Racial Reconciliation (Day 1) | Laing Lectures 2024. Regent College (Vancouver BC). https://www.youtube.com/watch?v=3jB3aB9FiLo. Downloaded: 03/12/2024.

of color— The cultural momentum behind these "preferences" is strong, but it cannot be documented.[487]

An example of covert racism in the West, and specifically, America, involves school quality—Schools in the predominately White, or Black, or Hispanic parts of many cities are qualitatively different. For example, Dr. Yancey, who attended high school in the Hispanic part of the city he grew up in, noted that students were prepared to build homes. But White schools prepared students for college. Whereas there is nothing wrong with "blue collar" work (in my book, *Living Missionally Beyond Sunday,* I wrote that all legal, legitimate work, is sacred, because work is a sacred ordinance in Scripture, meaning, work was stitched into the lining of creation by the Creator, cf. Gen. 2:15; Eph. 2:10); Professor Yancey, however, is both correct and timely in his emphasis on the fact that people who go to college, run the country— "If we did not have segregation, schools would train people for all fields of employment and college."[488] Segregation "concentrates many dysfunctional elements into minority communities," resulting in people becoming "trapped" in environments from which they cannot "get ahead"[489] — These communities perpetuate poverty which isolates minorities, removing them from the kind of interpersonal relations needed for advancement.

The space required to comprehensively develop multiple forms of covert racism in the West, and particularly America, e.g., the criminal justice system, explicitly, the death penalty, health care, the economy, the military, and immigration (to name just a few), would require another book, but the distinguishing of overt racism from covert racism is the primary purpose

487 Dr. George Yancey. "Christian Racial Reconciliation" (Day 3) | Laing Lectures 2024. Regent College (Vancouver BC). https://www.youtube.com/watch?v=B2qyoLY4I_0. Downloaded: 03/20/2024.

488 Ibid.

489 Ibid.

of this segment of Chapter 12.[490] We will now, therefore, move forward to briefly distinguishing covert racism from systemic racism.[491]

SEPARATING 'COVERT' RACISM FROM 'SYSTEMIC' RACISM

"We live in a racialized society"[492]
— George Yancey, Baylor University.

Woke Identity Marxism constructs Systemic racism on a foundation of superficial characteristics, e.g., skin color, ethnicity, shared language, and party affiliation (et. al., Critical Diversity) — In the spirit of anthropological theories from the 19th into the early 20th century, the Woke Ruling Elites redefined "racism" to fit their "colonialist inspired" construct of "systemic racism."

Systemic racism originated in the moral subjectivism of Woke Marxist Ideology's fallen imagination[493]— *"Systemic racism is a deceptive strat-*

490 For an exhaustive development/evaluation of multiple forms of covert racism, please see the extraordinary work of: Glen H. Stassen & David P. Gushee. *Following Jesus in Contemporary Context, Kingdom Ethics.* Downers Grove, IL.: Inter-Varsity, 2003.

491 "Systemic racism" is defined by the Ruling Elites to obliterate any hope of reconciliation between Woke Marxist, Repressive Tolerance, characterizations of the "Privileged" and "Underprivileged." But the distinction between "overt" and "covert" racism is not reified, it is reality, and racial reconciliation is possible.

492 "Racialized" means that "race" is inserted into a significant portion of our society and how it works.

493 The Heritage Foundation. "How to Identify Critical Race Theory." https://www.heritage.org/civil-society/heritage-explains/how-identify-critical-race-theory. Downloaded: 12/26/2023.

egy constructed by Progressive Left Elites, and Social Justice theorists, for the exploitation of the "Underprivileged/Oppressed." [494]

Whereas systemic racism was a concentration in Chapter 9, it is important to re-emphasize here that systemic racism, as an (reified) abstract construct of the Party eliminates, *a priori*, any opportunity for racial reconciliation.[495] But the confession of covert racism can lead to forgiveness and reconciliation, and the rebuilding of racial relationships. Of course, racism, like any other sin, will not be completely eradicated until Christ returns and a New Heaven and Earth appear as *visible* reality.

Nevertheless, traditional values (Judeo-Christian values) are centered in redemption, and reconciliation for all image bearers of our

---

[494] Discussed above in Chapter 9, under the final two sub-headings: "BUT WHAT ABOUT THE EMANCIPATION OF THE UNDERPRIVILEGED?" And "THE PROGRESSIVE LEFT'S BETRAYAL OF THE UNDERPRIVILEGED."

[495] To ensure clarity, my argument involving CRT's historical revisionism is, precisely: The roots of America's founding as a free Democratic Republic are traced to Plymouth, Massachusetts, and the signing of the Mayflower Compact. Following the Mayflower Compact, America's freedom is founded, and lived, on the bedrock foundations of the Declaration of Independence, The U.S. Constitution, and the Bill of Rights. American social and cultural institutions— Our shared beliefs, values, and patterns of social order are formed by freedom themes woven throughout our founding documents and through which serve religious, family, governmental, legal, economic, educational, healthcare, the arts— music, film industry, art galleries, museums— archives, and monuments, most of which are ostensibly rooted in traditional Judeo-Christian values.

Creator[496]— *Redemption and reconciliation have always been, from our nation's beginning, at the core of Western Culture's thriving.*[497]

A CRUCIAL OBSERVATION— "BLIND SPOTS"

"It has always been difficult for white people to empathize fully with the experience of black people. But it has never been impossible"
— James Cone, *The Cross and the Lynching Tree.*

Regarding the "cultural momentum" Yancey speaks of above, it is more evident to Black people than it is to White people. The author learned this as a sacred lesson while he was the pastor of a church in Oregon.

As the pastor of this church, I walked with many people of varied ethnicities in my congregation through difficult times; we shared genuine Christian love together. If anyone had questioned my sensitivity towards another human being's personal dignity, I would have been, to say the least, shocked.

A young Black professional man was an invaluable Board Member in our church. My friend was very accomplished; but far beyond his academic and professional achievements, his spirituality was characterized by

---

[496] This is the vision of Dr. Martin Luther King Jr.'s "The Beloved Community." Please see the highly recommended book: George Yancey. *Beyond Racial Division, A Unifying Alternative to Colorblindness and Antiracism.* Downers Grove, IL.: Inter-Varsity Press, 2022. And please view Professor Yancey's lectures: "Christian Racial Reconciliation," Laing Lectures 2024, Regent College: Christian Racial Reconciliation (Day 1) | Dr. George Yancey, https://www.youtube.com/watch?v=3jB3aB9FiLo. Downloaded: 04/05/2024.

Racial Reconciliation (Day 2) | Dr. George Yancey, https://www.youtube.com/watch?v=QKCPPLJGjSM; And Christian Racial Reconciliation (D3) | Dr. George Yancey, https://www.youtube.com/watch?v=B2qyoLY4I_0 Downloaded: 04/05/2024.

[497] See: APPENDENIX ONE: "CIVIL RELIGION AND THE SOUL OF OUR NATION: RECONCILIATION & REDEMPTION."

a conscientious, biblically refined wisdom. On one occasion, over coffee, I asked my friend about his perspective on a statement I had recently heard: "*Everything in America is a racially Black and White matter.*"

From a White perspective, I confessed to my friend that my initial impression was that the person making the statement had overstated his claim. My friend casually reached for a napkin from its place holder and drew a circle on it; he then divided the circle in a way that separated about 20% of the circle from the remaining 80%. He then proceeded to graciously explain to me that he had observed that sometimes I "overextend" myself to Black people in a way that I don't to White people. But at other times, I "overextend" myself to White people in a way that I don't to Black people. My friend then provided for me a couple of examples of my "overextensions" to both Blacks and Whites.

I was uncomfortable with this, but I needed to know why my friend interpreted my actions, as the pastor of the church, in this way. He placed the napkin between us, and he proceeded to shade the 20%, and leave the 80% clear. He then explained that the shaded portion is a "blind spot." While driving we need to clear our "blind spot" before changing lanes because otherwise, we may side-swipe another driver who happens to be in our blind spot. My friend concluded, saying, regardless of how much love exists in inter-racial relationships, Whites, because they are the majority and therefore, our society is constructed more to accommodate the "way they see life," have this blind spot, that is, this residual effect of our racist history— *Our "blind spots" are where subtle, covert forms of racism go unnoticed.*[498]

As leaders, especially Church Leaders, engage in creative, imaginative, and tested ways of creating environments conducive to racial reconciliation, leaders need to keep this lesson regarding "Blind Spots" at the forefront of their minds. (*Please observe that "Blind Spots" are the result of insensitivity— Aside from any racial offense, the majority population of any nation will see the culture they built differently from the minority population among them. Therefore, whatever the cause of insensitivity, it is a common human infirmity. Standpoint Theory is, as discussed above, a part of the Marxist delusion and therefore, it does not distinguish any legitimate racial profile, rather, its inane claims are invalidated by both Lyotard's "problematic of legitimation" and Wittgenstein's insistence that ethics are "transcendental" —See Chapter 9).*

CREATING ENVIRONMENTS FOR RACIAL RECONCILIATION

Barbra Williams Skinner wisely observes: "Throughout Scripture — and throughout American history — we see God using the rejected and the despised to bring about social transformation and to address issues of injustice. I believe he can use the Black Church today to help heal and

[498] An important qualification re, "blind spots," has to do with how our society is constructed to accommodate the majority (Whites) and the "way they see life." "Blind spots" can be cleared to avoid covert racial actions or impressions. "Blind spots" have absolutely nothing to do with "Standpoint Theory," a Marxist Repressive Tolerant construct that is not based on human dignity, but superficial characteristics of one race as opposed to the other race— In other words, "Blind Spots" have nothing to do with colonialism or imperialism. ("Blind spots" have to do with the "noetic effects of sin;" thus, my stress on our racist history).

transform our dividedness."[499] Church Leaders, and/or other like-minded people, working together towards racial reconciliation, would be wise to acknowledge the Black Church's leadership.

Dr. Martin Luther King Jr.'s vision of, "The Beloved Community," continues to survive (and thrive) through the work of two eminent Black Christian Leaders: Dr. George Yancey, and Dr. John M. Perkins:

GEORGE YANCEY
A MUTUAL ACCOUNTABILITY MODEL

"Because sin divided our nation, it will take a special work of God's grace to fully unite us"
— George Yancey.

Professor George Yancey argues that "colorblindness" and "antiracism" are failing to resolve racial problems. Yancey charges that colorblindness ignores racialized cultural issues,[500] and antiracism creates more hostility and polarization than good (of course, redemption and reconciliation are not even on antiracism's radar[501]).

Professor Yancey offers an alternative approach to racial relations where all parties contribute and are mutually accountable to one another. He provides empirical rationale for how collaborative conversations in a mutual

[499] Barbra Williams Skinner, President of Skinner Leadership Institute. The Black Church and the Promise of Racial Reconciliation. In: *Response*. Seattle Pacific University. Winter 2009 | Volume 32, Number 1 | Features. https://spu.edu/depts/uc/response/winter2k9/features/black-church.asp. Download: 05/13/2024.

[500] Recall, "Racialized" means that "race" is inserted into a significant portion of our society and how it works.

[501] Redemption and Reconciliation are not on antiracism's radar because Professor Ibram Kendi, among others (e.g., The revisionist history of Nicole Hannah-Jones, The 1619 Project: A New Origin Story), presupposes systemic racism.

accountability model can reduce racial division; history and societal complexity mean that different participants may have different kinds of responsibility, but all are involved in seeking the common good for society to thrive.

Avoiding unilateral decisions that close off dialogue, Yancey casts a vision for moving beyond racial alienation toward a lifestyle and movement of collaborative conversation and mutuality. For those who desire to get off the path of "colorblindness" and/or "antiracism," Yancey's approach presupposes the inherit dignity of all human beings as founded on their special creation in the image of God. Consequently, rather than being told how to think—e.g., "You do what we ask, and we will create this perfect society,"[502] — people engage in "collaborative conversations."[503]

Reflecting on his book, *Beyond Racial Division: A Unifying Alternative to Colorblindness and Antiracism,* Yancey stresses that he does not tell each church, each community, each denomination, etc., how to solve racial problems, but rather he offers resources, and questions based on his extensive research, and encouragement for each church, community, denomination, etc. to work together to discover resolve to racial problems.[504] Only by means of holding one another accountable are we able to discover, together, resolve for our racial alienation— A Christian based approach presupposes that we all struggle with a sin nature (Romans 7:7-25) and therefore, we make ourselves accountable to one another (through collaborative conversations) for the sake of our high purpose of racial reconciliation.

---

502 Astoundingly, colorblindness and antiracism presuppose that the Underprivileged/Oppressed do not struggle with a sin nature; instead, the source of a sin originates with the white privileged (recall this notion is centered in Marcuse's Repressive Tolerance).

503 Professor Yancey is a prolific author. The outline below centers on his work: *Beyond Racial Division: A Unifying Alternative to Colorblindness and Antiracism.* Downers Grove, IL.: Inter-Varsity Press, 2022.

504 Dr. George Yancey| Christian Racial Reconciliation (D3). https://www.youtube.com/watch?v=B2qyoLY4I_0. Downloaded: 04/05/2024.

Towards racial reconciliation, George Yancey places significant emphasis on the skill, and needed wisdom, of negotiation. Yancey stresses our need to strive for "win-win" solutions— People who feel as though they have lost, have nothing to work for. Professor Yancey queries: "What if you get 80% of what you want or 100%? In negotiations, you are going to give up at least 20%. What is better, strive for 100% and spend your time fighting? Culturally, that's what we are doing now. In the Summer of 2020, the protesters got 100%— Are they satisfied with that? Are we good now?[505]

Professor Yancey's book, *Beyond Racial Division: A Unifying Alternative to Colorblindness and Antiracism,* provides definitive instructions on how to create "A Mutual Accountability Model" for churches, denominations, and institutions/organizations to redemptively engage in the urgent need of racial reconciliation. The Mutual Accountability Model features: "Foundations of the Mutual Accountability Model," "Empirical Work on Healthy Relations," "How to Win Arguments in Social Media," "How to Convince People," "Steps in Using a Mutual Obligation Approach," "Mutual Accountability Lifestyle," etc.[506]

By way of introducing Dr. George Yancey and his biblically saturated work, particularly, his Mutual Accountability Model, my hope is that churches, communities, and denominations will see the need to fully incorporate Dr. George Yancey's impressive body of work into their vision for Racial Reconciliation. If this is your hope as well, please:

(1) Add George Yancey's Web Site to your Bookmarks: https://www.georgeyancey.com/

---

[505] The body of "The Fifth Foundation" is a quote from Dr. Yancey's Christian Racial Reconciliation (D3).

[506] Dr. Yancey's: *Beyond Racial Division: A Unifying Alternative to Colorblindness and Antiracism.* Downers Grove, IL.: Inter-Varsity Press, 2022.

(2) Among Dr. Yancey's outstanding books, ensure that your group has sufficient copies of: George Yancey. *Beyond Racial Division, A Unifying Alternative to Colorblindness and Antiracism.* Downers Grove, IL.: Inter-Varsity Press, 2022.

(3) View with your group, George Yancey's Laing Lectures, 2024, Regent College: Christian Racial Reconciliation (Day 1) | Dr. George Yancey, https://www.youtube.com/watch?v=3jB3aB-9FiLo. Downloaded: 04/05/2024.

In Day 1, Yancey discusses the problem. Christian Racial Reconciliation (Day 2) | Dr. George Yancey, https://www.youtube.com/watch?v=QKCPPLJGjSM.

In Day 2, Yancey discusses what won't work. Christian Racial Reconciliation (Day 3) | Dr. George Yancey, https://www.youtube.com/watch?v=B2qyoLY4I_0. Downloaded: 04/05/2024.

In Day 3, Yancey discusses what will work. Because of Christian men, like George Yancey, and John M. Perkins, who disregard *antiracism* and its message of systemic racism, and instead bow to God's will, and are used by Him towards the lighting of the paths of those committed to racial reconciliation, *"There is hope that our past does not predict our future"* — A.D. Thomason.[507]

[507] A.D. "Lumkile" Thomason. *Permission to Be Black: My Journey with Jay-Z and Jesus.* Inter-Varsity Press, 2021.

DR. JOHN M. PERKINS COMMUNITY TRANSFORMATION

Historically, the church has been the only entity on earth that exists for the benefit of all of its nonmembers.[508]

John Perkins asserts, "When we put the needs of the church ahead of the needs of those we are trying to reach with the gospel, we end up accommodating our heresy and hypocrisy. We need to empower the poor to reach the middle and upper classes of society."[509] Throughout the history of the church, those who have been beneficiaries of the grace of God have been called to reveal Christ's poverty to their neighbors; the outcasts, the vulnerable and the poor.

Perkins' Christian Community Development Association observes that isolation is the single greatest source for the perpetuation of poverty in major urban areas; the poor are isolated from the city's major service systems. When people with influence in society *relocate* to the inner city, they can help connect the poor with the marketplace, the church, educational institutions, and the political sphere.

The Christian Community Development Association's term for the empowering of the marginalized is *redistribution*. Mary Nelson cites John

---

[508] Archbishop William Temple is cited for this observation in *Towards an Evangelical Public Policy*, 232.

[509] John Perkins was the keynote speaker for the 'New Wine, New Wineskins' Spring Conference, April 10-14, 2007, in Portland, Oregon. The Conference was hosted by the Institute for the Theology of Culture, Portland, Oregon. The theme of the conference was: "For the Least of These."

Perkins' remarks in his *Beyond Charity* by way of the thinking behind redistribution:

> In the 1960s the motto of community development was "Give people a fish, and they'll eat for a day." In the 1970s it was "Teach people to fish, and they'll eat for a lifetime." In the 1990s the focus has turned to "Who owns the pond?" Perkins goes on to say, "The challenge for Christian community-based economic development is to enable the people of the community to start local enterprises that meet local needs and employ indigenous people."[510]

Redistribution for the common good is about empowering the marginalized to enact social and economic justice on their own behalf. Working for economic and social justice for the common good is not a solo effort. Partnerships with like-minded people and organizations are needed to end isolation for the poor and significantly contribute to the common good and transformation of culture.

CO-OPERTIVE CONFRONTATION OF SOCIAL PROBLEMS

Partnerships with like-minded people and/or organizations are critical for the funding of projects for the common good and consequent cultural transformation. Therefore, the local church must not allow fear of damage to their personal integrity to keep them from partnering with others committed to their goals, reforms, and projects.[511] John Perkins and

---

[510] Mary Nelson, "Redistribution, Empowering the Community," *Restoring At-Risk Communities*, 139-40.

[511] See Chapter 3, for a definition and historical context for co-belligerent relationships.

the Christian Community Development Association have effectively led community transformation in Mendenhall, Mississippi through carefully (wisely) establishing the right partnerships to confront particular social problems/needs.

Perkins has organized co-ops for poor African Americans. The Federation of Southern Co-ops is dedicated to the development of local resources and local income: "When we look at the poor getting poorer through the self-perpetuating cycle of ignorance, poor health and lack of opportunity, two truths are evident: (1) money must be made available to develop potential, and (2) the community itself must develop its potential to utilize and multiply economic resources."[512]

Perkins teamed with the Farmers' Home Administration to help house the poor: "The overall goal of indigenous community vitality" brings economic empowerment to the poor. He has worked with tutorial programs and educational assistance particularly in helping the poor discover their own economic independence: "Federal handouts don't help. People themselves must be their own economic salvation."[513]

The People's Development Incorporated is a co-op dedicated to helping the poor with housing needs. Through this ministry, Perkins' strategy is to "seed" every neighborhood with two or three Christian families to bring about community change. The People's Development Incorporated works for school integration. In the South, the last to integrate have been the churches.[514] The People's Development's contributions to economic and social justice include a general store, legal aid for the poor, a medical center for the poor housed in a formerly segregated medical building in down-

512 John Perkins, New Wine Spring Conference: "For the Least of These," April 10-14, 2007, Portland, Oregon.

513 Ibid.

514 Ibid.

town Mendenhall and staffed by a physician who is a committed part of Perkins' Voice of Calvary Ministries in Mendenhall; the Voice of Calvary Health Center in Jackson, Mississippi, a Christian Youth Center, and the first Bible Institute in Mendenhall and Jackson.

In 1982, Perkins and his wife, Vera Mae, returned to Southern California. His daughter, Elizabeth writes, "Of course, they chose to live on a street known for its cocaine dealers and stabbings."[515] Through partnerships in Los Angeles the Perkins established the Harambee Christian Family Center to meet the needs of children in Pasadena, California. The needs of children in Los Angeles are different from the needs of kids in rural Mississippi, gangs and drug dealers were picking up children at an early age. Many children were dropping out of school and getting into trouble with the law. Harambee started a tutoring program in the evening and many children responded.

Perkins began buying up the crack houses in the neighborhood and turning them into ministry centers. He started business training centers and eventually, he established a prep school. Perkins' strategy is to raise up in Christ some of the gifted kids who would subsequently change their neighborhoods. Perkins and his wife now live in Jackson, Mississippi where they established the Spencer Perkins Center for Reconciliation and Youth Development (named in honor of their late son).[516]

---

[515] Elizabeth Perkins, *Let Justice Roll Down*, 82.

[516] The author has extracted this segment of introducing John Perkins from his book: *Following Jesus to Burning Man, Recovering the Church's Vocation.* Lanham, MD.: Rowman & Littlefield, 2011.

JOHN PERKINS CENTER FOR: RECONCILIATION, LEADERSHIP TRAINING AND COMMUNITY DEVELOPMENT[517]

Although Dr. John Perkins dropped out of school in the third grade, he is an internationally known author, speaker, and teacher on cultural transformation, racial reconciliation, and leadership and community development; he is among preeminent evangelical voices having originated in the American Civil Rights Movement.[518] The esteem and contributions of this great man have not gone unnoticed, he is the recipient of fourteen honorary doctoral degrees to include: Wheaton College, Gordon College, Huntington College, Geneva College, Spring Arbor University, North Park College, and Belhaven College. Other academic honors include Seattle Pacific University's naming of Dr. Perkins, "distinguished visiting professor at Seattle Pacific University.[519]

Dr Perkins has both authored and co-authored more than twelve books to include: *One Blood: Parting Words to the Church on Race* (2018), *Let Justice Roll Down,* and *Beyond Charity.* And John Perkins has served on the boards of World Vision, Prison Fellowship, National Association of Evangelicals, Spring Arbor University, and "more than a dozen others."[520]

The John Perkins Center training and mentoring for Seattle Pacific University students as part of the Center's student-led ministry teams engaging in reconciliation and community development in and around

---

[517] John Perkins Center. https://spu.edu/administration/john-perkins-center. Downloaded: 05/25/2024.

[518] John Perkins Center for: Reconciliation, Christian Leadership Training, and Community Development, Seattle Pacific University, https://spu.edu/administration/john-perkins-center/about/john-m-perkins. Downloaded: 05/25/2024.

[519] Ibid.

[520] Ibid.

Seattle, Washington.[521] Additionally, students further equip themselves through adding a minor in Reconciliation Studies to their major. Students will uniquely prepare themselves to learn, and serve together, in Urban Involvement, Urban Plunge (experiential learning about homelessness in Seattle) and the JPC (John Perkins Center) Pilgrimage which takes place in the Summer and lasts a week. In this week-long venture, students participate in a justice journey studying history at important Civil Rights and memorial sites, engaging stories, and participating in guided reflections. Throughout the week, students participate in discussion series, and look at how race shapes experience.[522]

JOHN PERKINS: RECONCILIATION AND COMMUNITY DEVELOPMENT

John Perkins Center for: Reconciliation, Christian Leadership Training, and Community Development, Seattle Pacific University, https://spu.edu/administration/john-perkins-center/about/john-m-perkins.

The Christian Community Development Association: INSPIRE. TRAIN. CONNECT. Centers in Perkin's three R's: Reconciliation, Redistribution, and Relocation. https://ccda.org/.

---

[521] John Perkins Center: Student Involvement: https://spu.edu/administration/john-perkins-center/student-involvement. Downloaded: 05/25/2024.

[522] Ibid. Under the subheading: Scholarship, academic partnerships through the John Perkins Center offer a Reconciliation Studies Minor that prepares the student to participate in the work of reconciliation through their field of study. And a Global and Urban Ministry Minor that equips the student to understand the theological and contextual realities in today's world. https://spu.edu/administration/john-perkins-center/scholarship. Downloaded: 05/25/2024.

The Mendenhall Ministries: A Model of Rural Christian Community Development Since 1962. John & Vera Perkins: https://mendenhallministries.org/.

Perkins: Voice of Calvary Outreach Programs: "*Changing the Narrative, Reaching Our Full Potential in Christ.*" https://vocm.org/

Harambee Ministries: Discipleship, Scholarship & Leadership: https://www.harambeeministries.org/.

The following select books by John M. Perkins, and co-authors as mentioned, are resources related to racial reconciliation, leadership, and community transformation. It is suggested that cohorts (e.g., missional teams/and/or individual missional entrepreneurs[523]), led by a facilitator, gather to discuss selected readings by both John Perkins, and Charles Yancey, in the context of Yancey's Mutual Accountability Model, and Perkins' expansive ministry, "Reconciliation and Community Development."

Disciplemaking, majoring in Missional living, Racial Reconciliation, and theological formation, would then be fully facilitated. Alongside of the Racial Reconciliation library the author recommends, again, that *The Woke Opiate, and Living Missionally Beyond Sunday, be purchased together for the purpose of framing the starting point for the confrontation of Woke Identity Marxism by one church, and one community at a time throughout Western Culture.*

[523] Please see: Living Missionally Beyond Sunday, "and all peoples on earth will be blessed by you," Gen. 12:3b., Chapter 6: Principles— (Stage #5), "The mDNA Of Missional Congregations" and Appendix 1— "Stage 5: Disciples Making Disciples — 'Teaching Them To Obey.'"

BOOKS BY JOHN M. PERKINS:

https://www.amazon.com/s?k=Books%2C+John+M.+Perkins&crid-=18HUTQ56QJGTR&sprefix=books%2C+john+m.+perkins%2Caps%2C176&ref=nb_sb_noss_2.

John M. Perkins. *Let Justice Roll Down.* Baker Books, 2012.

"His brother died in his arms, shot by a deputy marshal. He was beaten and tortured by the sheriff and state police. But through it all he returned good for evil, love for hate, progress for prejudice, and brought hope to black and white alike. The story of John Perkins is no ordinary story. John Perkins' story is a story of redemption— John Perkins redeems broken lives, and communities by transforming them through the power of the Gospel into new life, new disciples, and communities of hope." — (Partial Publishers' Description).

John M. Perkins. *One Blood: Parting Words to the Church on Race and Love.* Moody Publishers, 2020.

"Perkins rightly states that true reconciliation with our brothers and sisters 'from every nation' has been long overdue, and we continue to witness disastrous results.... Dr. Perkins's insight and guidance on this subject are well worth considering by today's church leadership as well as individual members of the body of Christ" — Rick Warren.

John M. Perkins. *Dream With Me, Race, Love, and the Struggle We Must Win.* Baker Books. Reprint. 2018.

"At a time when the racial divide in the United States is widening into a chasm, I cannot think of a more needed message than this book"—Philip Yancey, bestselling Christian author/speaker.

John M. Perkins. *Beyond Charity: The Call to Christian Community Development.* Baker Books, 1993.

"A powerful call to action to bring reconciliation and restoration to broken communities" — (Publishers Statement).

John M. Perkins. *Count it All Joy: The Ridiculous Paradox of Suffering.* Moody Publishers, 2021.

"We think of suffering as the worst of all evils. Our culture tells us to avoid it at all costs. But can suffering produce growth in us when we learn to endure it…then value it…then allow God to redeem it?" — (Publishers Description).

John M. Perkins. *With Justice for All: A Strategy for Community Development.* Baker Books 2011.

"I am persuaded that the Church, as the steward of this gospel, holds the key to justice in our society. Either justice will come through us or it will not come at all." John Perkins's optimistic view of justice becoming a reality starts and ends with the Church. *With Justice for All* is Perkins›s invitation to live out the gospel in a way that brings good news to the poor and liberty to the oppressed— (Publishers Description).

Wayne Gordon & John Perkins. *Making Neighborhoods Whole: A Handbook for Christian Community Development.* Inter-Varsity Press. 2013.

"For nearly thirty years the Christian Community Development Association has been a resource for people seeking to do prophetic, nonpaternalistic urban ministry. In Making Neighborhoods Whole: A Handbook for Christian Community Development, CCDA cofounders Wayne Gordon and John Perkins, and other veteran and emerging leaders, revisit key principles and lessons learned." —Sojourners, May 2014.

John M. Perkins with Karen Waddles. *He Calls Me Friend: The Healing Power of Friendship in a Lonely World.* Moody Publishers, 2019.

From the Back Cover: Sometimes I'm asked, "What should we do? How can we make a difference?" This book is my answer.

John M. Perkins & Wayne Gordon. *Leadership Revolution: Developing the Vision & Practice of Freedom & Justice.* Baker Books, 2012.

"The next generation hungers for strong, visionary, ethical, and passionate leaders. Where do we start in this day where we lack leadership at all levels? The authors of this breakout book contend that leaders of tomorrow are among us, but they need to be identified, trained, and empowered. John M. Perkins casts the biblical vision that has started a movement. Wayne Gordon has rolled up his sleeves at the grassroots level to spark the transformation of a Chicago neighborhood. Together (and with friends) they founded the Christian Community Development Association. Now they put in this book the stories and lessons of discovery, growth, mistakes, success, and lives changed. They are ready to hand batons of leadership, especially for poor and under-resourced communities, over to the next generation. With this book, they do just that!" — (From the Publisher's Description).

John M. Perkins, Editor. *Restoring At-Risk Communities: Doing It Together and Doing It Right.* Baker Books, 1996.

This comprehensive handbook to urban ministry introduces and shows how to implement a Christian community development program.

Charles Marsh & John M. Perkins. *Welcoming Justice: God's Movement Toward Beloved Community.* Inter-Varsity Press, 2018.

"Together, Perkins and Marsh are attempting to restore the vision, both conceptually and practically, showing how theology can indeed be lived out in a multicultural society despite its deeply stained past. I know of no better time to attempt such a project, and no team better equipped to accomplish it." — From the Foreword by Philip Yancey.

APPENDIX ONE

THE SOUL OF FREEDOM: RECONCILIATION & REDEMPTION

"Should our Republic ever forget this fundamental precept of governance," John Jay wrote about the importance of faith for virtue, *"men are certain to shed their responsibilities for licentiousness and this great experiment will surely be doomed."*[524]

Themes of redemption are inextricably woven throughout the fabric of our nation's story. Civil religion is the cornerstone of our Republic. The Ten Commandments hang over the head of the Chief Justice of the Supreme Court. In the House and Senate Chambers appear the words, "In God We Trust." On the walls of the Capitol dome appear the words, "The New Testament according to the Lord and Savior Jesus Christ."

The Washington Monument memorializes the "father of our nation." Our nation's "father" is invisible; nowhere on the outside or inside of the

[524] Guinness, *A Free People's Suicide,* 117.

monument is a picture of George Washington. The Monument's structure points towards the heavens and the profound *faith* Americans have in the religious heritage of our nation. Engraved on the metal cap on the top of the Washington Monument are the words, "Praise be to God," and numerous Bible verses line the walls of the stairwell. And the Eighty-Third Congress set aside a room in the Capitol Building exclusively for the private prayer and meditation of members of Congress.

When one visits the Lincoln Memorial, they first see the strong hands of our nation's "savior" who redeemed and restored the Republic and set the captives (the slaves) free. Inside the Monument, the walls are filled with Scriptures referring to redemption, reconciliation and resurrection, themes foundational to our nation's *hope*.

And was it Providence, that Martin Luther King Jr. delivered his, "I Have a Dream" speech in front of the Lincoln Memorial, as though he proceeds from the "Great Emancipator" and applies his finished work in the form of the Civil Rights Movement to those most in need: the marginalized, oppressed, and the disenfranchised? From redemptive themes in children's fairy tales such as Snow White and Cinderella, to Julia Roberts and the story of redemption in "Pretty Woman," to Denzel Washington and "Eli's Book," to the great monuments, the U.S. Capital Building, and the Supreme Court Building in Washington D.C.

APPENDIX 2

THE PROBLEM OF EVIL

"If you are sure that this natural world is unjust and filled with evil, you are assuming the reality of some extra-natural standard by which to make your judgment"
— C.S. Lewis.

The Eighteenth-Century Scottish Empiricist, David Hume, inquires, "Is God willing to prevent evil, but not able? Then is he impotent? Or is he able but not willing? Is he then malevolent? Is he both able and willing? Whence is evil?"[525]

All orthodox theology hangs on two primary truths: God is *able,* and God is *willing— God is the sovereign, almighty God over all creation, visible and invisible, and God is good.* This is the Christian theological position concerning the "problem of evil," as posed by Hume (among many other skeptics).

---

[525] Anders Kraal. *The of God In David Hume.* Cambridge University Press. 2024.

Regarding empiricism and vast depths of knowledge, David Hume is very formable, but concerning metaphysics (and theology), the renown Scottish philosopher is very vulnerable— Hume appears oblivious to man's sinful condition and hence, his moral culpability concerning evil. And as well, Hume appears incredulous concerning evil itself— "Whence is evil?" Since God is the Creator of all things visible and invisible, do we then conclude that God created evil? (So, Hume appears to imply).

WHAT IS EVIL?

The essence of sin is we human beings substituting ourselves for God, while the essence of salvation is God substituting himself for us. We… put ourselves where only God deserves to be; God… puts himself where we deserve to be"
— John Stott.

"The Fall" of humanity is an historical event recorded in, Genesis 3:1-7[526]—God gave Adam and Eve moral freedom in the Garden "to glorify God, and to enjoy him forever."[527] God imposed only one restriction on Adam and Eve: They were free to eat the fruit of any tree in the garden, except one: "The Tree of Knowledge of Good and Evil."

But the Serpent, that is, Satan, deceived first Eve, then Adam, into conceiving God's commandments as [too] restrictive, instead of righteous means and ends towards their ultimate freedom through knowing God and glorifying Him forever. Adam and Eve's desire for personal autonomy, unbounded freedom, to decide what is good and what is evil *for themselves* results in their transgression against God.

---

[526] The Fall of man is an *actual* historical event with metaphysical consequences, as described above.

[527] The First Question of the Shorter Westminster Catechism: Q. 1. What is the chief end of man? A. Man's chief end is to glorify God, and to enjoy him forever.

Once they transgressed God, they attempted to hide from Him when they heard Him entering the Garden. And the Lord God called to the couple, "Where are you?" (3:9). Now, God is both omniscient and omnipresent, He knows all, and He is present everywhere. Therefore, "Where are you?" is phenomenal language; nothing is being pointed to regarding God, rather, the question is telling us about mankind, the "crown of God's creation" (Gen. 1:27); mankind is *lost* in the sense of a broken relationship (re: *the special relationship by creation*— Gen. 1:27) with God because of sin. The image of God is still present, for "man" is referred to in Scripture, as "man" after the Fall, but the *imago dei* (the image of God) in humanity is "marred" in three significant ways—Our separation *unto* God (sanctification) is reversed, we are then separated from God (Eph. 4:18), and our intimate *awareness* of God is lost (Eph. 4:17-19), and our right *standing* before God (Eph. 4:20-24), is exchanged for servitude to anyone or anything that takes the place of God in our lives.

The human condition brings us face to face with the problem of evil: "This is the verdict: Light has come into the world, but men loved darkness instead of light because their deeds were evil" (John 3:19).

What is evil? Augustine answers this question by first positing God is good, and the creation he has brought into being is good (Gen. 1:3-31). But if God is good, and his creation is likewise, then, "Whence is evil?" Or, in other words, what is the origin of evil? Augustine's answer is: "Evil has no positive nature; but the loss of good has received the name 'evil.'"[528] Evil is the privation of good: "The truth is that evil is not a real *thing* at all, like

[528] Augustine. *The City of God.* Edited: Whitney J. Oates. *Basic Writings of Saint Augustine.* Vol. Two. Grand Rapids, MI.: Baker Book House, Reprinted: 1992. XII, Ch.9.

God. It is simply good *spoiled.* That is why I say there can be good without evil, but no evil without good."[529]

If evil has no existence apart from good, and therefore, it is not a thing, as is good, then how do humans commit evil acts? Augustine answers: "For when the will abandons what is above itself, and turns to what is lower, it becomes evil—not because that is evil to which it turns, but because the turning itself is wicked."[530] Thus, a person does not choose evil, as though it is a thing, but rather, they "can only turn away from the good, that is from a greater good to a lesser good (*re:* Augustine's hierarchy) since all things are good."[531] Evil then is an illicit reach for the "Beautiful and the Good"—"And I strained to perceive what I now heard, that free-will was the cause of our doing ill."[532]

Human nature is predisposed to desire the perverse, instead of the "Beautiful," and depravity instead of the "Good" (Rom. 3:10-18; 23). But though human freedom is the source of evil, it is also the source of virtue—courage, faithfulness, and compassion (among a myriad of other human virtues) are expressed through the character of free moral beings. Therefore, although moral freedom allows for moral evil, it also allows for the greater good in our world.

Alluding to Luther's *theologia crucis* (theology of the Cross), Jürgen Moltmann penetrates to the reality of living in a world wherein what men intend for evil; God ultimately intends for good:

---

529 C.S. Lewis. *The Letters of C.S. Lewis to Arthur Greeves* (1914-1963). Edited by Walter Hooper. New York: Collier/Macmillan, 1986. 465.

530 Augustine. *The City of God.* XII, Ch.6.

531 Gregory Koukl. "Augustine on Evil." http://www.str.org/free/commentaries/apologetics/evil/augustine.htm page 3 of 6 pages. Downloaded: 05/13/2004.

532 Augustine. *Confessions.* Edited: Whitney J. Oates. *Basic Writings of Saint Augustine.* Vol. One. Grand Rapids, MI.: Baker Book House, Reprinted: 1992.

> Since I first studied theology, I have been concerned with the theology of the cross... It is the basic theme of my theological thought. No doubt this goes back to the period of my first concern with questions concerning Christian faith and theology in real life, as a prisoner of war behind barbed wire... Shattered and broken, the survivors of my generation were then returning from camps and hospitals to the lecture room. A theology which did not speak of God in terms of the abandoned and crucified one would not have got through to us then.[533]

John Stott agrees with Moltmann: "I could never believe in God if not for the Cross because in a world full of injustice, I could never believe in a God who could not identify with it; a God who was immune from it."[534] God has not abandoned us to ourselves rather, he became flesh and lived among us; he endured suffering and moral evil as one of us and for us.

These three sections, and twelve chapters, and final two appendices, conclude The Woke Opiate, The Progressive Left's "Long March Through The Institutions" — *"I Rest My Case."*

[533] J. Moltmann. *Dergekreuzigte Gott. Das Kreuz Chrisals Grund und Kritik christlicher Theologie.* Müchen, 4th edn. 1981. 7. Quoted in: Alister McGrath. *Luther's Theology of the Cross.* 180.

[534] John Stott quoted by Tim Keller. Sermon: Mark 14:53-65. Copywrite Redeemer Presbyterian Church. www.redeemer.com.

BIBLIOGRAPHY

Animal Farm (A Synopsis). https://www.imdb.com/title/tt0047834/plot-summary/. Downloaded: 06/16/2023.

APPENDIX E. Letter to Governor Jay Inslee (June 2020). State of Washington, Office of Equity Task Force (Final Proposal). June 12, 2020. Downloaded: 03/28/2023.

Arnn, Larry P. President, Hillsdale College. "Orwell's 1984 and Today," 2. *Imprimis,* Hillsdale.EDU. December 2020, Vol. 49, No. 12. https://imprimis.hillsdale.edu/wp-content/uploads/2020/12/Imprimis_December_8pgweb-1.pdf. Downloaded: 05/08/2024.

___________. "The Life of Hillsdale College: Why Have Elite Colleges Gone Bad?" Gmail-The Life of Hillsdale College Why Have Elite Colleges Gone Bad. pdf. Page 2 of 4 pages. Downloaded: 04/06/2024.

Associated Press. "Family of Teen Killed in CHOP Zone: Seattle Enabled Danger." https://www.usnews.com/news/best-states/washington/articles/2022-07-19/family-of-teen-killed-in-chop-zone-seattle-enabled-danger. 07'19/2022. Downloaded: 10/21/2022.

Augustine. *Confessions.* Edited: Whitney J. Oates. *Basic Writings of Saint Augustine.* Vol. One. Grand Rapids, MI.: Baker Book House, Reprinted: 1992.

________. *The City of God.* Edited: Whitney J. Oates. *Basic Writings of Saint Augustine.* Vol. Two. Grand Rapids, MI.: Baker Book House, Reprinted: 1992 XII, Ch.6.

________. *The City of God.* XII, Ch.9.

Augustyn, Adam. Three-Fifths Compromise. United States History. The Editors of *Encyclopaedia Britannica.* (The most recent edition of my source was revised and updated by). https://www.britannica.com/topic/three-fifths-compromise. Downloaded: 08/14/2023.

Azerrad, David. Hillsdale College. "Civil Rights in American History," Lecture 9, "Identity Politics Today." https://online.hillsdale.edu/courses/civil-rights-in-american-history. Downloaded: 07/26/2023.

Bell, Derrick A. *Race, Racism, and American Law.* Boston, MA: Little, Brown, and Co., 1984.

Black, Henry Campbell. *Black's Law Dictionary.* Fifth Edition. St. Paul, MN.: West Publishing CO. 1979. 638.

Bolotnikova, Marina. *Harvard Magazine.* "What is Critical Race Theory?" https://www.harvardmagazine.com/2016/03/bu-law-professor-khiara-bridges-teaches-critical-race-theory-at-harvardlaw#:~:text=Critical%20race%20theory% 20grew%20out,by%20racist%20 interests%20and %20assumptions. Downloaded: 10/26/2002. 03/22/2016.

Breshears, Jefrey D. *American Crisis, Cultural Marxism and The Culture War: A Christian Response.* Centre Pointe Publishing, 2020.

Buchanan, Ian. *A Dictionary of Critical Theory.* (1st Ed.) Oxford University Press. 2010. https://www.oxfordreference.com/display/10.1093/oi/authority.20110803100414515;jsessionid=51A066FFA2AB87 82E85350295629B46B. Downloaded: 04/27/2023

Bussey, Barry W. *Law and Religion, Religious Liberty, Religious Freedom.* "Fides et Libertas," 2011. Fides_et_Libertas_2011.pdf. Downloaded: 04/09/2024.

Buswell, Jr, J. Oliver. *A Systematic Theology of the Christian Religion.* Grand Rapids, MI.: Zondervan, 1962. Vol. 1.

Calderon, Dolores. "One Dimensionality and Whiteness." *Policy Futures in Education.* Volume 4, Number 1, 2006.

Campbell, Henry. Black. *Black's Law Dictionary.* Fifth Edition. St. Paul, MN.: West Publishing CO. 1979.

Capitol Hill Seattle Blog— Community News for All the Hill." "CHOP: One year later — The East Precinct is Abandoned and the Protest Zone Forms." Posted: June 9, 2021. https://www.capitolhillseattle.com/2021/06/chop-one-year-later-the-east-precinct-is-abandoned-and-the-protest-zone-forms/. Downloaded: 10/21/2022.

______________________. "Who ordered the abandonment of the East Precinct?" — Update. Posted 11/18/2020. https://www.capitolhillseattle.com/2020/11/who-ordered-the-abandonment-of-the-east-precinct/. Downloaded: 10/21/2022.

Charen, Mona. *Useful Idiots, How Liberals Got It Wrong in the Cold War and Still Blame America First.* Washington D.C.: Regnery Publishing, Inc. 2003.

Chesterton, G.K. "The Five Deaths of Faith." Part 2. Chapter 6. https://www.worldinvisible.com/library/chesterton/everlasting/part2c6.htm. Downloaded: 06/03/2024.

Coates, Ta-Nehisi. *We Were Eight Years in Power: An American Tragedy.* New York, NY: One World Publishing, 2017.

Codevilla, Angelo M. "The Rise of Political Correctness." November 28, 2016. Originally published in *Claremont Review of Books,* November

8, 2015. https://claremontreviewofbooks.com/the-rise-of-political-correctness/ Downloaded: 06/16/2023.

Dawkins Richard. *River Out of Eden, A Darwinian View of Life.* New York: Basic Books, August 1996.

de Figueiredo, John M. MD, ScD. Yale University School of Medicine. "Distress, Demoralization and Psychopathology." *The European Journal of Psychiatry.* Vol.27 no.1 Zaragozaene. March 2013. https://scielo.isciii.es/scielo.php?script=sci_arttext&pid=S0213-61632013000100008. Downloaded: 05/06/2023.

Ekins, Emily. Cato Institute. 08/2020. "Most Americans Are Scared Stiff To Talk Politics. Why?" https://www.cato.org/commentary/most-americans-are-scared-stiff-talk-politics-why

Elder, Alasdair. *The Red Trojan Horse, A Concise Analysis of Cultural Marxism.* CreateSpace Independent Publishing Platform. 2017.

Fee, Gordon D. *The First Epistle To The Corinthians.* Wm. B. Eerdmans; Revised edition 2014.

Figure 17. Statement from the Governor's Committee on Disability Issues and Employment (GCDE). 2020 Office of Equity Task Force, Final Proposal.

Fogel, Robert William. "The Phases of the Four Great Awakenings." https://press.uchicago.edu/Misc/Chicago/256626.html. Downloaded: 05/13/2024.

Freire, Paulo. "The Pedagogy of the Oppressed." Edited: Myra Berman Ramos. Translated: New York: Continuum. 1968.

Friedrich, Carl J. Introduction, in G.W.F. Hegel. *The Philosophy of Hegel,* ed. Carl J. Friedrich. New York, NY: Random House, 1954, xiv.

Fulton, John. "Religion and Politics in Gramsci: An Introduction," *Sociological Analysis* 48 (1987): 197-216.

Genocide and Mass Murder Since 1900. "Statistics on Democide," https://www.hawaii.edu/powerkills/NOTE5.HTM. Downloaded: 09/13/2023.

Geraghty, Jim. Senior Political Correspondent, National Review. "Burning Cities." https://www.nationalreview.com/the-morning-jolt/burning-cities/. August 2020. Downloaded: 10/21/2022.

Goins-Phillips, Tre'. "Cambridge Dictionary Bows to 'Woke Activists,' Changes Definition of 'Woman.'" https://www1.cbn.com/cbnnews/us/2022/december/cambridge-dictionary-bows-to-lsquo-woke-activists-rsquo-changes-definition-of-lsquo-woman-rsquo Downloaded: 12/15/2022.

Grenz, Stanley J. & Roger E. Olson. *20th— Century Theology, God & the World in a Transitional Age.* Downers Grove, IL: IVP Academic. October 25, 1993.

Guignion, David. "What is the Dialectic?" | Plato, Kant, Hegel, Marx | Keyword https://www.youtube.com/watch?v=RY_rGJUpwsM. Downloaded: 11/28/2022.

Guinness, Os. *A Free People's Suicide, Sustainable Freedom And The American Future.* Downers Grove, Ill.: Inter-Varsity Press, 2012.

Hamblin, James, Katherine Wells, and Adam Serwer. *The Atlantic.* May 13, 2020. Social Distance Podcast: The Racial Contract. https://www.theatlantic.com/health/archive/2020/05/the-racial-contract/611614/. Quoted in 2020 Office of Equity Task Force, Final Proposal.

Hanson, Victor Davis. "American Citizenship and Its Decline. Lecture 3: The Disappearing Middle Class." https://online.hillsdale.edu/courses/american-citizenship-and-its-decline. Downloaded: 11/28/2022.

________________. "American Citizenship And Its Decline." Lecture 5— The Rise of Tribal Politics. https://online.hillsdale.edu/courses/american-citizenship-and-its-decline. Downloaded: 12/08/2022.

Hegel, Georg. *Phenomenology of Mind.* Translated by J.B. Baillie. New York: Harper and Row, 1967.

Hennessy-Fiske, Molly. "George Floyd died a week ago, rocking Minneapolis and its mayor." https://www.latimes.com/world-nation/story/2020-05-31/george-floyd-died-a-week-ago-rocking-minneapolis-and-its-mayor. May 31, 2020. Downloaded: 10/21/2022.

Herman, Paul. *Manchesterhive.* "Our post-Christian Age, Historicist-Inspired Diagnoses of Modernity, 1935" in *Post-Everything.* DOI: https://doi.org/10.7765/9781526148179.00008

Online Publication Date: 17 Jul 2021. Downloaded: 05/13/2024.

"HISTORY." Black Codes. https://www.history.com/topics/black-history/black-codes. Jim Crow Laws. https://www.history.com/topics/early-20th-century-us/jim-crow-laws

Hoag, Alexis. Harvard Law Review, Blog. "Derrick Bell's Interest Convergence and the Permanence of Racism: A Reflection on Resistance." August 24, 2020. https://blog.harvardlawreview.org/derrick-bells-interest-convergence-and-the-permanence-of-racism-a-reflection-on-resistance/. Downloaded: 10/07/2022.

Hobson, Theo. British Church Ministry Network. Copywrite: 2012-2024. https://baptistcmn.com/three-things-must-happen-for-a-moral-revolution-to-occur/. Downloaded: 05/11/2024.

Horkheimer, Max. *Traditional and Critical Theory.* New York, N.Y.: The Continuum Publishing Co. 1972.

__________________. "Traditional and Critical Theory." Translated By: Matthew J. O'Connell.

https://books.google.com/books?hl=en&lr=&id=YiXUAwAAQBAJ&oi=fnd&pg=PR3&dq=horkheimer+traditional+and+critical+-theory&ots=uxUGjo6xp0&sig=CnhUgMYORCyZgTi9jAlAJzB-

IvE#v=onepage&q=horkheimer%20traditional%20and%20crit. Pages 197-98. Downloaded: 11/14/22.

Huxley, Aldous. *Brave New World.* New York: Harper &Brothers, Publishers, 1932.

Internet Encyclopedia of Philosophy—A Peer-Reviewed Academic Resource. "The Frankfurt School and Critical Theory." https://iep.utm.edu/critical-theory-frankfurt-school/. Downloaded: 11/01/2022.

Jarvis, Danielle. "Joe Biden Signs Respect For Marriage Act Into Law, Jeopardizing Religious Liberty." December 14, 2022. https://soulpurposemag.com/joe-biden-signs-respect-for-marriage-act-into-law-jeopardizing-religious-liberty/. Downloaded: 02/24/2023.

Jeffries *Stuart.* *Grand Hotel Abyss: The Lives of the Frankfurt School. The Frankfurt School: A Timeline. September 29, 2017.* https://www.versobooks.com/blogs/2844-the-frankfurt-school-a-timeline. Downloaded: 11/04/2022.

Jones, Nikole Hannah, Director. *New York Times Magazine's* 1619 Project. Thus, America was founded on slavery, not freedom. https://www.nytimes.com/column/1619-project./. Downloaded: 08/05/2023.

Kelly, Robin D.G. "The Rebellion Against Racial Capitalism," interviewed by Jeremy Scahill, *The Intercept* (2020).

Kendi, Ibram X. "Antiracism, Anticapitalism, and the Eugenicist Origins of IQ & SAT Tests." Democracy Now! https://www.youtube.com/watch?v=_oQXki0hG9w. Downloaded: 04/12/2024.

_____________. *How to Be an Antiracist.* One World—First Edition, 2019.

Kilner, John F. *Dignity and Destiny. Humanity in the Image of God.* Grand Rapids, MI: William B. Eerdmans, 2015.

Kizer, Walter C. Jr. *What Does the Lord Require? A Guide for Preaching and Teaching Biblical Ethics.* Grand Rapids, MI.: Baker Academic. 2009.

Kolakowski, Leszek. "What is Left of Socialism?" October 2002. *First Things. https://www.firstthings.com/article/2002/10/what-is-left-of-socialism.* Downloaded.

Koukl, Gregory. "Augustine on Evil." http://www.str.org/free/commentaries/apologetics/evil/augustine.htm Downloaded: 05/13/2004.

_____________. *The Story of Reality, How the World began, How It Ends, and Everything important that Happens in Between.* Grand Rapids, MI.: Zondervan Publishing, 2017.

Lawrence, Keith. Aspen Institute and Terry Keleher, Applied Research Center, for the Race and Public Policy Conference (2004). *Chronic Disparity: Strong and Pervasive Evidence of Racial Inequalities.* And Maggie Potapchuk, Sally Leiderman, Donna Bivens, and Barbara Major *Flipping the Script: White Privilege and Community Building.* (2005).

Lewis, C.S. *God in The Dock, Essays on Theology and Ethics.* "Myth Became Fact." Edited by Walter Hooper. Grand Rapids, MI.: Wm. B. Eerdmans Publishing Co. 1970.

_________. *Mere Christianity.* Bk. I. San Francisco, CA: Harper, 1952.

_________. *The Abolition of Man.* "Appendix, Illustrations of the Tao." New York: Collier Books, Macmillan Publishing Company, 1947.

_________. *The Letters of C.S. Lewis to Arthur Greeves* (1914-1963). Edited by Walter Hooper. New York: Collier/Macmillan, 1986.

Lindsay, Jim. "Antonio Gramsci, Cultural Marxism, Wokeness, and Leninism 4.0" https://www.youtube.com/watch?v=VdsSIWh_VkQ. Downloaded: 09/26/2022.

____________. "Dismantle," Social Justice Usage. https://newdiscourses.com/tftw-dismantle/ Downloaded: 08/07, 2023.

____________. "Disrupt," Social Justice Usage. https://newdiscourses.com/tftw-disrupt/ Downloaded: 08/07/2023.

____________. *The Marxification of Education: Paulo Freire's Critical Marxism and the Theft of Education.* New Discourses. December 6, 2022.

____________. "The Marxist Roots of DEI— Session 1: Equity." https://www.youtube.com/watch?v=xbby7yFrIxM. Downloaded: 03/25/2023.

____________. "The Marxist Roots of DEI - Session 2: Diversity" | James Lindsay https://www.youtube.com/watch?v=C-aarD-dFm4. Downloaded: 04/13/2023.

____________. "The Marxist Roots of DEI— Session 3: Inclusion." https://www.youtube.com/watch?v=IsX8zPuSVRk. Downloaded: 04/25/2023.

____________. "Tolerance: Social Justice Usage." Under the subtitle: "New Discourses Commentary." https://newdiscourses.com/tftw-tolerance/. Downloaded: 04/27/202.

López Esmael, *Community Engagement Coordination for the Washington State Office of Equity Force.* 2020 Office of Equity Task Force, Final Proposal. Marin Health and Human Services. https://www.marinhhs.org › files › boards › genera.

Lukács', György. *History and Class Consciousness.* 1922 Publication. The Frankfurt School.

Luther King Jr., Martin. *Where Do We Go From Here? Chaos or Community.* Boston, MA: Beacon Press, 1968.

Lyotard, Jean Francois. *The Postmodern Condition: A Report on Knowledge.* Minneapolis, MN: University of Minnesota Press, 1979.

Marcuse, Herbert. A Critique of Pure Tolerance. 1965. https://la.utexas.edu/users/hcleaver/330T/350kPEEMarcuseToleranceTable.pdf. Downloaded: 04/19/2023.

____________. *One-Dimensional Man.* 2nd ed. Boston, MA: Beacon Press, 1991. (First published 1964).

______________, Robert Paul Wolff, and Barrington Moore, Jr. A Critique of Pure Tolerance. 1965. https://la.utexas.edu/users/hcleaver/330T/350kPEEMarcuseToleranceTable.pdf. Downloaded: 05/02/2023.

Martin, Jay. *The Dialectical Imagination*, Berkeley: University of California Press, 1996.

Marx, Karl. "Afterword to the Second German Edition," in *Das Kapital* (1873), in *Capital: A Critique of Political Economy: Volume One.* Translated by Ben Fowkes. London: Penguin, 1976.

_________. "The Victory of the Counter-Revolution in Vienna." *Neue Rheinische Zeitung,* 136. November 1848, https:///www.marxists.org/archive/marx/works/1848/11/06.htm.

Marxist Project, The. "Fundamentals of Marx: Dialectics." https://www.youtube.com/watch?v=GNHzVeC7jeY. Downloaded: 11/28/2022/.

McKinsey & Company. "What is Diversity, Equity, and Inclusion?" August 17, 2022. https://www.mckinsey.com/featured-insights/mckinsey-explainers/what-is-diversity-equity-and-inclusion. Downloaded: 03/27/2023.

McRoberts, Kerry D. *A Letter from Christ, Apologetics in Cultural Transition.* University Press of America. 2011.

________________. *Living Missionally Beyond Sunday, And All Nations Will Be Blessed Through You (Gen. 12:3b).* Sydney, Australia: Ark Publishers. 2023.

Mohler Albert. Podcast: "Thinking In Public." Subject: "Critical Theory and the Cynical Transformation of Society." Interview: James Lindsay. https://www.youtube.com/watch?v=de7j0npQu-4. Downloaded: 06/26/2023.

Moltmann, J. *Dergekreuzigte Gott. Das Kreuz Chrisals Grund und Kritik christlicher Theologie.* Müchen, 4th edn. 1981. 7. Quoted in: Alister McGrath. *Luther's Theology of the Cross.* 180.

NFL Football Operations. Four Pillars of Inspire Change. https://operations.nfl.com/inside-footballops/social%20justice/socialjustice/#:~:-text=OUR%20Mission,public%20in%20working%20towards%20solutions.&text=This%20opens%20in%20a%20new%20window. Downloaded: 01/05/2023.

Office of Equity Task Force, Final Proposal (2020). "Definition of Equity & Guiding Statements for the Office of Equity." Downloaded: 03/28/2023.

________________________, Operating Principles. Adopted: August 19, 2019. Download: 08/15/2023. Noah Miller. Updated 12/14/2022. Reviewed by Kyle Perterdy. https://corporatefinanceinstitute.com/resources/esg/esg-score/. Downloaded: 03/31/2023.

________________________, Final Proposal. 2020. "Systems Change." Downloaded: 03/28/2023.

________________________, Final Proposal. 2020. "Systems Transformation: Toward an Equitable, Just, and Sustainable Future." Downloaded 03/29/2023.

________________________, "Our Greatest Hopes for the Office of Equity." https://healthequity.wa.gov/sites/default/files/202201/EquityOfficeTFFinal%20Proposal%20%28final%29.pdf. Downloaded: 03/28/2023.

Orwell, George. *1984.* Berkley, Penguin Random House, LLC. 1949.

Pearcey, Nancy, Forward: Gregory Koukl. *The Story Of Reality, How The World Began, How It Ends, And Everything Important That Happens In Between.* Grand Rapids, MI: Zondervan. 2017.

Packer, J.I. *Knowing God.* Ch. 5: "God Incarnate." Downers Grove, IL.: Inter-Varsity Press. Anniversary Edition, 1993.

Perkins, Tom. "The Guardian" (A News Website). "Most Charges Against George Floyd Protesters Dropped, Analysis Shows." April 2021. https://

amp.theguardian.com/us-news/2021/apr/17/george-floyd-protesters-charges-citations-analysis. Downloaded: 05/05/2023.

Phung Huynh, Linh, Project Manager, Esmael Lopez, Community Engagement Coordinator, Hannah Fernald 2020 Office of Equity Task Force, Final Proposal. Administrative Coordinator.

Pluckrose, Helen. "On confronting Critical Theory/Solutions with David Ansara." Podcast #32. https://www.youtube.com/watch?v=xC-MUa7pMA8/ Downloaded: 09/28/2022.

____________________, & James Lindsay. *Cynical Theories. How Activist Scholarship Made Everything about Race, Gender, and Identity.* Durham, NC: Pitchstone Publishing, 2020.111.

RacialEquityTools.org, MP Associates, Center for Assessment and Policy Development, and World Trust Educational Services. https://www.racialequitytools.org/ Downloaded: 07/19/2023.

Ramaswamy, Vivek. Interview: "DOJ To Crack Down on 'Threats' To School Boards." America's Newsroom, FOX News. October 10, 2021. https://twitter.com/VivekGRamaswamy/status/1447352486914891777. Downloaded: 07/27/2023.

Roberts, Kevin D. *America Must Reclaim What The Left Has Attempted To Destroy.* The Heritage Foundation. July 25, 2023. https://www.heritage.org/americanfounders/commentary/america-must-reclaim-what-the-left-has-attempted-destroy. Downloaded: 03/11/2024.

Robertson, Ian. February 2019. *"George Orwell's Preface to the Ukrainian Edition of Animal Farm | The Orwell Foundation".* *www.orwellfoundation.com.* Retrieved 6 March 2021. Quoted in Animal Farm. https://en.wikipedia.org/wiki/Animal_Farm. Downloaded: 06/19/2023.

Robertson, Sebastian. KING 5 News, "Proposal Would Cut $49 Million from Seattle Police Budget as Officers Leave in Record Numbers." Published: 10/19/2020. Updated: 10/20/2020. https://www.king5.

com/article/news/local/seattle/seattle-budget-committee-to-consider-proposed-police-budget-cuts/281-8fd1edd9-5fe8-41a3-92c6-3f01c-b6e6bc3. Downloaded: 05/05/2023. Downloaded: 05/05/2023.

Rolf, Wiggershaus. *The Frankfurt School*, Cambridge: Polity Press, 1995. In: Internet Encyclopedia of Philosophy—A Peer-Reviewed Academic Resource. "The Frankfurt School and Critical Theory."

Rozado, David. "The Great Awokening As A Global Phenomenon," regions: English-speaking West, continental Europe, Latin America, sub-Saharan Africa, Persian Gulf region and Asia." https://arxiv.org/ftp/arxiv/papers/2304/2304.01596.pdf. Downloaded: 07/07/2023.

Rufo, Christopher F. *Imprimis.* "Critical Race Theory: What It Is and How to Fight." https://imprimis.hillsdale.edu/wp-content/uploads/2021/04/Imprimis_Mar_3-21_6pgNM.pdf. March 2021. Vol. 50. Number 3. Downloaded: 10/22/2022.

Rummel, R.J. Center for National Security Law, Charlottesville, Virginia, and author of *Death by Government.* New Brunswick, NJ: Transaction Publishers,1994.

Russian Revolution of 1917: The Essential Reference Guide. https://publisher.abc-clio.com/9781440850936/18 Downloaded: 11/29/2022.

Schaeffer, Francis. *A Christian View of the Church.* The Complete Works of— A Christian Worldview. Vol. 4. Westchester, ILL.: Crossway Books, 1982.

_______________. *The Church at the End of the Twentieth Century.* The Complete Works of Westchester, ILL.: Crossway Books, 1982.

Schaefer, Robert. "Scholars have begun to expose 1619 Project and CRT as dangerous frauds." https://www.telegram.com/story/opinion/2021/08/10/scholars-have-begun-expose-1619-project-and-crt-dangerous-frauds/5425904001/ August 10, 2021. Downloaded: 08/21/2023.

Schwartz, Ian. "Seattle Mayor Durkan: CHAZ: "Block Party Atmosphere, Could Turn Into Summer of Love." https://www.realclearpolitics.com/video/2020/06/12/seattle_mayor_durkan_chaz_has_a_block_party_atmosphere_could_turn_into_summer_of_love.html. 06/12/2020. Downloaded: 10/21/2022.

Slack, Kevin. *How Liberalism Became Despotism. The War on the American Republic.* New York: Encounter Books. 2023.

__________. Hillsdale College. "The American Left: From Liberalism to Despotism." Lecture 4: "Civil Rights and Black Power." https://online.hillsdale.edu/courses/american-left. Downloaded: 03/11/2023.

__________. Hillsdale College. "The American Left: From Liberalism to Despotism." Lecture 8: "Radicals March Through the Institutions." https://online.hillsdale.edu/courses/american-left. Downloaded: 03/11/2023.

Smith, Robert S. "Cultural Marxism: Imaginary Conspiracy or Revolutionary Reality?"

https://www.thegospelcoalition.org/themelios/article/cultural-marxism-imaginary-conspiracy-or-revolutionary-reality/. Downloaded: 2022.

Stanford Encyclopedia of Philosophy. Critical Theory. First published Tue Mar 8, 2005. https://plato.stanford.edu/entries/critical-theory/. Downloaded: 11/01/2022.

______________________________. "Identity Politics." *First published Tue Jul 16, 2002; substantive revision Sat Jul 11, 2020.* https://plato.stanford.edu/entries/identity-politics/. Downloaded: 11/12/2023.

Stassen, Glen H. & David P. Gushee. *Following Jesus in Contemporary Context, Kingdom Ethics.* Downers Grove, IL.: Inter-Varsity, 2003.

Steinmetz, Katy. *TIME – INEQUALITY.* Kimberlé Crenshaw. "She Coined the Term 'Intersectionality' Over 30 Years Ago. Here's What It

Means to Her Today" February 20, 2020. https://Time.com/5786710/Kimberle-Crenshaw-Intersectionality/ Downloaded: 10/07/2022.

Stott, John. Quoted by Tim Keller. Sermon: Mark 14:53-65. Copywrite Redeemer Presbyterian Church. www.redeemer.com.

The Heritage Foundation. "How to Identify Critical Race Theory."

https://www.heritage.org/civil-society/heritage-explains/how-identify-critical-race-theory. Downloaded: 12/26/2023.

The Oxford Dictionary The Coalition for Racial Equalities and Rights. "Racism in Scotland."

The Coalition for Racial Equalities and Right. https://www.crer.org.uk/what-is-racism#:~:text=The%20term%20'racism'%20is%20often,explanation%20of%20a%20complex%20issue.

Tudehope, Damien. "What's left of Western Culture? Just about Everything," *The Spectator,* 9 October 2017, https://tinyurl.com/y4jdlbhg.

Voltaire, Francois Marie Arouet. 1880. *Le Sottisier.* Paris: Librairie des bibliophiles. Wentworth Press. 2019.

Waltke, Bruce. "Reflections From The Old Testament On Abortion." The presidential address at the 27th annual meeting of the Evangelical Theological Society, December 29, 1975.

Ward, Michael. C.S. Lewis On Christianity. Lecture 2: "Good and Evil." https://online.hillsdale.edu/courses/c-s-lewis-on-christianity. Downloaded: 12/19/2022.

Ward, Myah. POLITICO. "Blackburn to Jackson: Can You Define 'The Word Woman?' 03/2022. https://www.politico.com/news/2022/03/22/blackburn-jackson-define-the-word-woman-00019543. Downloaded: 09/14/2022.

Washington State Office of Equity. Summary Proposal. Page 1 of 6 pages. Downloaded https://healthequity.wa.gov/sites/default/files/202201/

Equity%20Office%20TF_Final%20Proposal%20Summary%20%28ADA%20compatible%29.pdf. Downloaded: 3/23/2023.

Wittgenstein, Ludwig. *Tractatus Logico-Philosophicus.* Translated by D.F. Pears and B.F. McGuinness. London: Routledge, reprinted, 1994.

Wood, Peter W. *1620, A Critical Response to the 1619 Project.* New York: Encounter Books, 2022.

World Economic Forum's website. February 2021. Quoted in: USA Today: https://www.usatoday.com/story/news/factcheck/2022/02/22/fact-check-thousands-black-lives-matter-protesters-arrested-2020/6816074001/. Downloaded: 02/23/2023.

Wright, N.T. *The Resurrection of the Son of God.* Minneapolis, MN.: Fortress Press, 2003.

Yancey, George. *Beyond Racial Division: A Unifying Alternative to Colorblindness and Antiracism.* Downers Grove, IL.: Inter-Varsity Press, 2022.

______________. "Christian Racial Reconciliation" (Day 1) | Laing Lectures 2024. Regent College (Vancouver BC). https://www.youtube.com/watch?v=3jB3aB9FiLo. Downloaded: 03/12/2024.

______________. "Christian Reconciliation" (Day 2), https://www.youtube.com/watch?v=QKCPPLJGjSM. Lang Lectures 2024. Download: 03/16/2024.

______________. "Christian Racial Reconciliation" (Day 3) | Laing Lectures 2024. https://www.youtube.com/watch?v=B2qyoLY4I_0. Downloaded: 03/20/2024.

www.ingramcontent.com/pod-product-compliance
Lightning Source LLC
Chambersburg PA
CBHW071416090426
42737CB00011B/1478

* 9 7 8 1 7 6 3 6 4 6 8 0 3 *